THE WEST WING

The Television Series

ROBERT J. THOMPSON, SERIES EDITOR

THE
WEST WING

*The American Presidency
as Television Drama*

EDITED BY

PETER C. ROLLINS

AND

JOHN E. O'CONNOR

SYRACUSE UNIVERSITY PRESS

Copyright © 2003 by Syracuse University Press
Syracuse, New York 13244–5160
All Rights Reserved

First Edition 2003
    05 06 07 08   6 5 4 3

Frontispiece: A partial cast of *The West Wing (left to right):* Richard Schiff (Toby Ziegler), Allison Janney (C. J. Cregg), Dulé Hill (Charlie Young), John Spencer (Leo McGarry), Martin Sheen (President Jed Bartlet), Rob Lowe (Sam Seaborn), Janel Moloney (Donna Moss), and Bradley Whitford (Josh Lyman). Copyright © 2000 Warner Bros. All Rights Reserved.

The paper used in this publication meets the minimum requirements of American National Standard for Information Sciences—Permanence of Paper for Printed Library Materials, ANSI Z39.48–1984.∞™

Library of Congress Cataloging-in-Publication Data
The West Wing : the American presidency as television drama / edited by Peter C. Rollins and John E. O'Connor.
p. cm.—(The television series)
Includes bibliographical references and index.
ISBN 0–8156–3026–3 (alk. paper)—ISBN 0–8156–3031–X (pbk. : alk. paper)
1. West Wing (Television program) I. Rollins, Peter C. II. O'Connor, John E. III. Series.
PN1992.77.W44R658 2003
791.45'72—dc21
2002156732

Manufactured in the United States of America

Contents

Focusing on Issues

Language and Structure in *The West Wing*

Perceptions of *The West Wing*

Critical Responses: *West Wing* Press Reviews

Bibliographical Overview

Acknowledgments

The editors wish to make the following acknowledgements for photos. For the cover photo of the White House, we thank the White House Historical Association. (Full citation of credit accompanies the photo.) For the cast photo for *The West Wing*, we thank Laura Sharp of Warner Bros. TV Legal Department. We also thank the American Political Science Association for allowing us to reprint Dr. Staci L. Beavers' essay on pedogogy.

The journalists represented in this collection were most gracious in lending their voices. The article by Sharon Waxman was first printed in *George Magazine*. The article by Chris Lehmann first appeared in the *Atlantic Monthly*. The article by John Podhoretz first appeared in the *Weekly Standard*. We thank the authors and the publishers for their permission to use these colorful and insightful analyses.

Susan Rollins and Deborah Carmichael are to be acknowledged for their efforts in organizing a wonderful conference, The Presidency in Film and TV, in 2000 and for the follow up help with the editing and logistics for this anthology.

Contributors

Staci L. Beavers is an associate professor of political science at California State University San Marcos. Her research has appeared in journals such as *Publius: The Journal of Federalism* and *PS: Political Science and Politics*, and she currently serves as an associate editor for *The Social Science Journal*. She can be reached at sbeavers@csusm.edu.

Samuel A. Chambers is assistant professor of political science at Saint Mary's College of Maryland. His recent articles include, "Spectral History, Untimely Theory," *Theory & Event* and "Foucault's Evasive Maneuvers: Nietzsche, Interpretation, Critique," *Angelaki*. He has recently completed a book manuscript entitled *Time Is Out of Joint: Toward a Politics of Untimeliness*. He can be reached by e-mail at sachambers@smcm.edu.

Pamela Ezell teaches creative writing and literature into film at Chapman University in Orange, California, where she also produces a weekly television talk show, *Dialogue*, for PBS affiliate KOCE. She is also the director and producer of the award-winning short documentary, *TV Dream Homes: The Drawings of Mark Bennett*. She can be reached at ezell@chapman.edu.

Patrick Finn is a Social Sciences and Humanities Research Council of Canada Doctoral Fellow at the University of Victoria. His research has been published in a number of academic journals and he has had the opportunity to speak about his work in interviews in print, and on radio and television. He is currently editing two collections of scholarly essays and working on a book. He can be reached at pjfinn@uvic.ca.

Heather Richardson Hayton is a faculty member in the Literature and Writing Studies Department at Cal State University San Marcos. She has given several papers and interviews on *The West Wing* as well as Hollywood's attitudes following September 11. She is currently editing a collection of essays called *Translating Desire in the Middle Ages* and finishing a book on factional politics and medieval poetics. You can contact her at getmedieval@csusm.edu.

Christina Lane is assistant professor in the Motion Picture Program at the University of Miami. She is the author of *Feminist Hollywood: From* Born in Flames *to* Point Break (2000) and has forthcoming essays in *Kathryn Bigelow: Hollywood Transgressor,* edited by Deborah Jarmyn and Sean Redmond, and *Authorship: Trafficking with Hollywood,* edited by Janet Staiger and David Gerstner. She can be reached at clane@miami.edu.

Chris Lehmann is a feature writer for *The Atlantic* and a columnist for the *Washington Post.*

Myron A. Levine is a professor of political science at Albion College and the College's Justin L. and Marjorie Wardell Sleight and Norman R. and Alethea E. Sleight Endowed Professor of Leadership Studies. He is the author of *Presidential Campaigns and Elections* and coauthor of *Urban Politics: Power in Metropolitan America.* His articles have appeared in *Presidential Studies Quarterly;* his analysis of *Primary Colors* and *The War Room* appears in *The American Presidency in Film,* edited by Peter C. Rollins and John E. O'Connor. He can be reached at mlevine@albion.edu.

Michelle Mouton is assistant professor of English at Cornell College of Iowa. She has published on Victorian literature and culture in *Victorian Review* and *Studies in Popular Culture,* and she is currently at work on *Reforming Fictions: Gender, Agency, and Merit in the Victorian Parliamentary Novel.* She can be contacted at mmouton@cornellcollege.edu.

John E. O'Connor is professor of history at New Jersey Institute of Technology (NJIT) and a member of the Federated Department of History of NJIT and Rutgers University, Newark. He is cofounder of the Historians Film

Committee and was editor/coeditor of its journal *Film & History* from 1979 until 1991. Also with Peter C. Rollins he coedited *Hollywood's World War I* (1997), *Hollywood's Indian* (1998), and *The American Presidency in Film and Television* (2002). He is author/editor of *Image as Artifact: The Historical Analysis of Film and Television*, compiler of the 120-minute *Image as Artifact* video compilation, and author of *Teaching History with Film and Television*, all published or copublished by the American Historical Association in 1990. In 1991 the American Historical Association honored him with the creation of its annual John E. O'Connor Award for the best historical film or video production.

John Podhoretz is contributing editor to the *Weekly Standard* and a columnist for the *New York Post*.

Donnalyn Pompper is associate professor in the Department of Communication at Florida State University. Her primary areas of scholarly interest include how mass media texts are used for meaning making, as well as environmental risk communication, and gender issues in the workplace and in popular culture texts. She can be reached at donnalyn.pompper@com.fsu.edu.

Peter C. Rollins is Regents Professor of English and American/Film Studies at Oklahoma State University. He is the editor in chief of *Film & History: An Interdisciplinary Journal of Film and Television Studies* and coeditor of *Hollywood as Historian, Second Edition* (1998); *Hollywood's Indian* (1998); and *Television Histories* (2001). His *Columbia University Press Companion to American History on Film* (2003) is basic to the field. His films include *Will Rogers' 1920s: A Cowboy's Guide to the Times* (1976); *Television's Vietnam: The Real Story* (1985); and *Television's Vietnam: The Impact of Media* (1986). He received a Lifetime Service Award by the National Popular Culture Association and the American Popular Culture Association in 2001 and Lifetime Achievement Award from those organizations in 2002. For more information, contact www.filmandhistory.org and RollinsPC@aol.com.

Greg M. Smith is an assistant professor of communication and graduate director of the Moving Image Studies program at Georgia State University. He is editor of *On a Silver Platter: CD-ROMs and the Promises of a New Technology* (1999) and coeditor of *Passionate Views: Film, Cognition, and Emotion* (1999). His book *Movies, Emotion, and Mood: The Emotion System and Film Structure* is forthcoming. He can be reached at gsmith@gsu.edu.

Jason P. Vest teaches in the Department of English and American Literature of Washington University, St. Louis. His articles have appeared in the *Proceedings of the Society for Interdisciplinary Study of Social Imagery, Y2000 Conference, Multicultural Studies in American Television,* and in *Science Fiction Studies.* He can be reached at japaves@yahoo.com.

Sharon Waxman wrote for *George* magazine and is a columnist for the *Washington Post.*

THE WEST WING

Introduction

The West Wing, *The American Presidency as Television Drama*

JOHN E. O'CONNOR AND PETER C. ROLLINS

Most historians agree that during the twentieth century the role of the American presidency and the executive branch expanded significantly in relation to other institutions of American government—Congress and the judiciary. Despite several failed attempts at stripping the power from presidents through impeachment, the century was a period of fulfillment of growth tendencies begun by Theodore Roosevelt (1901–1909) with his trust-busting and his dynamic, personally driven foreign policy, and by Franklin Delano Roosevelt with his four terms in office (1933–1945) during which special powers were invoked—and new bureaucracies created—to address both the Great Depression and World War II. Rexford G. Tugwell, who himself played a role in FDR's brain trust and in its expanding of federal power, later reflected negatively on *The Enlargement of the Presidency* in his 1960 book. Arthur M. Schlesinger (1973) referred to the Kennedy presidency (1961–1963), which he knew from inside the White House, as "imperial." Then there were the scandals and power plays of the Nixon years (1969–1974). As the new century and new millennium began, responses to international tensions and terrorism seemed to bring executive powers—and concern for America's traditional separation of powers—even more to the forefront of public consciousness. Beyond the duties of office spelled out by the Constitution, the president is also head of his political party, responsible for raising money and helping his partisans win seats in Congress and in governors' mansions across the land. *A Glorious Burden* is what the Smithson-

1

ian Institution's Museum of American History called this expansion of power and celebrity in a permanent new exhibit on the presidency installed in 2000. One result has been an inevitable increasing general interest in what goes on both in front of the cameras and behind the scenes in the Thomas Jefferson-designed building at 1600 Pennsylvania Avenue.

Continuing the trend, it was 2002 when NBC News produced a special entitled *The Real West Wing,* hosted by its distinguished news anchor Tom Brokaw. The program brought viewers into the George W. Bush White House near the beginning of his second year in office. Viewers met a young college intern and several protocol functionaries. Cameras observed the president in the Oval Office, sat in on a meeting in the basement "situation room," and visited with the first lady in the residence upstairs. Vice President Dick Cheney was there, in from the secret quarters where he was living and working as a result of security concerns in the wake of the September 11, 2001, terrorist attacks on New York's World Trade Center and Washington's Pentagon building. The officials and staff seemed to relate to one another comfortably and gave the distinct impression that the Bush White House enjoyed a dynamic mix of caring people attuned to national concerns and committed to carrying out public policy. The president was portrayed as a family man, with a wife who seemed to be adapting well to a life so prominently in the public eye and with two daughters away at school, but nonetheless growing to adulthood in unique situations—as "first siblings." Many viewers of the special took in the White House tour as somewhat informed visitors, since they were already familiar with the location and the types of people who lived and worked there; they had already become intimates of Jed Bartlet and his staff through the popular television series entitled *The West Wing,* then in its third season. But creator of *The West Wing,* Aaron Sorkin, was dissatisfied with the Brokaw special. "The White House pumped up the President's schedule to show him being much busier and more engaged than he is, and Tom Brokaw let it happen—the show was a valentine to Bush." NBC's rival networks made such a bruhaha out of this family squabble at NBC that Sorkin was pressured to withdraw his remark and apologized to the much admired celebrant of "the greatest generation" ("*West Wing* Honcho Blasts Bush" 2002).

Sorkin's caveats about the Brokaw documentary notwithstanding, the general impression that the public had received from *The West Wing* series was clearly a sympathetic one, perhaps even more so shortly into the second season when a major problem arose questioning President Bartlet's health and his long-term ability to carry on in office. It seems the fictional president had been diagnosed with multiple sclerosis (MS) several years earlier, although as yet there were no severe symptoms. The issue was complicated by the fact that his condition had never been announced publicly, either before he became a candidate or at any time since (remember that Bill Clinton had not made his medical records public either). Now, just at the point when Bartlet was contemplating standing for a second term, the potentially career-ending news was coming out. Concurrently, in the real world, it was also election time for the White House. Clinton was nearing the end of his second term and the parallels that had been established between his real life and Bartlet's scripted situations—from the vagaries of congressional party politics to a threatened impeachment—would likely have to be changed to accommodate a new chief executive.

Critical Acclaim and Some Tough Sledding

The West Wing has been a resounding success with audiences and advertisers, but early reception was mixed. Most reviews of the show were positive, but there were some negative responses. Perhaps the most glowing review came from Sharon Waxman (2000) in *George* magazine—now defunct, but at the time a mouthpiece for John F. Kennedy Jr. and patrician liberalism. In her review, reprinted in part four of this book (see chap. 12), she points to the industry recognition the show had received in its first season—nine Emmy Awards to the single one garnered by the similarly acclaimed HBO series *The Sopranos*. She spells out the ways in which *The West Wing* characters could be read as counterparts of actual Clinton White House personnel: Sam Seaborn as George Stephanopoulis, C. J. Cregg as Clinton press person Dee Dee Meyers, and Josh Lyman as Clinton aide Paul Begala. Sorkin was adamant in rejecting such comparisons and insisting that he was writing *fiction*: "I make these people up." Meanwhile, Waxman notes that the show's leading star, Martin Sheen, continued to be an "outspoken anti-Republican." As Waxman summarizes her analysis: *The West Wing* was "the rarest of rarities," a "zeitgeist show, a reflection of the tenor of our times" (chap. 12, 206). Michael Wolff's (2000) review in *New York* magazine also praised the series, and also pointed out that Sheen and others of the cast were known to be "rabidly anti-Republican." Wolff predicted that Clinton's constitutional inability to serve a third term would surely "put pressure on the show to change" (44).

On the negative side were reviews that appeared in the *Weekly Standard* and the *Atlantic Monthly,* both reprinted in part four of this volume. In the first of these, published in the *Weekly Standard* in March 2000 (see chap. 14 in this volume), John Podhoretz comes down particularly hard on the series. He quotes from a cover story in *Brill's Content* (a short-lived investigative periodical) to the effect that *The West Wing* presents a "truer, more human picture of the people behind the headlines than most of today's Washington journalists" (chap. 14, 223). But then he dismembers the show piece by piece, arguing that the characters "aren't human beings—they're noble soldiers in a noble cause, and they have been washed clean of every impurity because of it" (223). He attacks the show as unrealistic: "There are no staff conflicts of any consequence . . . no turf battles between these White House aides. . . . No one is hungry for power, perks, or privilege" (224). He quotes a line from Bartlet's demanding wife to the President: you have "a big brain, a good heart, and an ego the size of Montana. . . . You don't have the power to fix everything, but I do like watching you try" (225). In the end, Podhoretz sees *The West Wing* as "nothing more or less than political pornography for liberals" (222–23) as the "ultimate Hollywood fantasy: the Clinton White House without Clinton" (222) and without its embarrassing scandals.

The second negative review, from the *Atlantic Monthly* (see chap. 13 in this volume), was entitled "The Feel-Good Presidency: The Pseudo Politics of *The West Wing*." It posits *The West Wing* as an imaginary "cultural platform for the revival of liberal politics in America" (chap. 13, 000). Taking pot shots along the way (for example, characterizing the give-and-take dialog style of the show as "encounter group policy making"), Chris Lehmann, an editorialist for the *Washington Post,* calls the series a "selective (yet ever didactic) liberal retreat into political fantasy" which has as its "tacit mission the revival of sagging liberal spirits" (214–15). What emerges, according to

Lehmann, is a "pointedly sunny weekly fable about the unassailable motives and all-too-human foibles of the nation's governing class which verges on the Capra-esque" (215). For both Podhoretz and Lehmann, then, *The West Wing* is not only unrealistic, but significantly skewed to the left. Even the most liberal viewers could not disagree.

A Diverting Cast of Characters

The writers for *The West Wing* developed a cast of characters that was intended to allow a multiplication of complex interactions among them in true ensemble fashion. As with other series developed around institutions, such as *Hill Street Blues, L.A. Law,* and *ER, West Wing* viewers were intended to identify with the individual characters and the ways in which they related to one another from week to week, developing a rapport and a deep sense of character over time. Chief among these characters, of course, was the commander in chief, although at the outset of the series it was thought that the president would remain in the background as a so-called "recurring character" who might appear in no more than one in five of the episodes. Most of the action would be carried on by key members of the White House staff, the denizens of the West Wing. But early on, especially after Martin Sheen was identified as the actor to play the president and the pilot episode worked so well, Sorkin expanded the role of the president. Interviewed on the *Today* show (October 18, 2000) early in the second season, Sheen referred to the program as "a prime-time civics lesson with a heart." Perhaps he related to the part so well because Sheen himself has participated in politics as an activist on nuclear and environmental issues and has appeared in public service spots advocating social justice for farm workers and for gun control. Asked by his early-morning interviewer if he thought his activism had "cost him," Sheen replied that he hoped so, "otherwise it would be impersonal and meaningless." President Bartlet also has a personal life, a wife who lives with him in the East Wing and three daughters. Dr. Abby Bartlet (Stockard Channing) is a real presence. An accomplished person in her own right as a physician, Dr. Bartlet is capable of acting in ways that distract her husband, the president, and everyone around him. Indeed, her concept of the first lady's role is more akin to that lived by Hillary Rodham Clinton, JD, than by Mrs. Laura Bush—as a conscience on special issues otherwise forgotten in the rush of beltway deals and compromises.

President Bartlet's communications director is Toby Ziegler (Richard Schiff). Described by some as "the conscience of the Bartlet White House," Ziegler argues to have the White House fight for a more effective law when Congress waffles on gun control; when a homeless Korean War veteran dies on the street (wearing the overcoat Ziegler had donated to the poor), it is Ziegler who arranges a funeral for him at Arlington National Cemetery. According to *The West Wing: The Official Companion* (hereafter cited as *TOC*), "more than anything, perhaps, he resembles a New Deal Democrat" (228). Interviewed on the television talk show *The View* near the start of the second season, Schiff indicated the interest that the Clinton administration had shown in the series. "The cast had been welcomed at the White House," he explained, noting that he was the only one of the main cast members not to have met Clinton personally (October 23, 2000). Commenting on the effectiveness of the Bartlet White House, Schiff has observed: "We're pretty lame as a group in terms of what we accomplish. It's very accurate and very realistic because so much of government is compromise" (*TOC*, 231). (Due to partisan comments by *The West Wing* actors and staff—especially Aaron Sorkin—the ensemble has *not* been welcomed by the George W. Bush White House, and an annual visit by the program was discouraged in the fall of 2002.)

The "second most powerful man in the country" is Leo McGarry (John Spencer). The man who convinced Bartlet to run for the presidency in the first place is now his chief of staff, "his best friend and confidant, a man who often seems to know what the President is thinking before the President does" (*TOC*, 303). John Spencer admits to being a "political junkie, fascinated by politics and the working machine" (*TOC*, 305). His character sits at the controls of White House operations. He is the one person on staff allowed to speak to the president one on one; he can, if necessary, tell him when he is wrong. McGarry is also the person responsible for keeping the White House personnel in line. Among them are Sam Seaborn (Rob Lowe), speech writer and Toby's deputy; Charlie Young (Dulé Hill), the president's personal assistant, who is at his side most of the time; and Josh Lyman

(Bradley Whitford), the deputy chief of staff who is "kept grounded" by his assistant Donna Moss (Janel Maloney).

Perhaps the character who most holds the show (if not the executive department, or at least the public's perception of it) together is press secretary C. J. Cregg (Allison Janney). Although barely visible in the pilot program and behind the scenes for most of the first season, C. J. has been at the center of almost every major episode. Unlike some of the other actors, Janney admits to being "not a political person," but calling the shots as far as White House public relations were concerned was something her character could handle. "If a person needs to be in control and in charge, I can do that" (*TOC*, 103). And whenever issues explode on the scene and reporters either are needed to promote or threaten to undermine administration initiatives, C. J. proves capable of deflecting criticism, confounding the malevolent, and offering the most favorable "spin" on volatile leaks, gaffes, and news stories.

Part One: Issues in *The West Wing*, Public and Otherwise

The scholarly essays of this collection are arranged in four sections, the first with four essays focusing on various issues that challenge the Bartlet presidency. First, Donnalyn Pompper notes the importance of *The West Wing* for promoting public understanding of procedures internal to the working of the presidency—issues that would be difficult, if not completely inappropriate, for journalists to raise. Viewers come away from *The West Wing*, Pompper notes, "feeling as though they have witnessed politics in action, unmediated by journalists." They may feel that they understand not only the things that happened, but details about *why* and *how* they happened, details about process to which reporters are not usually privy. Several episodes, in fact, deal with White House manipulation of the press, bargaining with reporters over the coverage of embarrassing issues, for example, or intentionally issuing multiple bad-news stories all at one time in order to avoid having negative coverage strung out over days or weeks—a Clinton staff technique. Since the 1960s, questions about what news emerges from the White House and how it is shaped for public consumption have become explosive political issues in themselves.

Christina Lane's contribution on the culture of gender and race in *The West Wing* focuses on the moral guidance that traditionally marginalized voices (e.g., women and blacks) provide in the series. Women play key roles. Even secretaries, such as Josh's secretary Donna, play a pertinent—if not a central—role. Lane describes Donna as "hyper aware, intuitive, confident, and an important voice of reason in the midst of chaos." In the last episode of the first season ("What Kind of Day Has It Been?"[1]) a racist sniper takes a shot at Charlie, the president's assistant, who happens to be black, and hits the president instead, requiring an emergency operation. When Charlie subsequently contemplates leaving his job for fear that his continued proximity to the president might constitute an added danger, his mind is changed by a West Wing encounter with an African American computer repairman with his wide-eyed young son in tow—a tangible reminder of what his position so near to the top must mean as a role model to youngsters of his race.

Myron Levine, who also provides a broad-based bibliographical essay for our volume, addresses "myth and reality in television's portrayal of the White House." He questions the image of a committed White House staff with no internal factions, no competition, and none of the "yes men" likely to arise in such "a culture of reverence, sycophancy, isolation and groupthink." Contrary to the series' portrayal, the modern vice president, in reality, is not "shut out" as is *The West Wing*'s Vice President John Hoynes (Tim Matheson), a ballot-balancing outsider from Texas who seldom appears in the show. Unrealistic as such portrayals may be, however, Levine joins many of the other authors in this anthology in concluding that *The West Wing* "presents a healthy corrective to the American anti-Washington impulse and an antidote to public cynicism."

In a long historical perspective, Heather Richardson Hayton asks whether the man and the president can be separated. As in the late months of the Nixon administration, when impeachment seemed inevitable, is it possible—perhaps even necessary—to distinguish attitudes of contempt for the man from deep respect for the office he occupies? On a more personal basis, can the father of a young girl separate his parental instincts from his political

---

1. *West Wing* episodes mentioned throughout this volume can be referenced alphabetically by title in the episode list in the "Works Cited" section at the end of this volume.

principles when his African American assistant asks her for a date? Location, character, and cinematography are used in various creative ways to portray a very old notion in modern dress, the concept of "the king's two bodies," which holds that such a separation is not only possible but is essential. The question also arises of the separation between the fictional president and contemporary politics: Hayton closes with a discussion of the impact the series may have had on the 2000 election, in which several members of the cast actively campaigned for Al Gore, the Democratic candidate whose political fortunes were inextricably linked to the Bartlet-like presidency of William Jefferson Clinton.

Part Two: Language and Dramatic Structure

Part two of this volume deals with cinematic language and dramatic structure in *The West Wing*. Samuel A. Chambers concentrates on the "textual implications" of a single episode, "Six Meetings Before Lunch," positioning it in the context of "broader questions raised in the realm of contemporary political theory." Specifically, he argues that the universe of political possibilities in *The West Wing* goes far beyond questions of "left" and "right," as characters "grapple" with questions of political agency and legitimacy and challenge the restrictive borders of the current political arena. One issue the episode focuses on is school vouchers, another is the idea of reparations for slavery. As dialog shifts and Sorkin evokes the issues, something distinguishable from the issues demands attention—it is the dialog itself, the way in which issues are worked through: "The process proves dramatically more significant than the end points" of the discussions. Chambers proposes "agonistic discourse" as a label for this process and examines other examples of how it works in a close exegesis. His reading clearly applies both to the series as a whole and to the constraints of our political system as we know it.

For Canadian scholar Patrick Finn, what sets Jed Bartlet apart from the previous residents of 1600 Pennsylvania Avenue is that he is a "public intellectual" who embodies his country's "primary principles." To explain the appeal of *The West Wing,* Finn turns to character development. The most significant appeal of Jed Bartlet, Finn argues, is his complexity. Bartlet's positions on issues are difficult to characterize, despite factors such as his Roman

Catholicism, which would seem to make him more predictable (and despite his status as a Nobel Prize winner, which might make him less so). His undecidedness in political debate represents a form of democracy that respects the rights of citizens to "make up their own minds."

Greg M. Smith concentrates on "In Excelsis Deo," the Christmas-themed episode from the first season, to examine how the series balances multiple plot lines with the necessity to maintain "a cohesive whole." One way a writer can have characters cover so much ground is by breaking up scenes into "snippets" in which several individuals can interact on a variety of different topics. An example Smith offers is a visit to a Georgetown bookstore by the president and several of his staff, where two or three different conversations punctuate their scanning of the dusty shelves. Sorkin's characters "tend to shift from one topic to another at a moment's notice," thus fracturing individual conversations into "snippets" as well and allowing multiple topics to be addressed. To compensate for this fractionalization and to add some continuity, the visual style of the series uses steadicam tracking shots, often with interchanging couples in conversation—a technique applied in Sorkin's other ensemble series, *Sports Night*.

The final chapter in part two offers Jason P. Vest's comparative analysis of two products of Aaron Sorkin—who wrote both *The West Wing* and the earlier feature film *The American President* (1995). The TV series, of course, with its multiple episodes, allows "a more nuanced" portrait of the presidency "as an institution." Pressures of the feature-film medium, especially time limitations, make it impossible to focus on minor characters or the nature of the presidential office; the "focus becomes the President's personality." Vest goes on to compare Sorkin's handling of scenes of similar situations in his motion picture and television scripts to demonstrate both the creative potentials of each medium and the special talent Sorkin brings to both.

Part Three: Perceptions of *The West Wing*

Pamela Ezell offers the first of three different perceptions of *The West Wing* in part three with an analysis of the "sincere" presidency of Jed Bartlet. She characterizes the fictional White House personnel as unrealistically "noble." They serve, she argues, "with the zeal of missionaries, the kindness of campus counselors, and the moral fiber of Sunday school teachers." Republican Ainsley Hayes (Emily Proctor), a character introduced "in an attempt to provide bi-partisan balance," winds up being impressed by *The West Wing* staff's commitment. "They're righteous, they're patriots, and I'm their lawyer," she tells disbelieving Republican colleagues as she decides to "jump ship" and go to work for Bartlet—albeit in a minority/advisory role. This sort of ardor Ezell contrasts with actual stories of self-serving, backstabbing staff conflicts within the Clinton and other administrations. (The short-lived experience of Republican journalist and strategist David Gergen in the Clinton White House comes to mind as a parallel.)

According to Staci Beavers, *The West Wing* is an effective tool for motivating students to learn about political realities. In areas such as "behind-the-scenes exploration of political decision-making," even the program's "left-leaning tendencies" can provide opportunities for students to think critically. The show also offers interesting representations of political associations, such as the "edgy relationship between White House press secretary C. J. Cregg and journalist Danny Concannon" (Timothy Busfield). Her contribution goes on to suggest numerous ways in which a judicious use of *The West Wing* references in the classroom could be instructive for students and teachers.

Michelle Mouton introduced a group of undergraduate college students to *The West Wing*. She had just taken them through a three-and-a-half-week intensive course relating contemporary Victorian novels to British politics of the nineteenth century. When the class turned to *The West Wing* after this exposure to literary politics, its response to the series was "largely negative." The novels, written in response to enlarging British suffrage, sought to persuade "new voters to trust and elect their social betters rather than members of their own class." Interestingly, as she describes it, "Victorian Parliamentary fiction, specifically, focuses on daily behind-the-scenes maneuverings of wealth, power, and personal ambition"—not unlike the way *The West Wing* presents the White House. But her students "read" *The West Wing* as not encouraging a positive political response, not "revising the cultural representation of power, race, and gender." According to Mouton, what they found important was what was left out: "voters' demonstrations, workers on strike . . . and politically active young women and men." Students found that *The*

West Wing, like the Victorian novels, validates "the codes, desires, and aspirations of the educated professional class." Those who oppose such codes will join the students as critics of the series; others who applaud the notion of noblesse oblige in American life will draw more positive conclusions. Either way, the critique offered by Mouton is well grounded in the consistent messages of *The West Wing*.

◆   ◆   ◆

The collection of articles published here should help attune readers to both the sensibilities necessary to appreciate the nuances of *The West Wing* and the warnings appropriate to avoid misreading them. The tendency toward an imperial presidency that Arthur Schlesinger noted in 1963 seemed even then to threaten to overturn the balance that the "founding fathers" built into the Constitution. But that balance had been expected, from the outset, to experience a fair share of tension and opposition—witness the warnings in *The Federalist* (1789) by authors Alexander Hamilton, James Madison, and John Jay. As Schlesinger has conceded, the structure of the three branches—executive, legislative, and judicial—"institutionalized conflict in the very heart of the American polity."

There is much to be learned if we approach such issue-laden television as *The West Wing* in a thoughtful manner, informed by both historical scholarship and media analysis that translates the politics of visual language. There is a paradox in the relationship between the White House and its representation in a fictional series for television. As citizens, we take increasing interest in presidential leadership; a series like *The West Wing* both capitalizes on our concerns and pushes us to think about governance as a human activity entrusted to the hands of ordinary people. Its message is sometimes troubling, but the long-term promise of the series is hopeful. Despite the partisan blinders of political ideology, despite the dangers of nuclear weaponry and the potential for mass destruction, and despite the health and psychological frailties of individuals, the American system will work. It will function for the greater good of the nation because of our reverence for law, the power of the American political tradition, and the commitment to service that inspires our best and brightest—a term too long out of favor. Furthermore, our public servants—for whom *The West Wing* is a microcosm—will stay the course for us if they sense that a vigilant public supports them. Although the series may be condemned as "idealistic," its characters and its clever techniques of camera work, lighting, editing, and mise-en-scène reflect America's best image of itself. In this respect, the series provides inspiration and hope while it entertains a loyal audience that desperately wants to believe in the nobility of the American dream.

It seems only fitting that director Frank Capra, the auteur behind such important political statements as *Mr. Smith Goes to Washington* (1939), *Meet John Doe* (1941), and the *Why We Fight* series of World War II orientation films (1942–45), is invoked by both Aaron Sorkin *and* his critics. In 1972, John E. O'Connor and Martin A. Jackson, founding editors of the journal *Film & History,* talked with Capra at a meeting of the American Historical Association, which Capra attended at his own expense rather than charging the fledgling scholarly journal a speaker's fee. Both editors were impressed by the continuing idealism and vision of this rags-to-riches embodiment of the American dream. As a celebrant of that vision—first in *Meet John Doe* and then most explicitly in "Prelude to War," the first installment in the *Why We Fight* series—Capra evoked the mythic image of America as a "lighthouse of freedom" in a darkening world. Like Americans after the horrors of September 11, 2001, Capra defined a world in which freedom and tyranny were in open conflict; the struggle required courage, commitment, and a moral vision. In our time, it seems clear that the fundamental attraction of *The West Wing* for Americans is its promise that, despite our failings and lapses, our system is still such a lighthouse. Such an appeal to our better selves is both refreshing and chastening.

THE WEST WING

FOCUSING ON ISSUES

1 | *The West Wing*

White House Narratives That Journalism Cannot Tell

DONNALYN POMPPER

Agrowing body of literature links journalism to America's political malaise. Researchers concur that Americans grow more cynical with every new generation. Only about half of the public votes in presidential elections (Perloff 1998, 333), and voters aged fifty and younger seem to have lost faith in the presidency (Kohut 2000, 28). There is growing evidence to suggest that the 2000 presidential election controversy has further alienated voters. Such disconnection between citizenship and governance raises questions about the role of the news media in a democracy. Rather than focusing on media effects—viewers' responses—this essay suggests that the very conventions and routines that define journalism conflict with reporters' ability to tell complete political stories. Thus, to supplement inconclusive political news accounts, audiences may attend to popular culture texts like NBC's *The West Wing* to fill in information gaps. Central to this essay is the confluence of media and politics in America—and the uneasy links forged through storytelling.

This premise is based on general agreement among mass media researchers that journalism fails in its attempt to mirror reality for audiences. First, it is argued that forcing reporters to behave like detached observers is impractical even though journalism's independence from politics is considered essential to a working democracy. Indeed, many scholars have critiqued journalism's vain attempts to achieve objectivity because news inevitably is a social construction. Despite journalists' efforts to produce objective accounts, they cannot overcome bias built into their industry's routines and conventions.

Second, it has been suggested that objectivity *should not be* a goal of journalism. Impartial reporting strips reporters of creativity and turns journalism into a mere technical trade absent of intellectual import (Glasser 1992, 179). A just-the-facts approach to journalism results in shallow news stories lacking in detail or rich, personal accounts. Furthermore, print reporters usually focus on working the *who, what, when,* and *where* into story leads and leave out the *why* and *how.* Carey posited that these story components usually require deeper explanation than space or time—both expensive commodities in journalism—will allow (1986, 149). Thus, political reporters offer audiences unfinished stories in omitting *why* and *how* details.

Third, researchers contend that news media accounts may be lacking because reporters omit details associated with the inner workings of news production. Journalists' narrative process conceals the manufactured qualities of news work such as the overreliance on authorities as news sources, newsroom conflicts among reporters and between reporters and editors, and deadline pressures. Furthermore, audiences are unaware of effects of symbiotic relationships between news workers who maintain credibility through "mutual determination of fact and source" (Tuchman 1978, 84). Perloff characterizes the president-press symbiosis as a "locked dynamic, transactional relationship" (1998, 97). Such conventions and routines are not deemed relevant by news producers and seldom make it into finished news stories even though these nuances might lend new dimensions to audience perceptions of issues and events.

Finally, political reporters cannot provide eyewitness accounts of national security behind the scenes at the White House because they are not privy to the inner sanctum of the nation's ultimate backroom. Even though political reporters develop high-ranking political insiders as news sources, national security laws and regulations override first amendment speech guarantees, restricting journalists' access. Furthermore, journalists seek only issues and events defined by enduring news values (Gans 1979, 42), and minutiae of West Wing staffers' ongoing strategy sessions and dynamics of personal relationships probably would not be considered newsworthy even if journalists had unfettered White House access. In fact, media watchers say that, without *conflict,* the Washington press corps "rarely tries to offer a rounded, human portrait of our leaders' character or motives" (Miller 2000, 89). In contrast, *The West Wing* executive story editor Lawrence O'Donnell told *Time* magazine that the show's scenes work only if the audience *understands* the conflict (Branegan 2000, 82). Consequently, *The West Wing* scripts offer simple explanations for complex issues so that audiences may understand policies. Such details central to conflict within the White House rarely make it into news accounts due to lack of space and airtime; the *how* and *why* that Carey characterized as "what we most want to get out of a news story and are least likely to receive" (1986, 149).

Surely, journalists do not intend to alienate audiences as they seek to fulfill their democratic role. More important, it is suggested here that a popular television drama can complement journalism by offering an entertaining and realistic view of the White House that sharpens images of the presidency and national politics. Launched in September 1999, *The West Wing* shows the back story by picking up where the formal news product stops. It probes the *how* and *why* of governance that the White House press corps does *not* report on. As stated in *TV Guide* magazine, "[*The West Wing*] is really about palace intrigue, about what we imagine goes on that doesn't make it into the news" (Robins 1999, 53). For one hour a week, Americans overcome political malaise and feel connected to the presidency in ways that formal journalism cannot facilitate.

Political Storytelling

Many Americans get their political news from the television medium, which has been called "the most important cultural artifact in modern American society" (McBride and Toburen 1996, 181) and "a central locus of activity in American culture and American politics" (Schudson 1982, 97). Indeed, television has captivated advocates and critics alike for its consensus-building potential and the ease with which it blends politics and entertainment. Such collaboration between writer and audience positions narrative as a form of rich, under-mined, cultural history.

Television has become a key political storytelling medium. The 1960 Kennedy-Nixon presidential debates launched television's reputation as the medium of choice for political narratives. Indeed, television has changed politics, redefined how we feel about it, and socialized us by educating us on the roles of the U.S. president and congressional representatives. Audiences learn more about politics from televised news than from newspapers, particularly when issues are complex. However, the new media environment and various types of genres like feature films, docudramas, talk shows, web sites, and popular music that the public uses for political information may be challenging traditional journalism's status as gatekeeper for political news. On the whole, politicians use television to showcase their credentials and expose their opponents' vulnerabilities. Thus, television has replaced communal storytelling sessions that organize social experience and transfer culture over generations.

Political narratives that rely on drama to bring together plot, character, scene, and purpose are quite useful for understanding culture. In the tradition of George Herbert Mead (1934), many scholars classify journalism's aesthetic function as a means of helping people interpret their lives relative to their nation, town, or class. Americans often turn to popular culture texts for information and behavioral cues beyond school and family resources, and much of what we know about the world comes from news narratives. Furthermore, people cannot register everything, so they rely on the news media to help them choose what they will attend to. Journalism perpetuates culture by crafting stories about politics that audiences can readily comprehend and use to make meaning.

Journalism is storytelling, and the news media have been characterized as "storytellers drawn to dramatic formulas and stereotyped roles" (Combs 1984, 96). Political stories especially tend to be linked to journalism's perceived "watchdog role" as a guardian of democracy. In particular, White House correspondents serve as a "guard dog" by reporting on major public issues. Indeed, American journalism traditions have been shaped within political coverage. By determining the range and content of public discourse, journalism helps to "make culturally consonant messages readable" (Schudson 1982, 98). Americans rely on news accounts to make sense of governance.

However, many steps in the news production process can compromise these democratic ideals, creating tension in the interplay between journalism and politics. It has been posited that journalism limits the public discourse by making "culturally dissonant messages unsayable" (Schudson 1982, 98). For example, some news media critics charge that journalists obscure the *real* issues when they are inconsistent with popular beliefs, overemphasize conflict, and offer unrealistic perspectives. Glasgow University Media Group (1976) researchers cautioned that the news media are unable to represent reality. By using drama, proximity, and timeliness values to define what is news, journalists have institutionalized bias in news production routines and conventions. In fact, some civic journalists recently discussed expanding news values to involve "even ordinary folks as valid sources" (Payne 2000, 5). Typically, journalism encourages people to be interested in politics as seen through the eyes of reporters.

Consequently, American journalists have come to regard themselves as authorities, and political reporters believe they are expert political analysts, best equipped to translate and interpret political acts for citizens unable to discern meaning unaided. Journalists' self-perceptions have been linked to the turn-of-the-twentieth-century rise of a reform movement when muckrakers revealed the seedy underbelly of industrialism, as well as to a shift in power from political parties to governmental managers with clearly defined administrative duties. By the 1920s, an autonomous corps of journalists began covering the president, and now the White House is coveted as the most prestigious journalism beat (Perloff 1998, 74). Operating at such an elevated station has catapulted political reporters such as Barbara Walters, Cokie Roberts, George Will, and George Stephanopolous to celebrity status. Even though journalists complain that political elections are treated too much like a horse race by framing political stories as sporting events and contests with winners and losers, few journalists would disagree that they are the most qualified mediators for political messages.

Overall, widespread public cynicism presents the greatest threat to the journalism-politics collusion. Among both elites and nonelites, a recurring theme of American political discourse is the perception that politicians are all corrupt and "in it for themselves" (Goldfarb 1991, 18). Carey posited that even though the press reports the facts and judges the relative effectiveness of claims, it does not go far enough (1986, 194). Similarly, voters recently told Pew Research Center pollsters that journalists focus too much on boring political strategies and do not go far enough in reporting on candidates' reputation for honesty (Kohut 2000, 28). Indeed, Americans are a cynical lot.

The West Wing tells stories about politics through use of a steadicam for an extraordinarily detailed and rapid narrative pace that journalists and their news products cannot offer. Themes of weary skepticism and complacence linked to traditional journalism stories give way to subjective depictions of a U.S. president (albeit a fictional one) and loyal staffers in The West Wing who are "passionate about principle, about government, about their jobs" (Poniewozik 1999, 96). These fictional Oval Office inhabitants consider public service a worthy, noble pursuit, and they work there because they hope to do good, not because of personal ambition. Overall, television shares political narratives that educate and enable the transfer of culture using a broad canvas. Many plotlines of The West Wing continue into future episodes and are reintroduced periodically, offering viewers sustained, extensive perspectives on complex, unfolding issues. Coupling this storytelling form with the types of stories audiences usually receive from journalists offers a more well-rounded account of governance than journalism alone provides.

Popular Culture and Politics

Popular culture has impacted politics in subtle yet important ways by disseminating and molding values, beliefs, and behaviors. The *manner* and *function* of governance itself, however, are seldom the focus in popular culture texts. Instead, much content of pop songs, romance novels, plays, and televised serials brushes against political issues by suggesting *attitudes* that bear political consequences. For example, the September 21, 1992, *Time* magazine cover featured a "Hollywood and Politics" headline and portrait of actor Candace Bergen as the lead character on the *Murphy Brown* television program, following a much-publicized single motherhood debate between a television mother-to-be and real vice president Dan Quayle. The debate skirted the women's rights issue by ridiculing Quayle instead. Brooke Gladstone's (2000) NPR report posited that even the film industry has limited governance discourse by focusing almost exclusively on the campaign story line that has very little to say about governing.

In contrast, The West Wing plots tackle federal governance head-on. As a referent for the real, *The West Wing* gives television viewers weekly behind-the-scenes peeks into the Oval Office and its outer cubicles, exposing the very human foibles of occupants and holding up for scrutiny the inner workings of the federal government. This elite culture of powerful decision makers tries to make sense of chaotic political life and intrigue. Scripts aim "not to tell what happens, but to reveal how it happens" (Wren 1999, 17). Unlike most films about high political offices, which focus almost exclusively on candidates who undergo unflattering transformations, *The West Wing* has been characterized as a "polidrama" (Berger 2000, 61) and "our national civics lesson" with "edu-content" (Branegan 2000, 82). *Newsweek* called it "intelligent" (Chang 1999, 80), and Matthew Cooper, *Time* magazine's deputy bureau chief and former White House correspondent for *U.S. News and World Report* and *The New Republic*, characterized the show as "more truthful than [political] reporting" (Miller 2000, 90). Such commentary runs counter to mass media researchers' usual critiques of television fiction for having "no mandate to reflect life in its episodes" (Greenberg 1980, 183). While Baudrillard (1988, 172) has lamented Americans' celebration of fantasy and images, it is suggested here that a fictional drama offers stories about governance that American consumers typically look for among journalists' stories but seldom find.

Hollywood, in general, has been criticized for failing to represent politics. Some have charged that Hollywood's artists are ignorant of political affairs, contribute to political cynicism, foster a liberal bias, and systematically disparage social values. Apparently, even NBC-TV executive John Wells was initially skeptical about *The West Wing* because of politics' poor image and a risk of turning off half of the audience by saying, "Washington, D.C., doesn't work" (Miller 2000, 91). *TV Guide* magazine also was doubtful at the outset of the new television season: "Conventional TV wisdom says fictional shows about politics don't work" (Robins 1999, 53). Yet, during its first season, *The West Wing* consistently posted high ratings—thirteen million "literate, upscale viewers every week" (chap. 12, 203)—and received critical acclaim in the form of eighteen Emmy nominations with nine awards, breaking the previous record of eight in a single season set by *ER* and *Hill Street Blues*. *The West Wing* also won three major awards at the annual Television Critics Association Awards in July. *George* magazine said the show was "currently embraced by the entire media and the political elite" (see chap. 12, 203).

It would seem that *The West Wing*'s creator, Aaron Sorkin, and his cast and crew have sought to overcome Hollywood's traditional inadequacies when dealing with politics by mingling with real politicians. To date, no screenwriter has devoted so much individual attention to the presidency as Sorkin. The NBC series' executive story editor, Lawrence O'Donnell, Jr., who once served as chief of staff of the Senate Finance Committee and is a former aide to New York democratic Senator Daniel Patrick Moynihan, pitched the show with Sorkin only after the box office and critical success of Sorkin's feature films, *The American President* in 1995 and *A Few Good Men* in 1992. Furthermore, *The West Wing* cast members hosted a pre-Democratic National Convention (DNC) party for politicos on the Warner Bros. set on the Sunday before the convention in August 2000 and then were themselves featured as stars at the DNC. Earlier that year, the cast took a road trip from Hollywood to Washington, D.C., in April to tour the White House and meet political figures like Secretary of State Madeleine Albright and Gene Sperling, head of the National Economic Council. *Time* magazine reported that actor Allison Janney, who portrays press secretary C. J. Cregg on the show, even stood at the White House press room podium and opened the midday briefing for White House spokesman Joe Lockhart. Actor John Spencer, who plays chief of staff Leo McGarry, also visited with his real-life counterpart, chief of staff John Podesta during the outing.

Furthermore, Sorkin retains political experts as creative consultants. Among the former White House insiders who work as *The West Wing* consultants are Patrick Caddell, President Jimmy Carter's right-hand man, and President Bill Clinton's first press secretary, Dee Dee Myers, who also currently serves as an MSNBC political analyst. Former White House press secretary Michael McCurry told *Brill's Content* magazine that *The West Wing* is "the first series in a long while that has treated those who work in politics . . . as human beings" (Miller 2000, 90). High-profile Republicans were added to the second season's cadre of consultants, including former Reagan and Bush press secretary Marlin Fitzwater and former Reagan speechwriter Peggy Noonan. Current White House staff members also offer Sorkin feedback on plots in the form of email messages. For example, in one episode of

The West Wing ("Take Out the Trash Day," Jan 26, 2000), a White House intern revealed to a family friend, who was a political foe of the Bartlet administration, that the chief of staff was a recovering alcoholic. Despite the fact that the disclosure threatened to damage the high-ranking official's reputation, he ordered that the intern be retained and not discharged even though, according to Sorkin, real White House staffers complained that the intern should have been fired (Tucker 2000). These interactions between artists and politicians enable *The West Wing* staff to create a reality-infused product and offer former and current White House workers an opportunity to participate in the process.

In comparing various popular culture treatments of politics, Combs suggested that Americans often turn to the mass media in addition to asking trusted family, friends, and coworkers for political information (1984, 5). Thus, it is not too much of a stretch to understand why television audiences might warm up to Martin Sheen as president of the United States. Sheen has been described as "Hollywood's most prominent . . . social activist" (Feuerherd 2000, 47), having been arrested sixty-one times protesting issues such as nuclear armament. Furthermore, Sheen has played a politician before, as chief of staff opposite Michael Douglas's president in *The American President,* as John F. Kennedy, Robert F. Kennedy, and John Dean, as a psychotic Senate hopeful aspiring to the U.S. presidency in the film version of Stephen King's *The Dead Zone,* and as narrator of Oliver Stone's *JFK.* Actor John Spencer told *TV Guide* magazine that he is a recovering alcoholic both in the series and in his real life (T. Johnson 2000, 50). Furthermore, it is not too hard for viewers to believe that the White House deputy communications director, played by Rob Lowe, accidentally slept with a call girl because the brat pack misadventurer achieved notoriety in 1988 after being caught on videotape in three-way sex during the DNC in Atlanta (one of the women was a minor). In fact, *George* magazine made Lowe and his role in *The West Wing* its September 1999 cover story, and *People Weekly* did the same in September 2000.

Thus, *The West Wing* offers viewers glimpses into how governance works in ways that other popular culture texts have not, and uses actual former and current political figures as consultants for authenticity in telling the stories.

Exposed Seams in Federal Government and Journalism

It has been argued that "all texts are ultimately political" (Storey 1993, 5), meaning that all narratives are shaped by an embedded, implicit worldview. Yet, *The West Wing* explicitly represents what goes on in the minds of political players and behind closed doors. Thus, viewers come away from watching the program feeling as if they have witnessed politics in action, unmediated by journalists. For example, *The West Wing* shows the many compromises that come with governance in the United States, including vote counting, arm twisting, and deal cutting. This is not the stuff of traditional journalism, as political reporters do not have access to it, nor is it usually the fodder of popular culture because political themes have enjoyed limited market sales appeal. *The West Wing* exposes the White House's seams—things that are traditionally concealed from public scrutiny—including important details about governance and the symbiotic relationship between politics and journalism.

News consumers enjoy sensational exposés of political figures and falls from grace, as witnessed throughout the Clinton-Lewinsky and Condit-Levy scandals. The only time Americans usually get to see behind the curtain, however, is when an insider writes a tell-all book. Such was the case with former Clinton staffer George Stephanopolous. *The West Wing* offers television viewers backstage glimpses complete with shop talk, White House trade secrets, dress rehearsals of the State of the Union speech, outtakes of radio addresses, and temper tantrums. A columnist for the *New Yorker* wrote that these details make for entertaining and informative stories: "The general citizenry is not privy to the fine details of spindoctoring and damage control in the White House—what we glimpse is probably the tip of the iceberg—but *The West Wing* makes viewers feel as if they had a ringside seat in the Oval Office" (Franklin 2000, 294). *Brill's Content* magazine also celebrated the voyeurism of watching what we are not supposed to see, calling *The West Wing* "not your average White House, perhaps—but then, how would we know?" (Miller 2000, 89).

The West Wing teleplay writers enable viewers to eavesdrop on the Oval Office, witnessing a myriad of contemporary social issues and dramatic complications faced by elite policy workers on the job. For example, plots involve love-hate relationships between the White House staff and press corps, partisan backbiting, and personal sacrifices for public service, as well as issues like substance abuse, interracial dating, and gender issues in the workplace. Through it all, White House staffers are portrayed as witty, sarcastic, and intelligent, yet frail, vulnerable humans who sometimes ride their bike into a tree while on vacation, humbly pray to God for guidance, argue with their ex-wives, work at being involved with their children in spite of hectic schedules, suffer from debilitating diseases, are jealous of their spouse's former lover, and solve crossword puzzles over morning coffee.

In addition, *The West Wing* examines many facets of presidential power from vantage points typically roped off from journalists. Historically, the U.S. government has been framed as a powerful congressional system, with a less-powerful president. But as presidents like Theodore Roosevelt enlarged the prestige of the presidency and Woodrow Wilson revived the precedent of appearing before Congress to deliver messages, and since the Bureau of the Budget was established in 1921, presidents have played greater roles in policy making and thus, much power has shifted from Congress to the president (Schudson 1982, 106). Consequently, the public persona of U.S. presidents has taken on near-mystical qualities. Some political theorists have attributed voter apathy to an ever-widening gap between average Americans who feel marginalized by a president who is out of touch with average people. *The West Wing,* however, paints the picture of a U.S. president who is quite human and approachable.

This dramatic television program and its spotlight on the White House's exposed seams sells. High-profile advertisers are attracted, hundreds of internet websites and online chats are devoted to *The West Wing,* and popular U.S. news magazines repeatedly showcase how the show is put together. The fictional, liberal Democratic president Josiah Bartlet, who moves through *The West Wing* as a functional, living archive of American political discourse, frequently is compared to a real president. *Newsweek* characterized President Bartlet as "folksy" (Chang 1999, 81) and the *Progressive* called him a "bimbo-less Bill Clinton" (McKissack 2000, 39). Indeed, *The West Wing* television president is represented as an outsider operating on the inside. He is an elite intellectual, well-educated Nobel laureate in economics, self-professed "leader of the free world" with the code name POTUS, who unashamedly entered a room booming, "I am the Lord, your God" during the "Pilot" episode. Yet, he is portrayed as accessible to staffers who shyly invade his privacy in the residence for an after-hours meeting as in the "Mandatory Minimums" teleplay. Furthermore, Bartlet is likeable and humble whilst Christmas shopping with staffers but refuses to allow the event to turn into a media photo-op in the episode "In Excelsis Deo." *Brill's Content* magazine suggested that President Bill Clinton spoke to forty million people only one night each year during the State of the Union broadcast, while Sorkin's President Bartlet on *The West Wing* speaks to thirteen million people every Wednesday at 9 P.M. "It's a prerogative the president can only envy" (Miller 2000, 88).

Other seams that routinely show in *The West Wing* are the power of the news media to alter public opinion and the central role of polls, statistics, and job approval ratings. Consequently, the White House staff attempts to manipulate the media as the Washington press corps wields its power to gather news. Nearly every episode features press secretary C. J. Cregg balancing her love interest with a journalist against her duty as White House public relations liaison, as well as carefully positioning issues for daily press briefings. Several episodes offer viewers a rare introspective on news production. For example, "Take Out the Trash Day" is about managing the media by issuing multiple bad news items on the same day to avoid negative news coverage over a long period of time. The "Let Bartlet Be Bartlet" episode defines news and illustrates damage control and bargaining with the news media in order to cover embarrassing issues. Similarly, viewers learn about controlling a news cycle in "The White House Pro-Am." And in another episode ("The Short List," Nov. 24, 1999), Bartlet defends his Supreme Court justice nominee to a retiring justice, complaining, that he has to contend with "an opposition Congress, special interests with power beyond belief, and a bitchy media." Overall, *The West Wing* press secretary consistently struggles with balancing openness and fairness with the media against protecting her boss from negative media treatment.

Finally, the traditionally obscure seams of White House crisis management sessions involving national security issues frequently are featured in *The West Wing* plots. Of course, such situation room meetings are routinely closed to the media, and consequently, the American public. Even though many may appreciate behind-the-scenes glimpses into an India-Pakistan border crises fueled by nuclear arsenal control, as in the episode "He Shall, From Time to Time," not all viewers have applauded the all-too-realistic view. For example, the American-Arab Anti-Discrimination Committee (ADC) cried slander after the October 6, 1999, episode "A Proportional Response," which featured a vengeful President Bartlet who wanted to bomb Syria after a fully passengered American jet was downed in the Middle East. The ADC representative said the fictional story blamed "a real nation and people in the most unfair manner possible" (Berger 2000, 61). Ironically, the pilot episode, which originally aired on September 22, 1999, featured a difficult decision that had to be made regarding what to do about Cuban refugees approaching the Florida coast on rafts. Even though the episode aired before Cuban refugee Elian Gonzales floated into Florida waters on an inner tube in November 1999, it may have affected viewers' response to Elian's story at the time of his arrival and again during reruns the following summer.

This drama series exposes the framework, or the seams, of the executive branch of federal government in an informative way that cannot be accomplished through journalism alone. Consequently, viewers also learn much about the news production process.

Blurred Lines Between Fact and Fiction

Television producers try to make drama appear real because it is in their economic interest to do so, and writers differentiate drama from documentary forms even though the lines sometimes are blurred. It is not difficult, however, to see how audiences might have difficulty finding the lines separating fact from fiction as represented on *The West Wing*. In fact, the *New Yorker* reported, "they make you feel as if the characters they're playing here actually existed before the show" (Franklin 2000, 290). Indeed, most of the actors on the show are instantly recognizable for roles they have played in other television dramas and Hollywood films. Some popular magazines, such as *Time* and *People Weekly*, have noted that of course *The West Wing* is not real, but the narratives it shares *are* based on real issues and events. Furthermore, debates are left fundamentally unresolved, giving audiences a sense of debates in progress. Such attempts to mirror the real underscore this essay's premise that *The West Wing*'s narratives can complement news by offering reasonable—if fictional—*why* and *how* elements that reporters' nonfiction stories often ignore.

Several members of the media have pondered the realness of *The West Wing*. *TV Guide* magazine seriously compared *The West Wing* to reality and criticized its minor inaccuracies, but concluded, "You don't watch a network drama the way you watch the History Channel. You watch to be engaged and entertained" (Tarloff 1999, 6). Some news media, however, have applauded the television drama for more closely matching Americans' ideal expectations for national government than what currently exists. For example, *Sojourners* reported, "If this is not how the White House actually is, it's how it should be . . . It might even seduce America back into believing government can be good" (Berger 2000, 61). A columnist for the *New Yorker* agreed, "if this isn't what the White House is like, it's what it *should* be like" (Franklin 2000, 290).

The West Wing creator Aaron Sorkin and his team create an aura of reality by weaving current events into plots and offering enlightening descriptions and explanations for complex issues that are difficult for journalists to address due to space and time constrictions. One popular magazine applauded *The West Wing* for conveying "the complexities of politics and decision-making in the real world where few things are black and white" (Berger 2000, 61). Several episodes have highlighted complex debates, such as use of statistical sampling to improve the U.S. census, shepherding legislation through Congress, environmental issues, domestic terrorism, hate crime and gun control legislation, gays in the military, school vouchers, drug abuse, labor disputes, anti-Semitism, Christian fundamentalism, living with physical handicaps, and "driving while Hispanic."

Interest groups also encourage television writers to offer viewers a fuller version of reality. For example, diversity in Hollywood was one complex social issue that was made very real for Sorkin. The NAACP charged that *The West Wing* and many other television programs of the 1999–2000 season lacked diversity. A *TV Guide* magazine columnist reasoned that the real White House was more diverse than *The West Wing* ("A Question of Color," Jan. 22–28, 2000, 52). Sorkin apologized in *Newsweek*, saying, "I genuinely appreciate the tap on the shoulder from the NAACP, and they're quite right in being upset" (Chang 1999, 81). Subsequently, changes were made mid-season and more African American actors appear on *The West Wing*, including Dulé Hill as Charlie, President Bartlet's personal aide. Such modifications underscore the attempts of *The West Wing* writers to offer viewers a real (albeit mediated) experience. Thus, viewers, television critics, interest groups, and the news media itself encourage *The West Wing*'s creative team to continue blurring the lines separating fact and fiction. Such a conclusion strengthens this essay's contention that popular culture complements journalism.

Deconstructing journalism is an exercise that John Fiske characterized as encouraging readers to "treat news texts with the same freedom and irreverence that they do fictional ones" (1987, 308). This essay has suggested that journalism routinely marginalizes audiences by subscribing to Procrustean conventions and practices that leave little room for details that audiences may need in order to fully comprehend political issues. Thus, the popular culture forms of news and a television drama series can be complementary, together offering audiences more complete stories about politics. By showing viewers the types of dealings that go on behind the Oval Office's doors, which typically are closed to the Washington press corps, *The West Wing* fills gaps in stories that reporters are prevented from reporting and offers *why* and *how* details that journalists are not likely to cover.

Others have argued that Americans generally feel alienated from participating in democracy because of a widening economic gap between elites and average people. Presidents and their families are political embodiments of the moral and material American Dream myths, and "the media's glimpses into how they live either confirms or denies that they are living up to that trust" (Combs 1984, 100). Thus, enabling the spheres of fact and fiction to overlap, *The West Wing* offers audiences a means for democratic engagement that journalism alone cannot.

2 | The White House Culture of Gender and Race in *The West Wing*

Insights from the Margins

CHRISTINA LANE

Following the tradition of "quality programs" such as *NYPD Blue* and *ER,* Warner Bros.' *The West Wing* dramatizes the moral ambiguity and complex, layered relationships between the private and public spheres. Drawing on numerous "quality" conventions and styles, the NBC program employs ensemble casting, mobile camerawork, densely packed visual fields, hot splashes of light, accelerated pace, and narrative velocity in order to dramatize the complex questions it asks (Coe 1991; Nehamas 1990; Feuer et al. 1984; Gitlin 1983). *The West Wing* launches a number of contradictory positions while maintaining, through three-dimensional characterization and mastery of dialogue, a moral center that subtly and precariously stands up to repeated challenges.

The iconic setting of the White House—and the distinct personality of President Bill Clinton's indication of what a presidency might be—lent themselves well to such a genre and informed *The West Wing*'s conventions as they evolved during the first two seasons. As a former Clinton deputy assistant put it, the variety and range of conflicts a president has to deal with is "mind-numbing," and the commitment to deep examination and intelligent debate demonstrated by Clinton on a daily basis was astonishing (Reeves 2000, 132). *The West Wing* is compelling for the nuanced way it sifts through such "mind-numbing" and morally ambiguous details to find an ethical center, a center that is remarkably refreshing without catering to simplistic notions of right and wrong, hero and villain, guilt and blamelessness. The series pilot established these stakes when Communications Director Toby Ziegler (Richard Schiff) declared in an open staff meeting, "I agree with Josh and I agree with Sam and I agree with C. J. and you know how that makes me crazy." It is the program's ability to value so many sides of an argument—and the concession to the insane yet necessary nature of this decision-making mode—that pushes the ideological envelope.

The West Wing takes not merely as its end point, but rather as its *point of departure,* a progressive, multifaceted, highly politicized understanding of gender and racial relations. The series demonstrates such an understanding by granting narrative authority to its secretarial (or "assistant") characters, all of whom are female or African American, and by suggesting that a commitment to feminism drives those white, male characters who currently hold positions of power. An entire essay could be devoted to the assertive characterization of press secretary C. J. Cregg (Allison Janney), for example, or to the feminist interventions of the first lady, Dr. Abigail Bartlet (Stockard Channing); this essay shall focus, however, on the presentation of what might be peripheral characters in another television context. *The West Wing* endows these characters with deeply charged moments that traverse power, privilege, and social categories of identity by rejecting hierarchical relationships between high-level officials and low-level assistants.

This attention to marginalized social positions occurs in an opening sequence of the first-season episode "Let Bartlet Be Bartlet." Elation strikes the president (Martin Sheen) as he realizes that several openings on the Campaign Finance Reform Committee might enable him to make some radical nominations. As a cadre of staffers surrounds him in an effort to guide him away from his idealist instincts, the camera comes to a distinct pause and moves into a shot/reverse shot structure between Bartlet and chief of staff Leo McGarry (John Spencer). Bartlet's eyes sparkle with glee as Leo unsuccessfully tries to douse the fire. The editing structure continues as Josh (Bradley Whitford) makes his attempt to dissuade the president. What is important about this scene is that the frame, both in shot and reverse shot, extends beyond the two debaters. Next to Josh, taking up an entire half of the shot, stands C. J., watching the conversation with intense interest. And on the reverse, next to Bartlet, stands Charlie Young, his African American personal assistant (Dulé Hill), who occupies just as much space as C. J. and looks on with just as much interest. Their presence, which is connected through graphic matches that position both C. J. and Charlie in the same place in the frame, could be described best not as background nor peripheral but in fact essential reaction shots to the conversation. They serve as a crucial reminder of the disenfranchised groups who are ultimately affected in an issue such as campaign finance—those who have less political or economic power to influence the selection of their leaders. Through mise-en-scène and editing, then, Bartlet's primary objective assumes political urgency.

Knowledge and Insights from the Margins

One of the predominant strategies of *The West Wing* is to place moral authority into specific character sites that would normally occupy the background in the halls of power. Charlie and, even more frequently, Donna, Josh's secretary (Janel Maloney), often see events and issues in ways the main characters do not, and they are afforded the opportunity to impart that alternative insight to white male characters. In fact, all of the professional pairings on the program (Josh/Donna, Bartlet/Charlie, Bartlet/Mrs. Landingham, Sam/Bonnie) culminate into significant moments when the conventional power structure flip-flops. Two examples illuminate this point: a sequence in which Donna holds the upper hand in "Let Bartlet Be Bartlet," and a scene from the second-season episode "The Midterms," which takes great care to highlight Charlie's point of view.

Scenes between Josh and Donna (Janel Maloney) during "Let Bartlet Be Bartlet" reinforce the secretary as intuitive and confident: she provides a voice of reason in the midst of chaos. These scenes begin with Josh entering the building from one of his meetings on the campaign finance reform issue to find Donna awaiting his arrival; she is poised and calm as other staffers race by her in a flurry of activity. A bit entertained by this, Josh asks, "Donna, how do you know to be standing there?" After replying, she proceeds to provide him with a requested memo outlining the debate on English as the country's official national language. As the scene plays out, he wrongly mistakes her thoroughness for incompetence and she lays into him as though she were *his* superior. He deserves her tongue-lashing, a common occurrence in their working relationship because of the combined professional and sexual tensions between them. The scene ends as she confides in him that office morale is suffering, suggesting that he mobilize staff confidence in the administration. Josh disparages her suggestion. Their following scene, two minutes later, however, brings Josh around to agreement with Donna's concern.

These scenes, and many more like them, endow Donna with an internal "intuition" about political issues and people of importance to *The West Wing*: she "knows" when and where Josh will arrive from his meeting; she "knows" where to go for the strongest rhetorical argument on a hotly contested issue; and she "knows" when interoffice politics are causing the work to suffer. As in this example, the camera work and lighting imply a deep televisual frame filled with ambiguity and confusion. But they suggest that Donna provides a searchlight through the confusion, by associating her with that depth and presenting her as a focal point in a mise-en-scène heavily populated and bustling. This example carries even more weight given that she has been introduced as a character who still needs to find herself. Her successes and her growing importance not just to the staff but also to the audience occur with great impact, with actress Janel Maloney having been added to the opening montage in the second season. This resonance is heightened in the second season's premiere, which relays her back story and presents Donna and Josh's first meeting through flashbacks. (She reveals that she is using the job to rebound from an exploitative romantic relationship.) Her growth comes across further when one compares her appearance in those flashbacks, as well as the Donna/Josh scene in "Let Bartlet Be Bartlet," with the later "Midterms" episode. In "The Midterms," Donna moves hastily through various regions of the office conversing with Toby as the camera arcs around her with mobility and freedom. Whereas previously she was usually the character most associated with stasis and solitude when she was not being pulled "in tow" by one of her higher-ranking employers, now she moves around with agency. The program's narratives suggest that she anchors the office's sense of moral duty, and its visuals increasingly supply her with the power to share her knowledge throughout the office complex.

It is in this "Midterms" episode that Charlie takes on a role as a moral center. Still reeling from the information that the shots fired at President

Bartlet were meant for him because of his interracial romance with Zoey (Elizabeth Moss), he experiences doubt as to whether he should remain at the White House. As the program draws to a close, Charlie finds himself in a room with an African American computer repairman and the repairman's young son. In a moment of reflection, he expresses his uncertainty about his job and confides that the assassination attempt has brought up his unresolved grief over his mother's death. The repairman remarks, "Charlie, you know what I think she would say if she was here right now? The same thing my father would say . . . if they're shootin' at you, then you know you're doing somethin' right." His words shift attention from the conservative priority of presidential protection to a more progressive perspective of long-range social progress.

Throughout the scene, Charlie maintains a clear connection with the boy, his attempts to keep eye contact heightened by the shot/reverse shot structure that proceeds from medium shot to close-up. These visual techniques foreground the fact that his choices carry ramifications that extend into the African American community—to include the future, a time by which this boy will grow to be Charlie's age. The lightning flashes produced by a passing thunderstorm intensify the melodrama, creating a moment of affect that underscores the recurring theme that a personal code of duty should serve larger political and collective goals. The scene bestows on these African American characters a brand of moral insight that is similar to Donna's; it also illustrates the way in which *The West Wing* looks for opportunities to connect local to global, personal self-involvement to long-range sociopolitical change, narrative complexity to moral consequence, and fictional policy to real-life ramifications.

Choosing "These Women"

This particular rhetorical strategy of privileging characters at the margins of power frequently drives *The West Wing*'s narrative, visual, and thematic structure. However, as many critics have pointed out, the series also relies on images of a white patriarch—our speech-making, risk-taking, bible-quoting Josiah Bartlet, who maintains ultimate authority over the vast array of "mind-numbing" moral, ethical, and political dilemmas that besiege any

Presidency. Admittedly, a strong tension exists between the series' centralization of feminist and racial concerns and its valorization of Bartlet's wisdom and power. With the number of scenes that crystallize into "frozen moments" of Bartlet's wide-sweeping analyses, the series needs to be seen in terms of its ideological multiplicity (see White 1992). One extended sequence at the end of the first-season episode "The Crackpots and These Women" illustrates these ideological tensions. Josh has spent the episode unhappily coming to terms with the realization that the National Security Council (NSC) has issued him a card that ushers him into safety with the president in the event of a nuclear attack on the nation's capital. He enters an end-of-the-day "chili party" in Bartlet's private residence still troubled by the idea of leaving his West Wing colleagues behind at ground zero. He approaches Bartlet and Leo and asks what they are talking about. Bartlet replies, "These women." The camera proceeds to weave around the room, focusing first on C. J., next on Mandy (Moira Kelly), and then Mrs. Landingham (Kathryn Joosten). Bartlet comments,

"Look at C. J. She's like a fifties movie star, so capable, so loving, and energetic."

LEO. "Look at Mandy over there. Going punch for punch with Toby in a world that tells women to sit down and shut up. Mandy's already won her battle with the President. The game's over but she's not done. She wants Toby!"

BARTLET. "And Mrs. Landingham. Did you guys know that she lost two sons in Vietnam? What would make her want to serve her country is beyond me but she hasn't missed a day's work, not one. . . . There's Cathy, Donna, Margaret."

Bartlet and Leo's spontaneous female fest pushes Josh to surrender his card. He declares, "I want to be a comfort to my friends in tragedy. I want to be able to celebrate with them in triumph. And for all the times in between, I just wanna be able to look them in the eye. Leo, it's not for me. I want to be with my friends, my family . . . and these women."

Is this scene an obvious ploy to engage audience emotion by providing back story and emotional commentary on "these women?" Is it a typical dramatic move to highlight the deep ties that bind this ensemble cast? Is it an attempt to amplify the show's themes of loyalty, duty, and perseverance? Is it governed by a series of traditional male gazes that linger on white male fantasies about women? Yes, of course it mobilizes all of these strategies; this scene, however, goes beyond them as well. In an environment where the antiquated phrase "women and children first" does not even apply because of the supreme importance of the president, Josh has made the unlikely decision to stick with the women—the women who would go last—through good tidings and turmoil, no matter what the cost. Josh is willing to potentially effeminate himself and to remain in a nonmale, nonauthoritarian, nondominant domain for the sake of friends and emotional nurture (which are feminized traditionally). His decision, and the feminist context in which it is reached, suggest that *The West Wing* makes efforts to revise traditional power relations and reorient its male characters toward a valuation of female resilience and community.

Indeed, the series continually articulates the philosophy that its male characters can redefine their personal relation to patriarchal structures in ways that might advance the causes of feminists, people of color, and the working classes. Josh's decision to align himself with the female characters offers one example of this self-repositioning. The final episode of the second season provides yet an even more poignant reinforcement of male feminist values. In this season finale ("Two Cathedrals"), Bartlet comes to terms with the death of his long-time secretary, Mrs. Landingham, as he decides whether to run for re-election. Through a number of flashbacks to Bartlet's initial interactions with Mrs. Landingham, when she worked as a secretary at his father's boarding school, the program directly connects *him* to the very marginalized, knowledgeable position of the secretary whom the program has come to value in the context of White House power relations.

In these flashbacks Mrs. Landingham convinces a teenaged Bartlet to fight for equal pay among the male and female employees at the school. In chatty banter that significantly mimics the contemporary dialogue between Josh and Donna, the secretary presents him with telling statistics about salary disparities, eventually winning him over to her cause. Suggesting that Bartlet has tapped into the same superior moral knowledge that she, as a female secretary, subscribes to, she declares, "You know I'm right. You know

I'm right. You've known it since I brought it up. You've known it since before that." He tries to detach himself from such knowledge by arguing, "I'm not a woman and I don't work here." In accordance with *The West Wing* typical ideological stance, however, he learns that he can identify with her on feminist terms no matter what prejudices he may have inherited.

In his attempt to advocate the women's cause, sixteen-year-old Bartlet goes to his father, a domineering man, an ultimate patriarch in this episode and several others. After suffering a blow from the father, Bartlet retreats, never summoning up the will to raise the pay equity issue and many other issues that have apparently arisen between the flashbacks and the present day. The fact that there is work left to do, and most specifically the work "on behalf of Mrs. Landingham," provides part of the complex motivation that drives the President to run for his second term.

These motivations, and the way they play out through the finale's storyline, are important for several reasons. For the first time, the series makes clear that Mrs. Landingham has helped mold Bartlet into the leader he is today, that it is his own alignment with the women of the world, and specifically the secretaries of the world, that propels him to conduct the work of the presidency. Her influence continues to make itself known in the feminist actions Bartlet takes in the White House. Furthermore, his interactions with his father indicate that Bartlet's own relationship to male power is ambivalent, an issue that will re-emerge through psychiatric sessions as the third season unfolds. Therefore, in this episode, a supposedly marginal secretarial role takes center stage, literally in fact, as the camera continually accentuates the space around the deceased Mrs. Landingham's desk and suggests that, even in her physical absence, she inspires him morally and spiritually.

Mrs. Landingham takes on the role of moral voice, one similar to the present-day character of Donna, when she defines her criteria for approving (or disapproving) Bartlet's political stance. For example, as the two characters discuss pay equity in one of the flashbacks, she remarks, "If you think we're wrong, then I respect that. But if you think we're right . . . and you won't speak up because you can't be bothered, then God, Jed, I don't even want to know you." *The West Wing* reiterates her privileged role as arbiter of knowledge when she visits him in "ghost form" after her death. ("You know, if you don't want to run again, I respect that. But if you don't want to run again because you think it's going to be too hard, or because you're going to lose, well, God, Jed, I don't even want to know you.") Therefore, when Bartlet stands in front of the press corps on the verge of announcing his decision to enter the presidential race, he is expressing his alignment with Mrs. Landingham's ethical viewpoint. *The West Wing* subverts dominant televisual conventions that relegate women to the realm of the unknown, and the unseen, positioning the president instead as a figure who must prove that he is worthy of being "known" by his secretary and "seen" by her ethereal, otherworldly presence.

The powerful montage that leads up to Bartlet's announcement that he will run is important not only because it is prefaced by Mrs. Landingham's visit, but also because it includes the presence of an African American janitor sweeping the National Cathedral floor after the secretary's funeral. As Bartlet makes his journey to the press conference in his limousine, the janitor finds a discarded cigarette butt among the rubbish on the church floor. Just as the president's motorcade passes by the cathedral, the working man makes the realization that this cigarette was cast by an indignant Bartlet, a connection that resonates as Bartlet makes his final decision to run again on behalf of the underrepresented working classes. Just as the series privileges its female and African American characters on a weekly basis, *The West Wing* suggests that its president has a great deal of work to do for the sake of bringing their power and moral authority to a place that is valued and embraced. It is in these moments that the series honors the histories of the second-wave feminist movements (with their struggles against male violence, sexual harassment, and pay inequity) and civil rights movements (with their commitment to equitable race relations and economic liberation for people of color). It insists on making those histories visible rather than subjugating them into the background of the primary (white, male) characters' lives.

Especially given *The West Wing*'s strong linkages between personal and political spheres, the series acknowledges the importance of 1960s social movements and insists that those movements now go further. Consider the following anecdote about a 2000 interruption of the cast and crew's night shoot in Georgetown. They were making a lot of commotion, and "a middle-aged lady came down to inquire about the noise. 'And by the way,' she said, 'why the heck doesn't the show have a secretary of state? And it should be a woman,' she added. The woman with the complaint was Secretary of State Madeline Albright" (see chap. 12, 212).

Because of the highly politicized nature of the program's binding of real-life conflicts to narrative ideologies, Albright's suggestion is not likely to lose its power and slip into a trivialized state of popular culture anecdote. Her positions as a (now former) political leader and feminist fan coincide in an insistence that *The West Wing* function as more than just a TV show and that her job function as more than just a "positive image" for women. Though the ideological direction of a prime-time drama is never predictable as it develops over its five-to-ten-year life span, this anecdote and this series' first two seasons reverently engage the second-wave feminist movement in its past, present, and future and ask in Bartletesque fashion, What's next?

3 | *The West Wing* (NBC) and the West Wing (D.C.)

Myth and Reality in Television's Portrayal of the White House

MYRON A. LEVINE

How realistic is the portrait of the White House painted by *The West Wing*? The Emmy Award-winning series draws much of its strength from its supposed verisimilitude. Although fictionalized, the setting and atmosphere of *The West Wing* are clearly meant to resemble the White House, especially the Clinton White House (although the major characters in the TV series are not explicitly modeled on members of the Clinton administration).

Much about the series, and the public reaction to it, has served to blur the boundaries between TV fiction and Washington reality. Creator and writer Aaron Sorkin has drawn on the talents of a number of former White House insiders, including Clinton press secretary Dee Dee Myers, Reagan press secretary Marlin Fitzwater, Reagan and Bush speechwriter Peggy Noonan, Carter pollster Pat Caddell, and Democratic political consultant Lawrence O'Donnell, for story elements and for the details that add to a realistic portrayal of the inner workings of the White House. After the 2000 election, cast members were invited to meet top officials in the George W. Bush administration. Martin Sheen, who plays the fictional president, Josiah "Jed" Bartlet, spurned the invitation. During the campaign, he had prepared commercials for the Democrats; Sheen had also dined with former president Bill Clinton. Later, in the immediate wake of the September 11, 2001, deadly attacks on the World Trade Center and the Pentagon, Sorkin prepared and aired a special *West Wing* episode ("Isaac and Ishmael") devoted to the issues of terrorism and racial profiling. In January 2002, NBC also positioned its special wartime documentary portrait of "The Bush White House: The Real West Wing" as a lead-in to a Wednesday evening *West Wing* broadcast.

But how realistic is *The West Wing*? In fact, much of *The West Wing*'s portrait is accurate and provides a much-needed counter to the anti-Washington stereotyping and presidency-bashing that is so much a part of pre-9/11 American political culture. Yet, *The West Wing* curiously omits common critical comments on White House staff operations and politics that are the subject of a good deal of both the popular and the political science literature.

An Idealized White House

The West Wing is first and foremost a television series that is designed to entertain, and not every element in each week's story line is meant to give an exactly accurate portrayal of Washington. As befits good television, each episode tells a story with a certain amount of melodrama; each also ends on an emotionally grabbing, oftentimes uplifting or cathartic, note. Consequently, Lesley Smith (2000) observes that the "show shifts from the logic of politics . . . to a logic of romanticism." *New York Times* television critic Caryn James (1999) likewise argues that *The West Wing* suffers from a "split personality"; the show's realism and sardonic insights are undercut by the "mawkishness," "emotional mushiness," and "inspirational uplift" of scenes designed to play to the viewing audience.

Still, whatever its shortcomings, *The West Wing* succeeds much as it was intended; it is enjoyable, interesting television that presents a highly positive and idealized view of public service and liberal presidential politics. Of the characters in his show, Sorkin freely admits:

> Yeah. They're fairly heroic. That's unusual in American popular culture, by and large. Our leaders, government people are portrayed either as dolts or as Machiavellian somehow. The characters in this show are neither. They are flawed, to be sure, because you need characters in drama to have flaws. But they, all of them, have set aside probably more lucrative lives for public

service. They are dedicated not just to this president, but to doing good, rather than doing well. The show is kind of a valentine to public service. (Sorkin 2000)

The series humanizes presidential aides, presenting staff members as persons with strong personal feelings, excellent work habits, immense loyalty, and high guiding values.

The series principle characters work for Democratic President Jed Bartlet, a man of courage and a commitment to strong liberal principles (who nonetheless will kneel in prayer). At times, Bartlet can temper his strong convictions with a healthy sense of political pragmatism. He is a caring father and a Nobel Prize-winning economist, to boot. A true intellect and scholar who quotes both classic philosophers and the Bible, he is in many ways above politics—so much so that in the episode "Noel," he even naïvely demands to personally sign all the White House Christmas cards, only to be informed that they number in the hundreds of thousands. By portraying Bartlet as an antipolitician, Sorkin has used the viewing audience's prevailing anti-Washingtonianism to paint a positive portrait of a liberal presidency. It is a vision of "executive liberalism" that is "at once principled and pragmatic" (see chap. 13, 215).

Bartlet's clear and consistent declarations of policy liberalism differentiate him from Bill Clinton, the president who, faced with Republican midterm congressional victories, forsook the initial liberal activist direction of his administration for more a limited set of "New Democratic" program initiatives. Chris Lehmann argues that *The West Wing* presents a "high-minded conscience-haunted upgrade of the Clinton White House" (chap. 13, 214), a "version of Clintonism with both moral gravitas and political backbone" (94). Conservative columnist John Podhoretz objects that *The West Wing* is nothing more than "liberal fantasy": "Human beings? These characters aren't human beings—they're noble soldiers in a noble cause, and they have been washed clean of every impurity because of it" (chap. 14, 223). *The West Wing* overstates and glamorizes the "adrenaline rush" or the charged atmosphere and sense of urgency experienced by cause-oriented White House staffers. Matthew Miller (2000) similarly scores that the White House, as presented in *The West Wing*, "feels overpopulated and overcaffeinated." This may make for emotive television, but fails to convey the true nature of what it means to work for the White House; it fails to show staffers "on the telephone or in tedious meetings—which is how real White House aides spend their days and nights" (chap. 14, 223). Yet as one former member of Clinton's White House press office observes, "believe it or not, working in the Clinton West Wing was more intense and all-consuming than *The West Wing* portrays" (Orszag 2001).

The West Wing also overstates the degree of camaraderie that characterizes White House staff relationships. Despite a shared sense of mission and loyalty to the president, there are conflicts among White House staffers that result from personal ambition, competition, and conflicting policy perspectives. Clinton staffer Paul Begala recalled the atmosphere of the Clinton White House to be very different from—and much less satisfactory than—that of the Clinton presidential campaign, as journalist Jeffrey Birnbaum reports in reviewing Begala's transition to the White House: "[I]n the White House, the work [compared to the campaign] was just as arduous if not more so, yet the familial feeling was gone. One reason was the sheer number of people. The White House is a much more impersonal place. Another reason was raw ambition. . . . Begala was not seized by any such personal drive, but he soon suspected that others around him were" (Birnbaum 1996, 212). Ambition and staff politics are recurrent features of White House life that, curiously, have little place in the stories of *The West Wing*.

If White House staff life is romanticized in *The West Wing* so is the character of President Jed Bartlet. Caryn James (1999) is particularly scornful of the rousing liberal speeches delivered by Bartlet, who is played by Martin Sheen "with such windbag bluster it's a wonder he ever got a vote." According to James, Bartlet is "a deus ex president arriving from fantasyland." The scripts even call for Bartlet to espouse liberal courses of action that no real-world president would dare undertake. For instance, in episode "Let Bartlet Be Bartlet," the president seeks to appoint genuine reformers to the Federal Election Commission (FEC), persons who will aggressively enforce campaign finance laws. The real world, however, is quite different; when it comes to the FEC, "expertise and political cronyism often vie as criteria for appointment" and appointments are "strongly influenced by the appointees' political connections and leanings" (Alexander 1992, 44). As the Federal

Election Campaign Act virtually mandates a three Democratic-three Republican balance among the commission's voting members, no president can afford the luxury of naming an commissioner from his own party whose independence would undermine the precarious political balance on the commission and hurt the party's fundraising efforts in the midst of a vital election contest.

Another example of Bartlet's outspoken liberal preaching is provided by the episode "Twenty Hours in L.A.," where Bartlet lectures a group of gray-haired men (and women) who have come to express their support for an anti-flag desecration constitutional amendment. These members of America's "greatest generation" talk about the importance of the American flag, what it represents, and of all the millions of Americans who carried it into battle. At first, the president listens and politely applauds; but quite soon, as an aide relates, he has that "look" on his face, as if he is thinking of a number of ways to kill himself. Bartlet can restrain himself no longer and even resorts to sarcasm in challenging what he sees to be the mistaken convictions of the assembled citizens: "This is a debate that is obviously going to continue in town halls, city halls, state legislatures, and the U.S. House of Representatives. There is a population in this country that seems to focus so much time and energy into this conversation, so much so that I am forced to ask this question—Is there an epidemic of flag burning going on that I'm not aware of?" As Bartlet walks to his limo, he continues to an aide, "I mean it, man. Is there an emergency-level outbreak of flag desecration that no one's kept me posted on?" Jed Bartlet is the idealized liberal antipolitician who must speak the truth.

In "The Midterms," at a White House meeting with radio personalities, Bartlet delivers an even more unrealistic broadside, this time to Jenna Jacobs (this episode's stand-in figure for controversial radio talk show host Dr. Laura Schlesinger, who, as a result of her own conservative moral preaching, has had the relevance of her educational credentials challenged by gay rights and other liberal advocacy groups):

JED. Forgive me, Dr. Jacobs. Are you an M.D.?
JENNA. Ph.D.
JED. A Ph.D.?

JENNA. Yes, Sir.

JED. In psychology?

JENNA. No, Sir.

JED. Theology?

JENNA. No.

JED. Social work?

JENNA. I have a Ph.D. in English literature.

JED. I'm asking you, 'cause on your show, people call in for advice and you go by the name of Dr. Jacobs on your show. And I didn't know if maybe your listeners were confused by that, and assumed you had advanced training in psychology, theology, or health care.

JENNA. I don't believe they are confused, no sir.

JED. Good. I like your show, I like how you call homosexuality an abomination.

JENNA. I don't say homosexuality is an abomination, Mr. President. The Bible does.

JED. Yes, it does. Leviticus.

JENNA. 18:22.

The President continues on an emotional rant where he asks Jenna if he can sell his daughter into slavery, put his chief of staff to death for working on the Sabbath ("Exodus 35:2 clearly says he should be put to death"), have the town stone his brother for planting different crops side by side, and burn his mother for wearing garments made from two different threads; he also asks if the Washington Redskins can play football as "touching the skin of a pig makes us unclean, Leviticus 11:7."

JED. Think about these questions, would you? One last thing, while you may be mistaking this for your monthly meeting of the Ignorant Tightass Club, in this building, when the President stands, nobody sits.

Jenna squirms in her seat and, under Jed Bartlet's persistent glare, finally rises.

This is pure Hollywood fantasyland. No real-life president would be so self-indulgent as to launch such a tirade and dress down a White House guest at a social event. A president can seldom afford to antagonize people, precipitate conflict, and polarize situations, even on matters of principle; a president may even feel the need for manners.

A Truthful Picture

The West Wing presents a glorified and overly noble version of the life and work of the White House staff and especially of the president. Yet, despite its excesses, this positive portrayal of White House life is largely deserved. By pointing to the human qualities, the hard-working dedication, and the ideological commitment of White House staff, *The West Wing* provides an important corrective to anti-Washington popular and journalistic assessments that see Washington officials as only interested in power and advancement.

The West Wing is also quite accurate in its observations concerning the limitations of presidential power and the difficulties of the presidential job. As the entire staff boards Air Force One to fly to the West Coast in "Twenty Hours in L.A.," Bartlet asks his aides if they "want to see the best part of having my job?" He grabs the intercom on the plane and tells the pilot, "Colonel, this is the president. I'm ready to go." This is one of the few times that he can order something and it actually gets done. As Richard Neustadt explained in his classic *Presidential Power* (1990), a president really possesses very little command power; instead, on important issues, a president must learn how to bargain with and persuade others whose cooperation he needs.

The difficulties of the job drain the president. In "Let Bartlet Be Bartlet," the president bemoans that he would just once "like to end the day feeling as good as I did when the day started." In "Twenty Hours in L.A.," Ted Marcus (played by Bob Balaban), a Hollywood mogul, gay activist, and party fundraiser (he's the host of a fifty-thousand-dollar-per-couple event at his mansion), tells the president to his face that he looks tired. Bartlet responds that he is, in fact, drained. His energies have been sapped by an exhausting day of coast-to-coast travel, by the pressures of the perpetual campaign, and by the need to respond to a never-ending string of political fires, including Marcus's threat to cancel the scheduled fundraiser should Bartlet fail to publicly condemn a congressional proposal seeking to ban gays in the military. The president's staff had been looking forward to the West Coast trip and the fun of a big Hollywood party; but, for the president, the trip offers little joy and relaxation.

The West Wing also deserves credit for portraying the complexity of issues, for showing that there are often competing concerns that allow no easy answer. This was a conscious calculation on Sorkin's part: "You know, one of the things I like about this world, or at least I like about the way we're presenting this world, is these issues are terribly complicated—not nearly as black and white as we're led to believe. There, by and large, aren't good guys and bad guys. You're talking bout very learned people capable of arguing both sides of an issue, and it's that process that I enjoy dramatizing" (Sorkin 2000).

Political calculations, a sense of pragmatism, and conflicting perspectives and principles mean that a president cannot always do the "right thing" as defined and demanded by outside interest groups. Bartlet, like any president, must see things from a larger vantage point. He extends Marcus the extreme courtesy of a personal visit and explains that there is no need to publicly denounce an anti-gays-in-the-military bill that has little chance of gaining congressional passage; Bartlet further notes that high-visibility public action by the president will only serve to mobilize antigay forces. Yet, Marcus is not appeased; he insists that Bartlet make a public declaration anyway, a symbolic gesture to the "people in my house [Hollywood]" who are "complaining that you take their money and run, without listening." When Marcus asks why the president simply will not say the right thing, Bartlet responds with another self-righteous put-down: "Because I know what I'm doing, Ted! Because I live in the world of professional politics, and you live in the world of adolescent tantrum!" Sorkin's idealized liberal president can even stand up to big-money liberal interests.

Despite the care that *The West Wing* takes to assure a discussion of the complexity of issues, Sorkin's liberal policy bias nonetheless shows through. Nowhere was this more apparent than in the special post-9/11 "Isaac and Ishmael" episode. Sitting in the White House cafeteria in the midst of an emergency security lockdown, the show's major characters take turns presenting diverse perspectives on such issues as terrorism, Islamic extremism, and racial profiling (so much so that *USA Today*'s Robert Bianco [2001] called the episode "a crashing and often condescending bore"). Still, despite this laudable effort at balance, the program gives inordinate focus to the question of potential discrimination against Arab Americans. The most dramatic segments of the show focus on chief of staff Leo McGarry (played by John Spencer) as he aggressively and quite improperly interrogates Raqim Ali (Ajay Naidu), an Arab American and low-level White House functionary who was present in the White House at the time of the security break. McGarry is outraged that the president's safety has been compromised; he knows that Ali is guilty. Yet, it is soon revealed that Ali is innocent; his name just happens to be the same as a name that appeared on a list of suspected terrorists. As *Washington Post* media critic Tom Shales scores, by the end of the show McGarry "was essentially apologizing to the kid" (2001a). The implications of "Sorkin's diatribe," according to Shales, "are unsettling—that even in this moment of pain, trauma, heartbreak, destruction, assault and victimization, Hollywood liberals can still find some excuse to make America look guilty."

Polling is another factor that is incorporated into White House strategic calculations—nowhere more so than in the poll-sensitive Clinton White House [1]—and is reflected in the television series. Yet, *The West Wing* also provides a valuable lesson on the use and misuse of polls. In "Twenty Hours in L.A.," director of communications Toby Ziegler (Richard Schiff) and deputy chief of staff Josh Lyman (Bradley Whitford) are given an education as to the intricacies of public opinion polls, especially in the reading of poll numbers that seemingly indicate the presence of strong public opinion but which, under closer scrutiny, prove to be little more than a "nonattitude." [2] Toby and Josh are worried about poll numbers pointing to the popularity of a proposed constitutional amendment to prohibit flag burning, poll numbers that are putting great pressure on the president to moderate his opposition to the measure. The two men meet Josephine "Joey" Lucas (Marlee Matlin), a

1. In *Behind the Oval Office* (1997), Clinton pollster and advisor Richard Morris describes a president almost obsessed with poll results.

2. A "nonattitude" exists when respondents give answers to pollsters' questions seemingly indicating the existence of public opinion, but further probing reveals that those answers do not necessarily indicate the existence of strong, stable, or meaningfully held underlying attitudes. For the classic work on nonattitudes, see Converse, "The Nature of Belief Systems in Mass Publics" (1964).

friendly Democratic political operative who is running a California congressional campaign. She is hearing impaired and speaks with the help of a signer, Kenny. Josh is attracted to her. Josh initiates the discussion of the poll results gathered by Al Kiefer, a Democratic pollster who has been pressuring the president to support a prohibition on flag burning:

> JOSH. I was just telling her about Kiefer's numbers.
>
> KENNY/JOEY. I've seen those numbers. We shared the California polling data.
>
> TOBY. And?
>
> KENNY/JOEY. Kiefer asked the wrong questions. His polls said that 80 percent of the people, when asked if they'd support an amendment prohibiting flag-burning, said yes, which is roughly the same amount of people that say they support sending litterbugs to prison. He never asked them how much they care.
>
> TOBY. Please, please say that you did.
>
> KENNY/JOEY. How good am I looking to you now?
>
> TOBY. That depends on the California numbers.
>
> KENNY/JOEY. Thirty-seven percent, or less than half of those who said they'd favor the amendment, rated the issue fairly or very important. Twelve percent, or less than a third of the group, said that the issue would swing their vote. The only place that this war is being fought is in Washington.
>
> TOBY. You're looking very good to me now.
>
> KENNY/JOEY. I thought so.

As this exchange reveals, the distribution of responses to a poll question (what opinion analysts call the "marginals") tell us very little about issue intensity, or just how much voters actually care about a matter. Despite the marginals that seemingly indicate that voters supported an anti-flag-burning amendment, the matter simply is not a salient or "burning" issue with many voters.

The *The West Wing* episode also shows that while White House strategy sessions often pay great attention to poll data, poll results do not necessarily drive a president's actions. In the case of the anti-flag-burning amendment, it was the philosophy and the principles of President Jed Bartlet, not the poll numbers, that ultimately proved decisive. Polling results do not dictate a president's position on an issues; rather, presidents use polling more as a tool to build public support—to test phrases, to refine rhetoric, to help identify friendly constituencies[3]—for the president's program.

The West Wing also presents a very provocative portrayal of the role of women in government. In *The West Wing*, women are not at the center of power but are marginalized in what appears to be essentially a man's world. As Lesley Smith (2000) has pointed out, while *The West Wing* occasionally "infiltrates" strong women into the president's team, it "quickly undermines their importance while maintaining their air time, reproducing the contemporary political sleight of hand that recognizes the need for visible female participation, but resists accompanying it with permanent power."

This televised representation may be not so much the result of a conscious or even unconscious bias on the part of the scriptwriters but a reflection of Washington reality. The show includes strong female characters such as press secretary C. J. Cregg (Allison Janney), Donna Moss (Josh's very assertive assistant, played by Janel Moloney), and even the Mandy Grunwald-styled political consultant Mandy Hampton (who disappeared when Moira Kelly left the show's cast). Yet, these women essentially occupy supportive, subordinate roles; it is men who dominate decision making in the White House. C. J., the most prominent woman on the president's team, "spins the White House view to the world, but has little role in deciding that view. She plays a mouthpiece, not a policy maker, the voice constantly asking the male team surrounding the President, 'What do I need to know?' " (Smith 2000).

In the Carter years, women's groups were outraged by the fraternity-like behavior of top Jimmy Carter staff members and by the exclusion of White House public liaison Midge Costanza, the top-ranked woman in the admin-

---

3. According to Heith (2000), presidents primarily use polling "to seek support for themselves and their own policy positions" (390), not to dictate the position that a president adopts on an issue. Polling is part of a "going public" strategy of "constituency building," where presidential staff identify the potential audience for a president's programs. Polling also allows a president and his staff to hone and test rhetoric and phrases (392). The Nixon administration, for instance, used its public opinion apparatus to identify just what issues it could use to mobilize the so-called Moral Majority (387). Clinton pollster Patrick Caddell (who would later be a *The West Wing* consultant) similarly employed surveys to find out if there would be a constituency for various elements of the president's energy policy (387–88).

istration and an outspoken advocate of women's issues, from inner White House circles. According to feminist activists, Costanza was treated shabbily in a reorganization effort led by chief of staff Hamilton Jordan. Jordan, who distrusted Costanza's commitment to advocacy, reassigned many of Costanza's public liaison responsibilities to others and had her office moved to the White House basement, after having failed in an attempt to have her exiled further to the Old Executive Office Building (Bachrach 1978; Walsh 1978). Costanza soon resigned.

Two decades later, Clinton press secretary Dee Dee Myers similarly complained of the attitudes of top male staffers in the Clinton administration. Despite her public visibility, when it came to decision making, she "was not in the first tier" (Birnbaum 1996, 171; also see 153–93). As journalist Jeffrey Birnbaum, in voicing Myers's complaint, explained: "The white boys' club would not let her in" (171). She had to push hard to win appointment as press secretary but was never given full authority; throughout her service in the White House, she was forced to share media responsibilities with communications directors George Stephanopoulos and Mark Gearan and with David Gergen, a press office hand from Republican administrations. Myers also complained that she lacked credibility with the press as she was excluded from key decisions made by the White House inner circle.[4] Given Myers's prominence as a consultant to *The West Wing,* it is not surprising that the series reflects her concerns over the status allowed White House women. Myers's critics counter, however, that Myers's own personal failings explain why she was not entrusted greater responsibilities: She did not handle the press as expertly as did other members of the administration. There was also a general unwillingness of top White House decision makers to share sensitive information with a person who would have to stand up daily to a barrage of questions from the press (although such concerns did not lead to Stephanopoulos's exclusion from top councils). Myers also did not enjoy

---

4. Birnbaum (1996) reports that Myers was largely left out of the decision-making loop (164) and was forced to play "second fiddle" (158) to White House communications director George Stephanopoulos. The prominence of National Security Advisor Condoleezza Rice in strategic decision making in the George W. Bush White House certainly must be regarded as an important exception to any generalization regarding the marginalization of women from top White House circles.

a good relationship with chief of staff Leon Panetta (Birnbaum 1996, 171–92).

As the staffing patterns and day-to-day operations of the presidency vary from president to president, it is no simple task to assess the degree to which *The West Wing* faithfully captures the structure and mood of the White House. *The West Wing* captures the sense that White House staffers have important work to do and that they are under siege by outside forces who do not share their president's concerns and interests. Yet, in important ways, the "organization of the White House defies precise generalization, for its form and structure are inevitably a reflection of the style and personality of the person it is serving" (DiClerico 1995, 217). To a great extent, the "way a president organizes his staff depends on *personality, experience,* and *circumstances*" (Cronin and Genovese 1998, 302, emphasis in original). Some presidencies, like that of George W. Bush, are structured hierarchically and run in businesslike fashion; others are organized more informally and work more fluidly, along the lines portrayed in *The West Wing.*

Franklin Delano Roosevelt (1933–1945) encouraged staff competition in order to drive information to the top and maximize presidential control (George and Stern 1998; Neustadt 1990). Disorderly, almost chaotic, the fluidity of his staff operations allowed a number of persons access to the president. Many management experts of the day, however, condemned the president's staffing approach for allowing a wasteful duplication of resources, something that Roosevelt could ill afford given the relatively small size of the presidential staff of that era.

Harry Truman (1945–1953), in contrast to Roosevelt, relied on a more formal approach to staffing, reorganizing reporting lines, for instance, in order to provide for more orderly and balanced participation in foreign policymaking. Dwight Eisenhower (1953–1961), too, largely took a hierarchical approach to staffing, almost standing "above politics," with a formalized chain of command and a stopper at the Oval Office door, chief of staff Sherman Adams. Such an approach reflected his military background and his respect for the chain of command. John Kennedy (1961–1963), in contrast, utilized a more collegial approach that valued the give-and-take among staff members with no clearly established hierarchy. There was no chief of staff standing between Kennedy and key advisors.

Under Richard Nixon (1969–1974), there was a return to hierarchical order, with chief of staff Bob Haldeman and domestic policy advisor John Ehrlichman comprising a "Berlin Wall" that other advisors seeking the president's ear found difficult to cross. During Ronald Reagan's second term, chief of staff Donald Regan enjoyed similar power. Under George Herbert Walker Bush (1989–1993), chief of staff John Sununu and Office of Management and Budget director Richard Darman dominated domestic policy.[5]

The style of a White House can even change during a presidency. When Jimmy Carter (1977–1981) assumed office, he purposely sought to avoid the isolation that had helped to produce Watergate; as a result, Carter allowed numerous officials direct access to the Oval Office. Like Kennedy, he saw himself at the center of a wheel with spokes connected to many advisors; there would be no stopper at the Oval Office door. But the result was confusion in assignments and an overload of the president with minor questions that could have properly been answered by others. By the end of his administration, Carter found that he had little choice than to formally designate Hamilton Jordan as chief of staff in order to impose more order on White House operations.[6] A similar change in White House management style occurred during the Ronald Reagan years (1981–89). The early Reagan White House lacked a strict hierarchy; instead responsibility was spread among a troika of top presidential assistants—James Baker, Edwin Meese, and Michael Deaver. During Reagan's second term, however, staff operations were considerably different as power was effectively lodged in the hands of a new chief of staff, Donald Regan (DiClerico 1995, 220; Neustadt 1990, 312).

Of course, *The West Wing* cannot represent all presidencies equally. Developed during the Clinton years, the series reflects the ambience and style of the Clinton White House (1993–2001), not the more structured, hierarchical, and businesslike manner of the Nixon, Reagan, and Bush presidencies.

---

5. For an overview of the different management styles of the presidents, see: Neustadt (1990, 131–35, 144–45 and 221–22); George and Stern (1998, 204–12); and Burke (2000, 417–42, especially 428–32).

6. The story of the confused state of the Carter White House is related by a member of his speechwriting staff, James Fallows (1979, 33–48).

The West Wing: What Is Missing?

What are the most important elements of White House operations, recurrent in the modern presidency, that are missing from Sorkin's sunny portrayal of the presidency? The political science literature points to the importance of internal White House politics: staff competition, conflict, factionalism, confusion, and the accompanying dangers of presidential isolation—all aspects of the Clinton administration and of other contemporary presidencies.

According to Lyndon Johnson's press secretary, George Reedy, the life of the White House staff is essentially that of the barnyard pecking order, where status and recognition depend on "one's relationship to the barnyard keeper" (Reedy 1987, 76). According to Reedy, there is only one fixed goal for White House assistants: "to gain and maintain access to the president" (88). Clinton secretary of labor Robert Reich further describes the importance of proximity and access in the highly competitive world of White House staff politics: "The decision-making 'loop' depends on physical proximity to [Clinton]—who's whispering into his ear most regularly, whose office is closest to the Oval, who's standing or sitting near him when a key issues arises . . ." (Reich 1997, 179, as quoted by Cronin and Genovese 1998, 308).

The assignment of White House offices determines just who enjoys access to the president and just who is moving up—and who is moving down—the White House hierarchy. Nixon presidential counselor John Dean described a White House in the throes of continuous reconstruction and remodeling, where the size, refurbishment, and relocation of offices all attested to the importance of its occupants (Dean 1976, 20–21). Carl Brauer describes the reasons that underlay the battle over White House offices:

> Although there are many top-level appointments to be had, there are few offices in the West Wing of the White House, and the competition for them among a President-elect's campaign staff can be shameless. "Never underestimate the value of proximity," [former Nixon advisor and New York Senator Daniel Patrick] Moynihan once remarked. Few presidential staffers have done so. "People will kill to get to an office in the West Wing," [top Reagan staffer] Michael Deaver told the journalist Hedrick Smith. "You'll

see people working in closets, tucked back in a corner, rather than taking a huge office with a fireplace on the EOB [Old Executive Office Building, which is just yards away from the President's office in the White House]."
(Brauer 1988)

The West Wing's upbeat portrait of White House staff ignores how the competition for access and favor helps to produce an advisory culture of reverence, sycophancy, and groupthink that can isolate a president from unpleasant voices of dissent, essentially from reality. Once staffers breathe the ethereal air of the presidency and see the world from that Parnassian vantage point, they will do anything not to lose their sense of privilege and importance. The result is that they become yes-men as no one wants to be the disturbing voice who pours cold water on the president's most cherished plans. The presidency is the "American monarchy," a royal court where "no one thrusts unpleasant thoughts upon a king unless he is ordered to do so, and even then he does so at his own peril" (Reedy 1987, 1, 97). No staff member will argue vociferously against the president's wishes, especially when he or she shares the president's larger agenda and when there are others who are more than willing to curry the president's favor by acceding to his wishes. In real life, White House staffers treat the president with "reverential" respect; in Sorkin's televised White House, in contrast, the reverence is there, yet "staffers treat President Bartlet like a mere co-worker" (Orszag 2001).

As a result, staff members often will not subject a president's desired course of action to critical inspection or vociferous dissent. There is extraordinary pressure among aides to be a loyal member of the presidential group: "The first strong observations to attract the favor of the president become subconsciously the thoughts of everyone in the room" (Reedy 1987, 12). Staff members bend their own views toward those of the president. In the worst case, they will sacrifice their independence and even their sense of ethics in their willingness to serve the president and thereby climb the White House ladder. As Watergate conspirator John Dean (1976) lamented, there was a sense among Nixon White House staff members that they were "reaching for the top" when they were really "touching bottom" (21). The Nixon White House, like all White Houses, had its share of "gophers" who were more than willing to do whatever was requested of them in order to hold their White House positions and the accompanying sense of power (1–2, 13–14).

Even on a matter as important as Vietnam, high-ranking advisors and members of the executive office of the presidency were overwhelmed by the awe and aura of the presidency; even top military advisors found themselves unable to face President Lyndon Johnson and contradict his policy wishes:

> Chester Cooper described how this process worked in a National Security Council meeting. "The President, in due course, would announce his decision and then poll everyone in the room. . . . 'Mr. Secretary, do you agree with the decision?' 'Yes, Mr. President.' 'Mr. X, do you agree?' 'I agree, Mr. President.' " During the process Cooper would frequently fall into a Walter Mitty-like fantasy: "When my turn came, I would rise to my feet slowly, look around the room and then directly at the President and say very quietly and emphatically, 'Mr. President, gentlemen, I most definitely do *not* agree.' But I was removed from my trance when I heard the President's voice saying, 'Mr. Cooper, do you agree?' And out would come a 'Yes, Mr. President, I agree.' " (Cooper 1970, quoted in Kearns [Goodwin] 1976, 338)

Selective recruitment, a shared sense of mission, and a desire not to be ostracized from the inner circle all compound the pressures toward groupthink, where White House aides find themselves unwilling to challenge the prevailing wisdom in the White House. The pressures that produce groupthink help to explain why even the faulty assumptions that underlay the Bays of Pigs invasion, the Vietnam escalation, and the Watergate break-in and cover-up were not effectively exposed in discussions among the White House inner circle (Janis 1982, 14–48, 97–130, 198–241).

Nowhere does *The West Wing* focus the potential for groupthink and the dangers of presidential isolation in a White House of yes-men (and yes-women). Instead, *The West Wing* portrays White House staff members as involved in a healthy interplay of ideas and strategic options and critical of the President's actions on various matters. *The West Wing* offers no comment on the limited nature of the interplay of ideas among staff members who all share a basic loyalty to the president and his agenda. Chief of staff Leo McGarry has no trouble speaking, in private, sharply and directly to the President Bartlet. McGarry is a political professional; he is respectful of the presidential office, but he can be forceful, and he is clearly nobody's yes-man. In the idealized world of *The West Wing,* there is no danger of presidential isolation.

Staff competition and politics are also fairly typical of the modern presidency; yet, *The West Wing's* airbrushed portrayal of the White House fails to explore the problems that staff factionalism poses for a president. The Reagan White House suffered the pull and haul of various factions led, at different times, by Ed Meese, Jim Baker, Michael Deaver, William Clark, Alexander Haig, and George Shultz. During Reagan's second term, first lady Nancy Reagan (of the East Wing) actively intervened in order to counter the influence of chief of staff Donald Regan and thereby, in her mind, protect the image and legacy of her husband (Neustadt 1990, 314–16). The Clinton White House, too, saw a battle between more liberal Democrats and more moderate New Democratic forces,[7] a division that was exacerbated when Clinton chose to bring in such outside advisors as maverick political consultant Dick Morris (who had aided Republican as well as Democratic congressional campaigns) and Republican "wise man" David Gergen. Staff members committed to traditional Democratic programs resisted Morris's efforts to tone down the class-warfare language and have the White House adopt a strategy of "triangulation"—Morris's view, especially after the Democrats' disastrous performance in the 1994 midterm elections, that the president should steer a middle course between the agenda of leftist-liberal Democrats and rightist Republicans. As Morris relates, "Clinton was in chronic conflict with his staff" (1997, 97), especially as George Stephanopoulos sought to keep the president committed to traditional Democratic policy goals.[8]

7. As Hale (1993, 1995) argues, Clinton's focus on moderate, middle-class-oriented programs was genuine and of long duration. As governor of Arkansas, Clinton had headed the Democratic Leadership Council (DLC). The DLC was a group of more moderate or centrist Democrats, predominantly from the South, who attempted to steer the party away from the big-government liberal orthodoxy of McGovern, Mondale, and Dukakis.

8. See Morris (1997, 12–13, 81–83, 93, 195) for his description of the staff factionalization in the Clinton White House.

As White House staffs have grown large and more difficult to manage, it is often the case "that staff members run about demanding action in the name of the president, but not always with the president's authorization" (DiClerico 1995, 216). As journalist Jeffrey Birnbaum caustically observed after reviewing staff operations during the President Clinton's first term, "In the Clinton White House, it was sometimes hard to tell who was in charge of the asylum" (Birnbaum 1996, 8). This problem, too, remains largely unexplored in *The West Wing*.

One other thing that *The West Wing* largely gets wrong is its portrayal of the modern vice presidency. *The West Wing* presents a dated view of the vice president as a person who is largely irrelevant to normal White House decision making. Vice President John Hoynes (Tim Matheson) is an outsider who is kept quite distant from the White House inner circle. He is seldom involved in key decisions or strategy sessions; indeed, Matheson's character seldom appears on the show. Once a rival of Bartlet's for the presidential nomination, Hoynes was recruited for the political assets he could bring to the party ticket; he continues to harbor his own presidential ambitions. (The show may indeed reflect reality, however, in depicting a great deal of friction between the presidential and vice-presidential staffs.)

This antiquated depiction misses the emergence of the modern vice presidency. Beginning with Walter Mondale, vice presidents (including George Bush and Al Gore, and even Dan Quayle to a lesser degree) have been figures of importance who served as key policy advisors to their presidents. Over time, the job of the vice presidency has grown, and vice presidents have come increasingly close to approximating "assistant presidents" (Cronin and Genovese 1998, 318, 323–38).[9]

The modern, significant vice president submerges his own policy views and political ambitions as the price for sharing in power. The modern vice president earns his new prominence by earning the president's trust. He gives the president his best advice. But he also clearly recognizes that, in case of a conflict in points of view, it is clearly the president's, not the vice president's, policy wishes that have the legitimate right to prevail. Indeed, Al Gore may

9. For other good articles on the emergence of a new vice presidency, see Pika (2000) and Light (1984).

have hurt his own presidential chances as a result of his sense of vice-presidential duty; after the failed impeachment vote he even led a public rally at White House for the besieged Clinton.

As the George W. Bush administration took office in 2001, one Washington commentator after the other observed the prominence and influence enjoyed by Vice President Dick Cheney, a prominence that even appears to have exceeded that enjoyed by Al Gore. The modern vice president is not shut out of the White House inner circle, as *The West Wing* portrays; instead, he obtains substantial policy-making responsibilities by earning the president's trust by demonstrating his loyalty and judgment. Dick Cheney enjoyed a double advantage here: He was a man of substantial White House and Washington experience who possessed important qualities needed to complement those of the Washington outsider, George W. Bush. Given Cheney's advanced age and health problems, the vice president could not be suspected of seeking to build his own independent record for a future run at the Oval Office.

One far-fetched *The West Wing* episode ("Twenty Hours in L.A.") presents Vice President Hoynes refusing to comply with the president's wishes to break an expected fifty-fifty tie vote in the Senate and thereby allow the enactment of an ethanol tax credit. Hoynes adamantly rejects the entreaties of the president's chief of staff and the president himself. He objects that such tax credits are worthless, that they favor business, that in his campaign for the presidency he had spoken out against them, and that as a Senator he had voted against them a number of times. If he voted for the credit now, the Republicans would make him "eat it for dinner," spoiling his future electoral ambitions. Maybe the only realistic detail of this story element is that the policy disagreement between the president and vice president is kept in confidence. But even here, Hoynes threatens to take the dispute public. In reality, no modern vice president, in private or public, would so forcefully and persistently challenge a president's wishes and thereby threaten his future relationship with the president. Instead, the vice president must function as a valued policy advisor and a trusted member of the president's team. The modern vice president may respectfully present his argument, but he cannot dig in his heels and so directly and forcefully challenge the president. As Walter Mondale explained the "rules" to his vice-presidential successor George

Bush: "Don't wear a president down. . . . Give your advice and give it well. You have a right to be heard, not obeyed. A president must decide when the debates must end" (Cronin and Genovese 1998, 332).

The West Wing: An Overall Assessment

There is much that is realistic in *The West Wing*'s picture of White House staff as a close-knit, hard-working, dedicated group of human beings motivated by loyalty, conviction, and a sense of patriotism; they do their best to resolve very difficult conflicts on issues where there exist no simple, just, and workable solutions. In this respect, *The West Wing* presents an essentially positive view of public service and a healthy corrective to anti-Washington stereotypes and public cynicism. With its discussion of issues coupled with much that is accurate and insightful in its portrayal of White House staff and contemporary politics, *The West Wing* does live up, in large measure, to the seemingly outlandish claim that it offers a weekly civics lesson; it is a presentation that both explains and inspires.

Yet, the show is didactic and suffers from serious omissions. While *The West Wing* clearly recognizes how external political concerns—fundraising, constituency pressure, polling, and the media—affect White House strategy and policymaking, the series curiously lacks a similar understanding of the internal politics of the White House staff. In its overly sunny and optimistic portrayal of an idealized president operating in a healthy White House atmosphere, *The West Wing* neglects the more unhealthy aspects of staff competition, factionalism, groupthink, and presidential isolation that also characterize the real West Wing. *The West Wing* is a piece of entertainment that focuses on politics in Washington and the nation; curiously, it turns a blind eye to the stories of staff politics and factionalism inside the White House.

4 | The King's Two Bodies

Identity and Office in Sorkin's West Wing

HEATHER RICHARDSON HAYTON

The "king's two bodies" refers to a time when people understood political sovereignty more explicitly as the notion of having a dynamic, individual ruler who can impose his will upon a land and, at the same time, the notion that he was simply a placeholder in a timeless office. The king's two bodies were both individual or local, and universal or timeless, as expressed most clearly in the cry "The King is dead! Long live the King!" (where the king is simultaneously the dead body of the former king, the personage of the new king, and the timeless office that both men only temporarily inhabit). Such a view held out the promise of a great, heroic leader—a man larger than life—who could overcome the limitations of the office, while also providing a real limit to the power of such a man to do damage to either state or office.

While great political historians like Ernst Kantorowicz (1957) have claimed that this bifurcated and complicated view of political rule was possible only because pre- and early-modern people had a view of rule by divine right,[1] we can see, in the "king's two bodies," many complexities held within

---

1. Kantorowicz's *The King's Two Bodies: A Study in Medieval Political Theology* is the seminal text for a history of this idea in political theory. For influential studies of the American presidency, and how it fits into a rhetorical or mythological paradigm having much in common with earlier British and continental models of sovereignty, see Thomas Cronin's *State of the Presidency* (1980), Jeffrey Tulis's *Rhetorical Presidency* (1987), and Clinton Rossiter's *American Presidency* (1960).

our own notions of political rule. Indeed, we are no less complex—or aporetic—in our views of the American president. Facetiously we could argue that, if anything, the "king's two bodies" has a special meaning to us in America precisely because we choose to have a placeholder for the king, elected every four or eight years, who must hold the timeless and sacred office as a "dead king" while at the same time, holding out the promise of being a "live one." Our notion of political sovereignty is even more contrary, though. As a people, Americans simultaneously doubt that our rulers can effect any change (they are simply placeholders after all) and yet hold out the hope that they can impose their individual will upon us, changing the very nature of that timeless office. Clinton Rossiter (1960), writing just as television had begun to play such an important role in shaping our cultural view of the presidency, argued that Americans do have an imperial view of the president: "If the president is a king, it is equally clear he is no mere constitutional monarch. For in an era in which many monarchies all over the world have disappeared, and the power of kings has declined, the power of the president has enormously increased" (17). Rossiter attributes the power of the presidency to its role as a symbol of democratic principles and the democratic process. Nonetheless, the very fact that the president has become both symbol and man upholds the notion of the "king's two bodies." Of course, this bifurcated view of political rule is nothing new; it informs the definition of the presidency from the very beginning, when George Washington reluctantly "held" office for a country in its troubled infancy and yet indelibly imprinted his image in our presidential mythography.

That mythography has been altered, however, by the rise of television and the media. Everything presidential—official duties or not—is now fair game for reporting on the television. Warren Rochelle (1999) points out that now "almost everything a president does that can be filmed . . . travel, speeches, dress, visits to McDonald's . . . is accentuated by television" (409). And what cannot be caught on film can certainly be re-created by talking heads on television. Political scientists argue that the "postmodern presidency" is characterized by a desire by the press and public to find the "real" candidate underneath all of the carefully staged media information, however futile that "real" leader might be (Jamieson 1988; Schram 1991; Tulis 1987). In what Sanford Schram calls the "infinite regress of appearances," presidential media is largely about demystifying the very image-making process that is simultaneously occurring (212). The symbolism of the man as office no longer satisfies the public because we can see its constructedness. Speaking of Nixon's and Reagan's legacy, Schram argues: "When the real cannot be identified, that which is reliably and consistently reproduced, like a pat performance, is taken to be credible. . . . While [political] models may have always created reality rather than reflected it, we are now encouraged to more self-consciously trade on this assumption" (214). Thus, "the king's two bodies" is also an apt metaphor for the way in which Americans understand private and public space, as well as the real and the artificial—both of which converge on the physical body of the president and within the West Wing of the White House.

This essay will be using the metaphor of the king's two bodies to address a range of mutually exclusive expectations attached to the American presidency. Specifically, it will focus on how Aaron Sorkin's phenomenally successful television series *The West Wing* manifests, challenges, and attempts to revise these beliefs for a generation of American voters. It may seem odd to use a thirteenth-century political metaphor to focus a discussion of late-twentieth-century cinematic presidents. However, in an interview with PBS, Sorkin himself acknowledges the connection between writing *The West Wing* and notions of kingship, saying "[t]here's a great tradition in story-telling that's thousands of years old, telling stories about kings and their palaces, and that's really what I wanted to do" (Sorkin 2000).

Yet, we also must acknowledge that Sorkin's series appears at a time when the American view of presidential rule is especially difficult to assess, precisely because we have a proliferation of "stories about kings and their palaces" coming from within and outside of the Beltway. Television and cinematic portrayals of the president (real and fictional) collide and compete for our attention with "real" presidential dramas such as the Clinton impeachment proceedings and Starr report. For example, in an article about the difficulty of telling the real politicians from the television ones, Brian Johnson (2000) points out that "when Warren Beatty was flirting with running for president, he gave a very well-received speech at the Beverly Hilton Hotel. But George Stephanopolous commented that, as great as it was, you couldn't help feeling this was someone playing the part of an actor thinking about running for president" (72). The situation has been further complicated by late-night comedy appearances by presidential hopefuls, past presidents, and even the sitting mayor of the city of New York—all of whom variously play or parody themselves. Rudolph Guliani's famous appearance as host of *Saturday Night Live*—including a sketch where he appeared in drag—is perhaps the most egregious blurring of the line between the kingly trappings of his role as mayor of New York and his own parodic imitation of that role. But presidential hopefuls Bill Clinton, Al Gore, and George W. Bush all appeared on late-night shows as well. In a multilayered parody of the presidential image, past president George Bush appeared in 2000 on *Saturday Night Live*'s "Presidential Bash," playing citizen Bush commenting on Dana Carvey's imitation of President Bush. Indeed, the blurring seems to have accelerated since 1992, when MTV first harnessed its own cultural influence to affect presidential politics by holding a gen-x version of the town hall forum and get-out-the-vote.

If all this late-night television pandering isn't enough, it seems the American public's consumption of presidential drama is furthered by an explosion of cable television shows that claim to go "behind the scenes" of history and retell, with authoritative demeanor, the "real story" behind presidential battles as public as Truman's decision to drop the bomb or as personal as Jefferson's relations with Sally Hemmings. The never-ending supply of presidential drama on television and the big screen seems at odds with most pundits claiming Americans are disenchanted with politics and no longer interested in anything but sound bites from our presidential candidates.[2]

However, that conventional wisdom has proven false yet again. If the popularity of such presidential dramas like *The West Wing, Running Mate,* or *The Contender* were not enough to convince you otherwise, take a look at recent surveys indicating that even brief comedic sketches and late-night political humor are making an impact on the way we understand politics. A Pew Research Center survey shows that these late-night sketches are, at some

---

2. For example, in 1999 the Center for Media and Public Affairs published a study on the images of government in television entertainment called "Government Goes Down the Tube." It showed that "[i]n the 1990s public officials had the worst image of any major occupational group on television, and civil servants weren't far ahead of them" (Executive Survey).

level, shaping national politics: 50 percent of those questioned say they regularly or sometimes get their information about candidates or the president from late-night comedy (including MTV). PBS *Online NewsHour* claims that number rises to almost 80 percent for viewers under the age of thirty, but according to the actual Pew Research Center report ("Audiences Fragmented and Skeptical" 2000), a full 27 percent of those are unregistered voters, and when asked to name the candidates and the states from which they come, 45 percent scored in the "low" knowledge range.

In an article appearing only one day before the election, the *New York Times* pointed out that "[t]he urge to mock our actual presidents is as strong as our longing, in the abstract at least, to revere the president. These impulses transcend party or ideology" (Scott 2000). Such a dual impulse is as complex and dichotomous as the metaphor of the "king's two bodies," and reflects, at an innate level, our desire to separate the man from the office.

Perhaps this is why Sorkin's *West Wing* is so interesting. His series refuses our impulse to separate man from office—refusing, at almost every level, to allow us to divorce the character of Josiah "Jed" Bartlet from his job as president of the United States of America. *The West Wing* forces us to see the people in the White House as real human beings who struggle with the "boundaries between public and private, in jobs where they are always on duty, and always in the spotlight" (Lewis 2001, 38). In fact, Sorkin regularly includes moments in the episodes that highlight the *impossibility* of separating the king's two bodies for either political or personal gain. One of the most evident examples is also a recurring one, and is based on Bartlet's role as *patria patrii*: father of three daughters, and father of the nation. There is no doubt that Sorkin consciously depicts Bartlet as a father of a daughter (rather than a son), for he borrows this telling detail from his earlier movie *The American President*.[3] But the power of the detail works on multiple lev-

---

3. In that movie, Sorkin has his president ask specifically whether the reason why "character" was not an issue in the election was because he was a recent widower raising a daughter. Although there is much similarity between *The American President* and *The West Wing*, Sorkin has moved the question of character and its relationship to presidential success further into the range of subtlety by reframing the question. In *The West Wing*, the questions are largely about ideology and office, and "character" gets mapped onto the staff.

els. Take, for example, the "Six Meetings Before Lunch" episode from the first season. In that episode, C. J. must tell the president that a reporter has harassed Zoe as she was leaving her college campus cafeteria—an intrusion made specifically off-limits by the Bartlet White House—and that in the ensuing confrontation between the reporter and the president's daughter, Zoe has lied. The news is upsetting to the president and he puts on his jacket, gets up to leave the Oval Office, and attempts to go "talk" to the press corps, to tell them to "leave his daughter alone." In a telling moment, C. J. forcefully tells the president of the United States to "sit down" and calm down.

As the dialogue and pacing of this scene shows, President Bartlet's role as upset father allows the audience to see him negotiate the fine line between being a loving, protective parent, and one determined to let his daughter grow up and lead her own life beyond him. Those two disparate parental instincts replicate his presidential (and ideological) instincts, whereby he tries to provide both individual liberty and social control for America. Sorkin uses the cinematic device of presidential parenthood to keep that difficult dance between personal freedom and political regulation present in our minds: as we watch Bartlet's instincts to protect Zoe from the intrusions of the press do battle with his rational desire to let her take some risks and find her own voice, we watch his administration struggle with the same dilemma on a national policy issue. But even beyond that, Sorkin purposely plays upon the merging and opposition of the king's two bodies by having Bartlet's instincts to protect Zoe (his role as man rather than office) supercede and threaten his role as president. It is C. J., after all, who forces him to return to his role as president and calm down.[4]

Sorkin establishes this father identity for Bartlet in the pilot episode. In one of the most moving speeches—real or fictional—Bartlet enters his own West Wing at the end of that episode and gives the "Lambs of God" lecture to a group of religious "zealots." But even here, Sorkin blends, or encourages us to confuse, the two bodies of the king. Bartlet has been in a bicycle acci-

4. As such, C. J. fits a pattern in Sorkin's dramas through which advisors and presidential staffers act as the "king's counselors"—those figures who historically shape the individual into the office—as well as acting as a mirror of the president. In the Lacanian sense, C. J.'s mirroring allows Bartlet to recognize his own identity and the limits of the king's "bodies."

dent and his staff has been trying to figure a way to make the faux pas look presidential by describing it as a "sudden arboreal stop." When we finally, after forty minutes, see Bartlet (played by Martin Sheen), he is wearing a workout suit and limping. He is not particularly tall, nor is he physically intimidating. Thus the very first image we have of the president is less presidential and more like a private man.

But things suddenly change in that wonderfully shot climax. Although Bartlet enters as a folksy and clumsy man (with perhaps a nod to President Ford?), he quickly turns into something out of *The Terminator*. Bartlet gives a two-minute, Bible-quoting, granddaughter-alluding chastisement to the group of religious folk who had been posturing and chastising the president's staff only moments earlier. We find out right before he kicks the group out of "his" room, that the bicycle accident was a direct result of the anger Bartlet felt at finding out his granddaughter has been sent a particularly violent piece of hate mail by members associated with the group. Sorkin uses the discongruity of the physical image to catch us all unaware: almost immediately the unintimidating man transforms into a very powerful and vengeful president, all under the guise of telling a story of grandfatherly affection and befuddled anger. It is no coincidence that the first image we receive of Sorkin's president is as a father. Nor should it surprise us that the episode ends with a Schlamme "long-shot" of the president behind his desk in the Oval Office, barking orders and looking suddenly very presidential; the audience is left wondering, "has he grown a few inches? He seems taller, somehow, and more regal."

Perhaps the most forceful image of Bartlet as father of the country and father of Zoe occurs in "Lord John Marbury." In this episode, Charlie asks the president's permission to go on a date with Bartlet's daughter. The episode is full of moments where the distinction between Bartlet as president and as father is blurred: Charlie asks for the president's permission—and for a night off!—in the Oval Office, Bartlet makes an ironic reference to himself as playing a part in *Look Who's Coming to Dinner* instead of playing the part of president, and when he finally does give Charlie his permission to date Zoe, Bartlet must then step into his presidential role by lecturing Charlie on the security dangers of dating the president's daughter. It is never made clear just which role, father or president, Bartlet is playing until after the event is over.

These are just a few of the examples of how Sorkin challenges our perception of the president as either the office or the man from the very first season. There are more such moments in each season, including from one of the most striking examples of that challenge: the award-winning episode "Take This Sabbath Day," where the president refuses to commute an execution. That episode ends with Bartlet and his priest praying in the Oval Office. The writing is excellent, and the episode is one of the best hours of television in memory. But what is telling in that depiction is that Bartlet asks the priest to call him Mr. President—arguing that in *this* room (the Oval Office), it helps to keep his role straight and to separate the man from the job. Obviously, that is not true, and his family priest calls him on such self-deception: the priest asks how Bartlet—a boy from his parish—can call the Vatican and ask to talk to the Pope. Obviously, it is Bartlet's role as president that allows him, as a private man, to seek spiritual counseling from the Vatican. Thus the ending, where the president is offering his confession and receiving penance, undoes any attempt (even unconscious) to pretend that the man can be distinguished from the office, or that the king's two bodies can be separated.

Location, Location, Location

I mentioned earlier that the "king's two bodies" is made manifest in two locations: in the body and character of the president, and in the physical space of the West Wing. Sorkin uses the liminal nature of the West Wing to emphasize the merging of identity and office throughout all of the episodes. We see this most clearly reinforced with the multitude of Schlamme's shots through long hallways, in and out of offices, and into spaces that are deemed off limits and restricted. Just as the president's body becomes the liminal container for the office of the president, so the West Wing becomes a liminal space. But like the body, the West Wing holds and protects the most sacred of spaces: the Oval Office, where the trappings of that office—the traditions, history, and institution of the presidency—are made manifest.

It has been argued that the series provides this "behind the scenes" look at the West Wing because American viewers like to be flattered, to think "that we are in the know . . . well-versed in Beltway shenanigans" (Wren 1999, 18). While there is something to be said for the American insatiability for trade secrets and "glimpses backstage," the series is *not* solely about voyeurism, nor does it place setting over content. Indeed, Schlamme reinforces the very opposite with his shots in and through the Byzantine halls, leading and sweeping into the Oval Office. When an episode wants to emphasize the dichotomy between private and public, between man and office, they do it by utilizing particular props in this room: the president's desk, the phone with different lines lit up (both usually shot from behind the desk as if the camera were the eyes of the president himself), the seal on the carpet and, perhaps most important, the long covered porch leading from the Oval Office into the residency. In more than one episode, the president's walk down to the residence has been used to signal to the audience Bartlet's shift from president to man at the end of a day—and more often, his *inability* to leave the office behind as he leaves the physical space of the Oval Office.

Part of the signature look of *The West Wing* series is the emphasis on shooting the Oval Office or the West Wing from outside looking in, as well as the use of strong backlighting and contrast to achieve the image of an "optimistic White house, a Camelot for the masses" (Oppenheimer 2000, 74). In 2001, one of the changes made to the set for *The West Wing* was to enlarge and widen the outside portico to shoot "seamless 'walking and talking scenes' " (Oppenheimer 2000, 82). Whether the shot is from outside of a window looking into the Oval Office, or whether it is a door suddenly closed or opened unexpectedly in front of the camera as a drunken reformer from Ukraine is kept from meeting with the president, the effect is to continually remind us that this space is contested. There are numerous other examples of how the series reinforces the "king's two bodies" with location, character, and cinematography. The relationship between Danny and C. J. in the first season, with Danny's continual entrance into "restricted" areas of the West Wing, becomes a metaphor for the private-public, man-office conflict. Indeed, the role of many of the staffers is to replicate the "king's two bodies" in their own conflicted lives. Sam's relationship with the prostitute and Leo's past drug use pose problems in their political careers precisely because it is impossible to convincingly separate private from public in the West Wing. Returning to Bartlet, however, we can see two very important examples of how the Oval Office, the West Wing, and the residence reinforce the duality of the "king's two bodies" with location.

One of the clearest examples of the two bodies of the president can be seen in the episode "Mandatory Minimums." Again at the end of the episode,[5] Jed Bartlet is being awakened in his bed in the residence first by Leo, then by each successive member of his staff. They convene in his bedroom at 11 P.M. to have a policy session and a pep talk. The president, disheveled and groggy, is sitting up in his bed, and the lighting for the room is lowered. Part of my fascination with this scene is that the president's residence, his bedroom within that residence, and his bed within that bedroom, are traditionally coded off-limits to everyone but the president (and the first family). Technically speaking, one is not allowed to enter the president's bedroom without permission, or unless it is a matter of state urgency. In fact, the whole space of the residency is constructed to allow the president some semblance of privacy. And yet, at 11 P.M., Bartlet is awakened to have a staff meeting in his bed—and this is no Clintonesque bad joke. While invading the most private of presidential enclosures, Sorkin has us find nothing sordid: just Jed Bartlet, in scruffy clothes, acting fatherly to his staff and setting a policy agenda for the days to come. We don't even see the first lady because she is conveniently out of the country, although we are reminded that she exists by Bartlet himself, who encourages his staff to do this "when Abby is around." The episode ends with Bartlet going back to bed and turning off the lights in the room. We see, as the camera draws out and the scene fades to black, that the president shares his bed with a pile of books and papers. Thus, even in the most private of spaces in the president's life, he still inhabits the king's "two bodies." It should also be noted that Bartlet makes a reference in this scene to the "armed guards" who are outside his door and wonders how his staff managed to get past them to invade his bedroom. The point of this example seems to be to remind us of our own inappropriate desire to see into the president's private side of the White House,[6] while at the

5. Sorkin has a penchant for reminding us of the duality of the president at the ends of each episode, almost as an apologia. I find this to be one of his most political, and recurring, statements in the series.

6. To continue the dual body analogy for Sorkin's *West Wing*, the White House represents the office and practice of the presidency, where our voyeuristic gaze is both inappropriate and disappointed.

same time rewarding us with a view that affirms that *good* presidents cannot ever separate the office from the man.

Another example of the way Sorkin uses location to address the king's two bodies is in a later episode ("And It's Surely to Their Credit"), when the first lady and the president try to schedule a conjugal visit. We are told it has been fourteen weeks since the presidential couple had sex—a detail and a subject matter that could easily have landed Sorkin in the company of the late-night routines frequently offered by Leno and Letterman. Inside the Oval Office, the president and the first lady schedule their tryst and almost engage in the act right there (but for the protestations of the first lady, who reminds the president that they are in the Oval Office). The two even comment facetiously on the fact that the residence is but a few steps away and how "convenient" that was for the founding fathers. But it is Sorkin who is facetiously commenting upon the separation of physical space as some sort of barrier between the man and the office. In fact, like the earlier example of the presidential bedroom as boardroom, we are comforted, as viewers, to find out that Bartlet loves his wife but also loves his job, if not more, then equally. The more difficult implications of that realization is that no neat distinctions between man and office, or between Oval Office and residency, can be made. But did viewers make that connection? This episode aired November 1, 2000, after Al Gore's very public "embrace" of Tipper and reference to the passion with which he loves his wife of over twenty-five years. This was a mere six days before the election.

Who Influences Whom?

Political philosophy has long articulated the notion of the "king's two bodies," whereby the king (or sovereign) was both a public office and a private man. The important function of such duality has been preserved in our notion of presidency and is reinforced by our own political rituals (the inauguration, state of the union speeches, official portraiture), as well as by staged media events ("candid" photos of first families, first family vacations, autobiographies and memoirs). Yet, with the rise of the cinematic president, and some may argue, long before that, the underlying philosophy of a separation between the public office and the private actions of the man in office have been intellectually and *visually* challenged.

Nonetheless, one of the seminal assumptions of the television series *The West Wing* is that such distinctions, although theoretically useful, are not only impractical, but an impediment to true leadership in America. Virtually every episode of the series grapples with the dilemma of the "king's two bodies" in the form of Jed Bartlet's ongoing efforts to act for, and in the spirit of, the office *and* as the certainly fallible man. Whether he admits it or not, Sorkin seems to be arguing for presidential iconoclasm. His virtual president refuses to serve solely the office or let the office serve solely himself, instead trying to merge both conceptions into one forceful image worthy of public veneration. Perhaps it is not surprising that the American public found more favor with a fictional president, whose efforts to remain two ideologically distinct and corporeal entities fail at every turn, than with either candidate in the 2000 election. The show's fall 2000 promos argued that Jed "was the President we could all agree on" (Auster 2001, 39). An article appearing on October 17, 2000, in the *New York Times* quoted John Wells, one of the executive producers of the show, stating that "Martin Sheen keeps outpolling the two presidential candidates" (Weinraub 2000).[7] In the final section of this chapter, I will examine the political effects of the blurring between fiction and reality that this show capitalizes on and encourages.

Whether Sheen did appear as a choice on any real election polls is unclear. But Wells's point in the *New York Times* article is perfectly apparent: with thirty-five million people watching the 2000 season opener, *The West Wing* had more viewers than either political convention or most of the pre-election coverage. Bumper stickers and buttons reading "Bartlet for President" began appearing midsummer and were as popular as their real counterparts.

Martin Sheen himself capitalized on Bartlet's popularity by campaigning against Proposition 36 in California, and for Al Gore in the Great Lakes

---

7. There was no poll of which I am aware that specifically asks about Bartlet versus Gore or Bush. Nonetheless, the quote was picked up by the *New York Times* and repeated in other mainstream media. Perhaps Wells was referring to the fictional polls in the ongoing plot line of *The West Wing*?

area. Sheen's commercial against Proposition 36 (which would mandate drug treatment rather than incarceration for first—and second-time offenders) appeared *during* the November 1, 2000, episode of *The West Wing*—further confusing the audience about whether he was speaking as Martin Sheen the actor or as Jed Bartlet the fictional president. Even early in the series' history, Sorkin and Sheen had to repudiate right-wing critics who claimed the pair's real life left-leaning politics were influencing the show. Much of the early press on *The West Wing* focused on whether the show catered to one political view more than the other, and as Fred McKissack points out, Sheen's past made him "already suspect" (2000, 39).[8] Thus, the "king's two bodies" can also easily apply to Martin Sheen and highlights how he personally transgressed the limits of the celluloid world by invoking the authority of the office of the character he portrayed.

Sheen also appeared with Gore on Jay Leno's *Tonight Show* one week before the election. In that appearance, we were again treated to a blurring of the line between reality and fiction as Gore jokingly staged himself as one of the writers of *The West Wing,* handing a revised script to Sheen as the actor walked onto Leno's set. Like the ad against Proposition 37, the Leno appearance coincided with that evening's airing of the *West Wing* episode in most of North America. It appears that proximity to the TV series, or to the character of Bartlet, seemed to promise some political cache for a *real* cause or candidate.

The blurring of lines between real and fictional presidents, plot lines, and locations continues, in fact, to be an issue for American and Canadian audiences. Immediately following September 11, 2001, *The West Wing* hastily shot a special episode ("Isaac and Ishmael") to "address" the 9/11 terrorist events. It was the first completely fictional television show to compete with more legitimate mainstream and cable news programs that had been devoting their time exclusively to 9/11 stories. However, in that episode, the plot had terrorists coming into America from a geographically

8. Most viewers found the show compelling and believable, if not always balanced, and by the 2001 season pundits were more concerned with how much of the "national civics lesson" audiences were picking up and whether the show was too believable. See Oxfeld (2000), Brill (2000), Lewis (2001), and Auster (2001).

incorrect Canadian city (Ontario to Vermont)—a fact not lost on our neighbors to the north. As Patrick Finn notes, for days following the airing of that episode, Canadian officials were quick to point out the show's error and insist on its "harmful stereotyping." Another example of such blurring can be seen in the press release sent from the State of New Mexico regarding an April 3, 2002, episode ("Stirred") about nuclear waste spillage. The AP ran a story about the shocking press release, which reminded viewers that "Wednesday's scheduled episode of 'The West Wing,' starring Martin Sheen as President Bartlet, is 'completely fictional' " (Clark 2002). According to the article, a spokesperson for the governor was quoted as saying "We're not trying to offend anybody's intelligence but they see vignettes and think that it could happen."

We are left to speculate whether or not this fictional television show actually influenced the minds of the voters in 2000. Positing short-term effects from *The West Wing* may be a dubious venture, despite efforts by the show's staff and some of the candidates to do just that in each season.[9] Nonetheless, I think a few suppositions can made, and there is room to argue for some links between the popularity of Sorkin's *West Wing* and voter behavior for the real 2000 election. Most prominent is the effect of the show on audience perceptions of what is "presidential," and that had immediate consequences for the two real candidates for president who were trying to look like enough

9. The most evident examples of the series' attempts to influence public thought can be seen in the timing of some episodes; for example, showing "The Midterms," an episode about not getting a clear mandate, in the middle of the Bush-Gore recount. But other examples of influence can be seen in the way mainstream media treats *The West Wing* episodes as if they were real events to examine the issues brought up on the series. From a cultural perspective, it is certainly impressive that *Good Morning America* (on a different network than the show, no less) spent fifteen minutes talking about *The West Wing* the morning after the 2001 season finale. It even translated the Latin Jed speaks in that episode "for the rest of us." In that same month, two separate political/policy wonk shows devoted time to multiple sclerosis and celebrities living with the disease, and defended Jed's lie of omission as if the events of the show were real. These examples show that *The West Wing* has the uncanny ability to upstage sitting presidents and to confuse our own political reality. Taken one step further, *Harper's Index* reported that President George W. Bush only received an average of nine minutes per night of coverage in his first fifty days in office, compared to Clinton's eighteen in the first fifty days (June 2001). I wonder how much coverage Jed Bartlet has received?

of whatever that might be to win the election. In hindsight, it is unlikely *The West Wing* actually helped either candidate in the election.

The demographics of the TV series' audience is an important factor in determining who might be influenced, if anyone, by the show's iconoclasm. NBC executives point out that in its first season *The West Wing* had the most upscale viewers of any show on network television, and those statistics have held for each season. In 2000, more adults aged eighteen to forty-nine who earned over $100,000 a year watched this show than they did any other regular series on television. *West Wing* viewers also have more advanced degrees, home computers, and Internet access than any other prime-time audience (Calvo 2000; see also Weinraub 2000).[10] In short, viewers of *The West Wing* were split evenly in how they fell into the demographic of each major candidate for exit polling immediately following the election: 11 percent more voters who had an income over $100,000 voted for Bush than Gore, but 12 percent more voters with an advanced degree voted for Gore than Bush. In terms of age, or Internet use, the statistics showed voters were split within 2 percent of each other for the two candidates (CNN Online, November 9, 2000).

While the television series obviously portrays a liberal president and much liberal ideology, the show is popular with Democrat and Republican viewers alike. Al Gore and the Clinton administration, however, were quick to register their affection for the show and to associate themselves with the show's idealism—if not actual positions. For example, while George W. claimed never to have seen the show, Al Gore offered his praise for the series. Joe Lockhart, a former Clinton press secretary, went on record in numerous interviews to comment favorably on the series, and there were reports of Albright and others asking for their "counterparts" to appear on a future episode (Branegan 2000, 82). The cast, along with Sorkin and Schlamme, also made appearances at democratic fundraisers and, most notably, at the 2000 White House Press Corps Dinner. It would seem, then, that any association with the fictional *West Wing* might help a democratic candidate win

10. Mike Nelson of NBC's publicity department confirms this statistic, and also points out that the show continues to attract a much broader (and older) audience than many of NBC's comedies.

the real presidency. Instead, that strategy may have backfired in the 2000 presidential election.

Despite "aggressive marketing" of the show during the final months of the presidential campaign cycle by NBC,[11] the series may have actually cost Gore some votes. Even as late as October 2000, major newspapers were claiming that Bartlet looked "more presidential than those actually running for the office . . . [he looked] a whole lot more believable than most politicians" (Long 2000). The *St. Louis Post-Dispatch* argued that voters should "vote with their remote" for Bartlet, the "president we long for—the president we deserve" ("Hail to the *West Wing*" 2000). As early as August 2000, Amy Wallace, from the *Los Angeles Times*, predicted that, despite the show's obvious influence on the image of the real president in viewers' minds, the show would have little partisan effect on the outcome of the election. But then again, no one in early August was predicting the race would be as tight as it was, with a statistically neglible margin between the two candidates and automatic ballot recounts triggered in Florida and New Mexico.

Well, almost no one. In that same article, Dan Schnurr, former communications director for John McCain's presidential campaign, argued that the series *would* have an effect on the electorate: "politics as entertainment definitely has an effect on the electorate. . . . It's overly simplistic to say that because voters have gotten used to being entertained by TV politicians, they feel more of a need to be entertained. But they're increasingly impatient. A natural human politician doesn't have a prayer" (Wallace 2000, 20). When commenting on the political impact of the recently released movie *The Contender*, Schnurr went on to argue that the movie might "distract the voters from the real presidential contest." He queried: "How . . . can you ask George Bush or Al Gore to compete with Jeff Bridges?" (20).

That is precisely what may have happened, although not in the way most political analysts predicted. Instead of movies like *The Contender* and TV series like *The West Wing* simply turning people off to the political process due to cynicism, it turned them off to the real candidates *by comparison*. In yet

---

11. NBC aired four reruns between the two national conventions as well as running previous episodes all summer. Five new episodes (including a doubleheader season opener) aired before the election itself.

another bifurcated view of the process, voter turnout in the 2000 election was higher than that in 1996 (51.2 percent compared to 49.1 percent) but lower than that in 1992 (55.1 percent), according to the Federal Election Commission. There are many factors that obviously play a part in an electoral win, and this was certainly the case with the 2000 election. But in a race as close as that one, with handfuls of votes changing the balance in some key states, we must take the influence of a highly politicized fictional president seen by thirty-five million viewers each week more seriously. Those who voted were distracted, at some level, if even by the idealistic promise of Bartlet. He seemed so much more *real* than Al Gore, or even Ralph Nader, that even Gore's attempts to fashion himself as the idealistic president Sheen plays on TV failed. *The West Wing* taught us throughout the preceding season, and reinforced most heavily in fall before the election, that perhaps we should not separate the man from the office, that the "king's two bodies" are really not distinguishable at all. Influenced by a fictional president loved by thirty-five million viewers each week, real-life voters were left with a choice in the 2000 election between a man and an office. A vote for Gore was a vote for ideology and office with room to find the man somewhere within that office; a vote for Bush was a vote for a likeable man who could grow into the office. Or perhaps it was the other way around; take, for example, one political analyst's comments in the aftermath of the election: "The yammering classes have decided that Gore's problem is a weird, deficient personality, and Bush's is a dull, incurious brain. I have sometimes suspected the reverse: That Gore is a nicer guy than imagined but not as smart as he would like everyone to think; and that Bush is smarter, but a lot less nice, than he seems. *The two men even out, in some irritating way*" (Morrow 2000; emphasis mine). So while we longed for Bartlet, the "real" president who was both man and office, brain and personality, we cast a split vote for two fictional kings.

THE WEST WING

LANGUAGE AND STRUCTURE

IN *THE WEST WING*

---

5 | Dialogue, Deliberation, and Discourse

The Far-Reaching Politics of The West Wing

SAMUEL A. CHAMBERS

The most straightforward way to get at the politics of *The West Wing* would seem to be to assimilate the politics of the television drama *about* American politics to the *terms* of American politics and current political discourse. This approach reduces the political question to the following: is *The West Wing* left wing, and if so, to what extent? Quite a bit can be said on this issue, especially when one considers the political affiliations of Martin Sheen, playing, some would say, the president that the American left wished Bill Clinton had been. This essay is not an effort to reject or refute such assertions, but it suggests that such an approach to finding the politics of *The West Wing,* although not necessarily invalid, cannot do justice to the political potential lodged deep within the text of the show, a text that acquires numerous layers as the show and its characters grow. Indeed, the political discourse within *The West Wing* exceeds the somewhat narrow terms of contemporary American political discourse; in this respect, the series may not only widen the American political spectrum but also open up the space of the political.

Demonstrating the series' broader conception of politics requires two related shifts in emphasis. First, the argument here focuses not upon the broad political positions that the Bartlet administration takes up, but on the textual implications of one specific episode, "Six Meetings Before Lunch." Making this shift requires a certain distancing of this analysis from other approaches. Second, in order to expose the far-reaching political implications of the show, this essay places the episode not in dialogue with the terms of American political discourse, but instead in the context of broader questions raised in the realm of contemporary political theory. A close analysis of the ongoing dialogues that anchor "Six Meetings Before Lunch" reveals a conception of political discourse that challenges both the deliberative democrats' notion of language as a medium of communicative action oriented toward the goal of consensus, and a pluralist theory that would define politics as the result of bartering and compromise (a model that does play a role in other episodes of *The West Wing*). What emerges through the interplay of continuing discussions in this episode is an open-ended model of political discourse not governed by teleological endpoints, but serving to maintain a space for plural politics. These specific arguments about the implications of the episode will support the general thesis that *The West Wing*'s political possibilities greatly exceed the questions of left and right, as Aaron Sorkin and his characters grapple with questions of political agency, legitimacy, and the very space of the political.

Kissing and Telling: Political Realism in "Six Meetings Before Lunch"

Jeff Riley, a former White House staffer, who worked in the West Wing for both the administrations of both George Bush, Sr., and Bill Clinton, wrote weekly reviews of the first season of the *The West Wing* for "Find Law Entertaiment." His review of "Six Meetings Before Lunch" (Riley 2002) can serve to introduce the episode and demonstrate precisely the sort of "realism" approach that this essay will eschew. That is, Riley seeks to use his own experience to provide a lens of realism for the television portrayal of the White House staff, and therefore his criticisms of the show almost always center on Sorkin's dramatic departures from "actual political reality." Riley continually reminds his readers that he worked in the "real" West Wing and "*that*" would never happen; "that" varies from what the president would say, where the press secretary would walk, and what furniture the staff would sit on, to the strategy of the staff and their actions in politics. Riley criticizes *The West Wing* when it does not mimic the actual practices of American politics. But it is precisely at that point of departure that the show starts to get interesting.

"Six Meetings Before Lunch" centers on two main dialogues: one between Josh, the deputy chief of staff, and Jeff, the president's nominee for head of the Civil Rights Division of the Department of Justice; and the other between Sam, deputy communications director, and Mallory, a grade school teacher who is the daughter of the president's chief of staff and is also a woman Sam hopes to soon be dating. Mallory and Sam hold a series of heated discussions over the topic of school vouchers, as Mallory has recently discovered a position paper (her father seems to have left it lying around) written by Sam that argues strongly in favor of vouchers. Josh and Jeff debate the issue of monetary reparations for slavery, for it seems that Jeff has recently lent his name to the dust jacket of a scholarly book that ardently defends reparations. The various stages of these two dialogues drive this episode, but interspersed between those discussions are other less momentous staff discussions (including how to get a pair of new panda bears for the National Zoo) and a series of key developments in the romantic relationship of Charlie, the president's personal aide, and Zoe, the president's daughter. Zoe is white; Charlie is black.

Riley focuses heavily upon the relationship between Zoe and Charlie, particularly the rather passionate kiss they share in the halls of the West Wing. He somewhat casually dismisses the dialogues, and does so at just those points where they start to depart from the typical practices of what "really goes on in the west wing of the White House." Riley tosses aside the *potentially political* aspects of the episode that try to do more than follow the actual daily practices of life in the West Wing. But he emphasizes those aspects of the episode that deal with social life—something which goes on perhaps alongside those practices but which does not prove central to them. Indeed, because "Six Meetings Before Lunch" spends so much time outside of those daily practices, Riley characterizes the overall episode as "a pretty weak show." And the weakness lies in the dialogues, which Riley describes as "stilted and staged" sounding as if they were produced by "members of opposing high school debate teams." [1]

1. I have never taught high school debate, but I do teach American politics to college students, and I do have them stage debates over currently significant topics within American politics. Never in my experience has their sometimes significant discourse reached the level of substance and sophistication as that articulated in Sorkin's text. Clearly Riley's high school had quite a debate team.

It is important to note that Riley turns out to be much more than just a critic, and his overall treatment of the show remains quite evenhanded. While challenging Sorkin for his lack of political realism, Riley clearly enjoys the show and finds much to like in it: he strongly praises this episode for taking on the delicate but important social issue of interracial dating. Riley's rather ironic mistake, from my perspective, lies in his decision to turn his focus toward questions of social norms (which are not, for that reason, unimportant) and away from politics. Unconsciously or not, Riley's review of "Six Meetings Before Lunch" has the effect of translating the issue of race out of the scene of politics and into a social and cultural problematic. Riley refuses to discuss the very much political (and unpopular for that reason) issue of reparations; he turns instead to the sociocultural question of interracial dating. While not downplaying the importance of this issue, the focus here is on the *politics* of the show. Riley's approach *depoliticizes The West Wing's* treatment of race not only by turning away from the question of reparations but also by suggesting that the issue of racial reparations proves either inappropriate or misplaced in a show about American politics. Certainly it seems unlikely that reparations will make it onto the national political agenda anytime soon, but what effect does Riley's argument have in suggesting that reparations ought to stay off even the agenda of a television show *about* American politics?

Part of the answer to this last question turns on deeper theoretical questions of politics and language. Riley sees something inherently uninteresting and intrinsically apolitical about two people sitting down and talking to one another. Such events only happen, it would seem, unnaturally; hence Riley's characterization of the dialogues in this episode as "staged," as if such things only occur when they are set up to do so. But what if it is possible to locate within the conception of political dialogue presented by Sorkin a certain alternative vision of democracy, a vision that exceeds the current scope of American politics? What if political discourse holds the possibility of reconfiguring democratic politics? Any beginnings of a response to these sorts of questions requires looking exactly where Riley says not to: the dialogues.

Political Speech and Deliberation

The dialogues within this episode prove significant both for their political content—which should not be dismissed simply for a lack of practicality—and for the political implications of their *form*. In other words, within Sorkin's "staging" of the dialogues in this episode, it is possible to locate another set of political possibilities. It is precisely here that the "discursive politics" of *The West Wing* begin to emerge. But in order to shed light on these possibilities it is first necessary to outline briefly the dominant model of political speech within contemporary political theory, for recent contemporary political thought has been marked by a return to language and an emphasis on the importance of political speech.

Theorists of deliberative democracy have shifted their attention to political speech as a way to respond to some of the most troubling uncertainties of the late-modern social and political world. Deliberative democrats have a number of significant worries about political life in the twenty-first century, but what bothers them most is the modern gap between morality and politics and the pereception that without a moral grounding for politics an abyss opens between mere opinion, on the one hand, and true knowledge, on the other. Democratic theorists of deliberation accept the fact that the political world can no longer be ruled directly by a specific political morality. In other words, morality or knowledge of transcendental truths can no longer serve as the foundation for politics. But how, they then ask, can we make sure that politics remains *governed* by some sort of general knowledge or morality? If religious or scientific truths no longer serve as the basis for politics, then how do we make sure that the political sphere does not fall into the "anything goes" abyss of relativistic nihilism?

Answers to such vexing questions lie, according to the deliberative democrat par excellence, Jürgen Habermas, in a reconstruction of Kantian moral theory through the medium of intersubjective communication. Habermas disavows a positivist social science that would attempt to ground the validity of political or social norms in a crude correspondence with political morality (Habermas 1990, 67, 168; Disch 1997, 148). Nevertheless, Habermas still wishes to close the gap between knowledge and opinion, to seek some justificatory grounding for normative claims. Kantian moral theory appears to provide just such justification, through a philosophy of subjective universalism. That is, Kant grounds universal moral (and therefore political) principles in the "thinking ego"—in the structure of the individual will and in the categorical maxim to act in such a way that our actions could serve as a universal principle for all human beings (Kant 1965, 30).[2] But Kantian moral universalism, which might appear to offer a beacon of light to the darkness of late-modern politics, fails because it turns the dialogue of politics into a monologue of the subject's will. On its own, Kantian moral theory eliminates human plurality, without which there can be no politics. This is why Kantianism has to be *reconstructed* by the deliberative democrats.

They accomplish this final task by turning to a conception of language and dialogue that can restore human plurality to Kantian morality. Habermas wishes to redeem normative claims to truth, guiding principles for political action, not through the Kantian monologue but dialogically, through intersubjective communication. And Habermas insists that language provides the very medium through which to validate political norms. He writes: "the idea of coming to a rationally motivated mutual understanding is to be found in the very structure of language" (1984, 2:96). In attempting to coordinate their actions communicatively, individuals are able to *"master"* the structure of language from within it. Language for Habermas plays a crucial role for politics, because it serves the needs of political actors as a principle of guidance: "language is thereby introduced as a *mechanism* for coordinating action" (1984, 1:94, emphasis added). When conceptualized in this manner, language can bridge the gap between morality and politics, between knowledge and opinion.

Social norms can be validated through Habermas's model of communicative action, in which political actors use language as an instrument for the purposes of reaching agreement and taking action. This model of communicative rationality that can guide politics presupposes a rather specific conception of language; according to Habermas the inherent structure of language is oriented toward consensus. Habermas sets up the following criterion for political action: a political norm shall be considered morally valid

---

2. For a more thorough elaboration on the relationship between Habermas and Kant, see Villa (1996).

if it would meet with the free and consensual "approval of all affected *in their capacity as participants in practical discourse*" (1990, 66; emphasis in original). Habermas insists upon this natural mechanism of language to direct human beings toward consensus: "what raises us out of nature is the only thing whose nature we can know: *language*. . . . Our first sentence expresses unequivocally the intention of universal and unconstrained consensus" (1968, 314). Given this essential structure of language, political speech seeks consensus, and intersubjectively produced consensus provides us with the crucial principle that makes it possible to validate political norms *rationally,* yet without relying upon totalizing, metaphysical worldviews that are off-limits in disenchanted, secular, twenty-first-century politics.

In other words—those of Seyla Benhabib, another key figure in the theory of deliberative democracy—public dialogue provides "a procedure for ascertaining intersubjective validity in the public realm" (1992, 132). Political principles can be justified through a process of dialogue that strips those principles of their subjective element (their confinement to the realm of mere opinion) and allows them to aspire to the level of universality (the realm of truth). Benhabib calls this understanding of political speech an "authentic process of public dialogue," which has the effect of producing *valid* and *justified* political consensus (133). That is, public dialogue oriented toward consensus produces legitimate politics—"the validity rather than the social currency of a norm is the determining ground of . . . action" (Habermas 1990, 162).

The view of political speech that emerges from this body of thought has a number of striking and salient features. Most significant among them may be the following: the deliberative democrats elevate language to a vaunted place within politics. Language, in their theory, cannot be presupposed or dismissed as something simply incident to the process of political negotiation and bartering. The deliberative democrats thereby reject a pluralist model of politics, one that would take political outcomes to be merely the result of free competition among rival interest groups. Language, instead, must be understood according to the deliberative democrats as a tool of guidance for politics, and politics, in turn, must be identified as a search for agreement, consensus, and coordinated human action. Language serves the supreme function in politics of "form[ing] a *common* will in a communication directed to reaching *agreement*" (Habermas 1986, 76; first emphasis in original, second emphasis added). The final goal of all political dialogue must always be agreement and, eventually, pure consensus. Indeed, since the inherent structural *telos* of language proves to be mutual understanding, how could political dialogue aim at anything else? Habermas spells out this point with some emphasis, arguing not only that agreement serves as the goal of political speech but also that such agreement proves to be a self-fulfilling telos: "the power of agreement-oriented communication . . . is an end in itself" (1986, 77). Consensus serves not just as the telos of political speech but of politics writ large.

This transformation of politics through the medium of speech leads us—the name is no accident—to a more deliberative conception of democracy. But the particular model of democracy (its contours already appear obvious from the above discussion) of the deliberative democrats proves to be of less concern than two other specific implications of their work. First, they increase the relevance and heighten the role of language for politics, and second, they articulate one very specific and clearly delineated conception of political speech. The next section of this essay will take this paradigmatic model of political speech in contemporary political thought and use it as a point of reference for the conception of political discourse that emerges in the dialogues of "Six Meetings Before Lunch."

Discourse and Democracy in *The West Wing*

More precisely, this section will argue that Sorkin's vision of political discourse as it emerges within this episode grants a key role to language and speech in contemporary politics while it simultaneously rejects and refutes the deliberative democrats' inherent goal of consensus. And, it thereby implicitly surpasses their model of democracy. To try to make good on bold claims such as these necessitates a close reading of the dialogues themselves, to plumb them for their political possibilities. This requires, first, a brief summary of the content and movement of the dialogues before turning, second, to a closer investigation of the conception of discourse and democracy within them.

The key subtext of the dialogue between Sam (deputy communications director) and Mallory (school teacher and daughter of the chief of staff) on school vouchers and public education lies in their mutually acknowledged and mutually shared attraction. Their discussion begins on the evening of the Senate nomination of the White House's candidate to fill a seat on the Supreme Court. Sam and the rest of the staff have been working even longer hours than normal trying to get this difficult nomination through, and Sam plans for this evening to be his first real date with Mallory, and in general his "day of jubilee." Mallory crushes those expectations by beginning the dialogue with this line: "I despise you and everything you stand for." It seems that Leo, the chief of staff, has shared with his daughter Mallory a position paper written by Sam defending a school vouchers policy. Initially, Sam tries to deflect attention away from the entire political debate and focus on their planned date, but Mallory has no patience for such a strategy.

Instead, after plans for both the date and the celebration have been quashed, Mallory returns to Sam's office the next day to continue the discussion on purely professional terms; "I decided to see you during your office hours," she says. After much provocation from Mallory, who vigorously defends the value of public education and the absolute necessity of putting more federal funds into it, Sam finally takes up in dialogue the position articulated in the paper. He unleashes this speech: "Public education has been a public policy for disaster for forty years. Having spent around $4 trillion on public schools since 1965, the result has been a steady and inexorable decline in every measurable standard of student performance, to say nothing of health and safety. But don't worry about it because the U.S. House of Representatives is on the case. I feel better already." Their debate grows only more heated from here, with Mallory finding it hard not to be offended that a staff member of a Democratic White House (not to mention someone she had once been inclined to date) could possibly hold such ideas. Sam rails on against rich "liberals" who send their own kids to private schools while defending a public education system that offers nothing to poor children. Just when it seems that disaster, not consensus, can be the only result of this dialogue, Sam and Mallory decide to take a break for lunch. But before doing so, Mallory insists they stop by her father's office. Sam explains to Leo: "she says she always asks her father's permission before she has lunch with fascists." At this point, Leo informs Mallory that Sam actually opposes school vouchers, but it is his job to write papers that take up the other side's position. Sam explains in a speech to mirror the one above: "Mallory, education is the silver bullet. Education is everything. We don't need little changes, we need gigantic changes. Schools should be palaces; the competition for the best teachers should be fierce; they should be making six figure salaries. Schools should be incredibly expensive for government and absolutely free of charge to its citizens, just like national defense. That's my position. I just haven't figured out how to do it yet." This speech brings the dialogue to an end, as Sam and Mallory depart for lunch—perhaps their first date?

Overlapping and intersecting scenes in this episode weave in the other main dialogue, that between Josh (deputy chief of staff) and Jeff (Department of Justice nominee). Josh's job is to assure that Jeff's nomination makes it through the Senate Judiciary Committee safely and uneventfully—a job made much more difficult now that key Republican members of that committee have been made aware of Jeff's words of praise on the back of a recently released book favoring monetary reparations for slavery. Josh opens the conversation with a restatement of the facts, hoping perhaps that Jeff had been misquoted or that there was some other simple misunderstanding. He has no luck with this strategy, as Jeff goes well beyond his mere praise for the book in question to state his own strong support for the idea of reparations, even citing one prominent economist who has put a dollar amount on reparations, $1.7 trillion. Now, Josh tries harder than ever to steer the conversation elsewhere. Here is their brief exchange, which illustrates Josh's utter lack of success:

> JOSH. OK, listen, this is probably a better discussion to have in the abstract. Don't you think?
> JEFF. No
> JOSH. What do you mean?
> JEFF. I mean someone owes me and my friends $1.7 trillion.

Josh and Jeff just seem to move further and further from resolution or consensus.

From this point on, their dialogue, like Sam and Mallory's, becomes more fiery and impassioned, and at times less amicable. Josh gives up on finding an easy resolution to the problem of political appearances, and he engages more directly with the substance of Jeff's claims and the complicated, entrenched problems of race relations and their history in America. Josh and Jeff quarrel over the meaning and ramifications of the Civil War; they dispute the implications of reparations paid to Japanese who were placed in internment camps during World War II; and they debate the relationship between the holocaust and slavery. One might pithily say that in the end they agree to disagree, but this cliché would miss the point of the very discourse that they enter into and produce. In the end what they agree on is the importance of disagreement to politics and to democracy; they agree to continue discussing their disagreements, to continue disagreeing.

One could even press their dialogue to a certain theoretical limit and say that their dispute converges on a rejection of the idea of democracy as oriented toward political action based upon agreement and consensus. Josh had initially hoped that he and Jeff could find some common ground, a space of agreement, from which to move forward in their common cause of action. But no matter how much he backpedals, he only finds discord between them. And when Josh tries to move on to deal solely with the politics of the matter, saying "but let's talk about your confirmation," he simply cannot bring himself to do so; in his next breath he turns again to the substantive issues, "and while we're on the topic of the Civil War . . ." In short, this dialogue has no telos; the discussion reaches no consensus whatsoever.[3] Indeed, the dialogue has no real endpoint at all, for the episode closes with Josh and Jeff failing to agree on who should buy lunch. As his final move in this last dispute, Josh reminds Jeff: "there's going to be a lot of these meetings before your confirmation. Why don't you let me get lunch this time—you get it next time."

3. In trying to locate a point of agreement in this discussion, one could argue that Josh and Jeff do agree on what Jeff will say to the Judiciary Committee and that this point of consensus even closes the episode. I would emphasize two important aspects of Josh and Jeff's discourse in response to such an argument: (1) their agreement on political strategy still remains far removed from a Habermasian version of rational consensus that motivates and guides political action, and (2) the termination of this particular discussion cannot metonymically take the place of a conclusion to the discourse. As even the characters themselves suggest, and I point out in the text below, the larger discourse must and will go on, and it will continue to be marked by conflict and dispute.

The episode itself closes on this exchange, but one is nevertheless left with the distinct impression that the dialogue has not ended at all, that the political discussion and dispute will go on between these two even if the viewing audience never sees the character of Jeff Breckinridge again. Therefore, one cannot locate the purpose of the dialogue in an instrumental conception of political consensus. Instead, the meaning of the dialogue seems to lie in the process of discussion and dispute itself. Indeed, what appears to emerge from this process is the very idea of democracy as incomplete, provisional, and always agonistic. The very disputes that comprise this episode would seem to be constitutive of democracy. Jeff suggests as much in his final speech, which he begins by asking Josh if he has a dollar. It is plausible to wonder if Jeff plans to ask for the first downpayment on reparations, but he has something else entirely in mind. He explains: "Take it out. Look at the back. The seal, the pyramid is unfinished with the eye of God looking over it and the words 'annuit cÚptis,' 'He (God) favors our undertaking.' The seal is meant to be unfinished because this country is meant to be unfinished. We're meant to keep doing better, we're meant to keep discussing and debating, and we're meant to read books by great historical scholars and then talk about them—which is why I lent my name to a dust cover." So the purpose of the dialogues is never agreement as such; in fact, it makes no sense to say the dialogues even have a purpose in this limited, instrumental sense. The process proves dramatically more significant than the endpoints, which in hindsight seem, if anything, disappointing.

The importance of the process can be illustrated just as clearly by the case of the discussion/debate between Sam and Mallory. At first glance it might appear that their debate fits the deliberative democrats' model of democracy quite well, since Sam and Mallory's spirited dialogue seems to result in a happy state of consensus. And it is true that, in the end, they do agree. But it makes no sense to say—as the deliberative democrats would wish to do—that their political discourse allows them to reach agreement. The argument that they have reached agreement through political dialogue simply will not hold in light of the basic fact that they agreed in the first place. The dialogue could not serve to help them reach consensus, since their starting point was consensus. With the model of political speech defended by deliberative democrats, the purpose of political speech is exhausted in the

creation of consensus, so on the view proffered by that model, the entire series of exchanges between Sam and Mallory turns out to be superfluous.

Agonistic Discourse

But the reading offered here refuses to rest with such an interpretation, precisely because the dialogue did *do* something—indeed, something significant.
First, the conversation transforms the relationship between Sam and Mallory—both personally, but also in important political ways. In turn, the
process of the dialogue changes each of them significantly. One example of
this transformation appears in the third episode of the second season, "The
Midterms," which again finds Sam debating education with an intelligent,
attractive woman—this time a Republican. This episode opens with Sam
"getting his ass kicked by a girl," as Josh puts it, on a political debate television show. The "girl" turns out to be Ainsley Hayes, an up-and-coming attorney and Republican pundit. She does such an excellent job in the debate
with Sam that the president insists (over Leo's protestations) on hiring her to
work in the White House. Why does Bartlet insist on bringing a Republican
(and not even a left-leaning one, at that) into his White House? Because, as
Leo explains, "the president likes smart people who disagree with him," a
statement that re-emphasizes the vision and model of political dialogue as
centered on dispute and agonism (not consensus), a model that the show
continually fosters.

To return to the dialogue between Sam and Mallory, it seems clear that
their discussion does not guide or ground political action. That is, it does not
tell either of them exactly how to act or what to do next. Lisa Disch has
championed a vision of political speech in the work of twentieth-century political theorist Hannah Arendt that challenges the model of deliberative
democracy, a vision that can throw light on the significance of this dialogue.[4]
As in the discussion between Mallory and Sam, Disch argues, with respect to

---

4. I turn to Arendt, and to Disch's particular reading of Arendt, not in an effort to appropriate the political implications of this episode (or the show in general) for a specific model
within political theory, but rather to use concepts in contemporary political thought to shed
more light on the radical political possibilities within the show itself.

Arendt's conception of political speech, that "the peculiarity of [it] is that it produces no results" (1997, 156). Somewhat surprisingly, while Arendt rejects an instrumental conception of language as serving to achieve political consensus and orient political action, she still insists that speech lies at the heart of politics—paraphrasing Aristotle in saying that "speech is what makes man a political being" (Arendt 1958, 3). The significance of political speech, therefore, lies not in any capacity to provide a grounding for political action, but instead in its ability to offer a space for political dispute and contestation.

This essay proposes "agonist discourse"—a phrase that highlights the importance of disagreement, conflict, and struggle to politics and to discourse—as a name designed to capture this idea of political speech. An agonistic politics, as political theorists such as William Connolly (1991) and Bonnie Honig (1993) have tried to delineate it, emphasizes the importance of contestation and conflict to politics, and it resists the attempt to displace politics, to substitute administration and judgement for political battles. An agonistic theory insists upon preserving the democratic struggle: "to affirm the perpetuity of the contest is not to celebrate a world without points of stabilization; it is to affirm the reality of perpetual contest, even within an ordered setting, and to identify the affirmative dimension of contestation" (Honig 1993, 15). Discourse is agonistic to just the extent that it perpetuates the contest. Further, this agonistic element of discourse must be rigorously distinguished from *ant*agonism. Agonism implies a deep respect and concern for the other; indeed, the Greek *agon* refers most directly to an athletic contest oriented not merely toward victory or defeat, but emphasizing the importance of the struggle itself—a struggle that cannot exist without the opponent. Victory through forfeit or default, or over an unworthy opponent, comes up short compared to a defeat at the hands of a worthy opponent, a defeat that still brings honor. An agonistic discourse will therefore be one marked not merely by conflict but, just as important, by mutual admiration—something we see clearly in both dialogues from the show.

Agonistic discourse offers neither the validity of an epistemological or moral grounding to politics, nor the standard of communicative consensus to guide politics as proffered by the deliberative democrats. Instead, the idea of agonism in discourse emphasizes the role of persuasion and argumentation within a context of dispute, disagreement, and conflict. Indeed, the notion of agonistic discourse remains bound up with a similar conception of democracy as that articulated by Jeff Breckinridge. Disch interprets Arendt as follows: "in politics . . . when I say 'this is right . . . ' I neither expect that my assessment will be universally binding, as I might when I say 'this is obligatory,' nor that it will be [utterly or definitively] convincing, as I might when I say 'this is true,' but I do regard that assessment to be [political]" in a crucial way (1997, 156). To speak politically, to speak from within an agonistic discourse, is not to preach from a position of authoritative power, nor is it simply to tell the truth. It is, rather, to make a move that one hopes will be persuasive within the terms of a conflict or struggle *of* power—that is, not a struggle *for* power, as if power could be possessed in some simple way, but a power struggle, a power play, in which power relations within the discourse shift. The contest of power cannot reach a telos since neither participant can ever definitively have the power that is at stake within the discourse, and therefore, a politics of agonistic discourse must remain centrally concerned with that unfinished project of democracy, with the ongoing discussions and disputes that make American democracy what Jeff Breckinridge says it is meant to be. The idea of agonistic discourse illustrates how a nonteleological conception of political speech—that is, one that does not seek consensus—can still produce significant political effects. The emphasis, then, shifts from the endpoint of the dialogue to the process itself, a process that serves as an exemplar. Political speech ". . . works to sound out a conflict, not to consolidate a standpoint" (Disch 158). Sam and Mallory's dialogue operates within the realm of agonistic discourse precisely by "sounding out a conflict," even though—or better, perhaps *because*—the conflict in their particular case turns out to be merely apparent.

The dialogues in this episode exemplify agonistic discourse even more strikingly in the case of Josh and Jeff, because with their dispute one encounters not a mainstream issue of American politics (as education surely is), but a sensitive, complicated, and explosive topic. Any discussion of race relations in contemporary American politics reveals a deep-rooted, difficult-to-grapple-with, and politically dangerous issue. But the very idea of monetary racial reparations to the descendents of former slaves is absolutely incendiary, and falls nowhere near the current political agenda of American politics (just imagine Jim Lehrer asking presidential candidates about *that* during a national debate). So the radical nature of a conception of political dialogue *not* oriented toward consensus comes to the foreground within this dispute, since the very content of the dialogue between Josh and Jeff remains utterly marginalized in contemporary American politics.

One can put this point more succinctly: it proves extremely significant that they are even talking about reparations. But even this way of phrasing it misses part of the point, since it rests upon the distinction between the form of the dialogue and its content—the very distinction that this essay wishes to call into question. Form and content cannot be separated so neatly, since one partially determines the other. On the Habermasian model of communicative action oriented to consensus, the question of reparations could never even arise or be allowed onto the agenda, since complete agreement on this issue simply proves impossible at the present point in the continuing history of American race relations. Within the terms of agonistic discourse, however, a topic destined to elicit dispute seems right at home. So once again, the discourse between Josh and Jeff—and it certainly seems safe to call it an agonistic discourse—cannot be interpreted as aiming at agreement, particularly with such self-confident and entirely stubborn men as these two. Josh wants to think that the idea is simply preposterous, even trying to get Jeff to laugh at the notion of putting a real number on monetary reparations early on. But he quickly discovers Jeff's icy realism here.[5] Jeff believes not merely that the issue is not a laughing matter, but that it has historically been, and can today, be talked about in practical terms. Agreement between the two of them on this issue seems distant indeed.

Moreover, once this lack of possible consensus is established in the dialogue, it does not bring the dialogue to an end. Quite the opposite, in fact, the conversation really only gets underway at that point as each participant grows more committed to the discussion and more heated in his or her re-

---

5. Jeff Breckinridge's approach to issues of race seems to intersect at key moments with the important work of Derrick Bell. Bell argues for a theory of "racial realism" that places questions of economics at the core of the problem of race in America, downplays some of the merely symbolic victories for African American rights, and rejects the blind pursuit of integrationist goals as outdated legacies of a different political era (see Bell 1987; 1992).

sponses. So once again one sees dispute as essential to discourse and democracy—as, in fact, the starting point for democracy. Once again, we glimpse a vision of American democracy with agonistic discourse at its core, but one in which political speech cannot be submerged within a model of consensus.

Lunch Time: The Politics of *The West Wing*

In proffering this specific interpretation of "Six Meetings Before Lunch," and in turn a general reading of *The West Wing*, this argument does not wish to relegate the show to the somewhat narrow confines of academic political theory. To the contrary, elaborating on the meaning of the show within the terms of contemporary political thought is an attempt to broaden, not narrow, the significance and relevance of *The West Wing*. Indeed, the social, cultural, and political significance of the show cannot and should not be exhausted by its contribution to a series of academic debates, but this should almost go without saying since *The West Wing* (as everyone knows) is a major network, Emmy Award-winning, prime-time television program. Almost by definition, it speaks to a far larger audience than that which comprises the discourse of contemporary political theory. These points produce a rather direct reply to the question of why this analysis does not lock the show up in the ivory tower: such a move would be impossible. But it still proves necessary to articulate what the argument here already suggests: why a discussion of *The West Wing* in relation to democratic theory actually broadens the significance and multiplies the implications of an already wildly popular program.

The answer to that more trenchant question requires returning to this essay's point of departure in the mainstream approaches to the politics of *The West Wing*. As suggested from the start, and then demonstrated through the analysis of "Six Meetings Before Lunch," the politics of the show greatly exceed the current, exceedingly narrow terms of American politics. The lens of contemporary political theory offers a view of *The West Wing* outside, or perhaps beyond, the scope of American politics, so through this lens one witnesses a much richer, more provocative, and perhaps even radical vision of politics.

Descriptions of the importance of that vision could take a number of different tacks, full elaboration of which must be subjects for further writing and research. But a few possibilities immediately suggest themselves. Certainly political theorists might be interested to explore and continue to reconstruct a dialogue between the articulation of democratic politics within *The West Wing* and the writings and arguments of democratic theorists. Sorkin's text, especially, speaks to those debates in important ways, some of which have already been suggested here. More boldly, one might wish to explore the challenges that these political possibilities within *The West Wing* offer to both the American viewing audience and the American electorate (especially to the great extent that they intersect). One can safely characterize the United States today as country in which citizens (especially compared to their European counterparts) seemingly never wish to discuss politics, as a country in which the word "political" has become a term of great disparagement, and a country in which the space of the political sphere grows more constricted by the day.

But what does it mean that such a country has made a show about politics one of its very most popular programs? What is the relationship of that possibly radical vision of politics to the obvious attractiveness of the show? Does *The West Wing* serve to open up those spaces of the political, to make the word politics itself less a term of derision and contempt and instead one of hope, of possibility? Whatever the answers to these questions, they will all depend on attending to the alternative political possibilities—some of which are outlined here—contained within *The West Wing*. That is, they will depend upon going beyond an analysis that reconciles the correspondence between the show's vision of American politics and the current practice of American politics.

6 | *The West Wing's* Textual President

American Constitutional Stability and the
New Public Intellectual in the Age of Information

PATRICK FINN

Contemporary philology studies the meaning of words and texts in relation to their history. By examining the ways in which textuality, history, and representation interact on *The West Wing*, the appeal of President
Jed Bartlet (Martin Sheen) can be shown to stem from his relation to
America's unique textual past. Key aspects of textuality can be usefully
mapped in this representation by borrowing the description of the public intellectual laid out by scholar/writer/reporter Michael Ignatief.[1] What is clear
is that the public intellectual—whose absence Ignatief mourns—now has at
least one new voice that operates as a digital repackaging or *remediation* of
the textual past.[2] The U.S. president carries a unique relation to textual work

---

1. My selection of Ignatief's general description of the public intellectual relies on his position as a journalist, policy maker, novelist, and academic. (Ignatief is currently director of the
Center for Human Rights at the John F. Kennedy School of Government at Harvard University.)
Further, his brand of liberalism dovetails nicely with that of Aaron Sorkin. Ignatief's position
ties directly to a perception of an unaddressed desire in the public sphere that is seen in part as
the academy's failure to engage the public. Debates about the role of the public intellectual in
Western society have reached a furor over the past few years. In particular, Russell Jacoby's
books (1994; 1987; 2000) have tracked the fall of the public intellectual and that figure's failure
to mount any real radical agenda, relying instead on hollow platitudes. A forum in the *Nation*
addressed these issues while allowing Jacoby to engage with several other writer/academics of
note ("The Future of the Public Intellectual" 2001). What all of these positions share is the no-

in his duties to the Constitution, one of the founding documents of the American people. This document is at once historical and textual. By becoming a living archive or stand-in for the country's textual past and future, the president is an inherently philological creature. In order to explore these assertions, we must apply certain methods.

By focusing on a unifying artifact, the people of the United States are able to find a meeting place for debate. Participating in the reading, interpreting, and modifying of the recorded words of the country's founders makes philologists of us all. By collapsing this communicative exploration into a compressed space, Aaron Sorkin (*The West Wing*'s creator) is able to deliver a president who is an embodiment of his country's primary principles. Here, Martin Sheen's character is planted within a mocked-up West Wing in order to act out a certain form of response to the current political situation. In this case, the public intellectual is no longer outside looking in, but is written into both the documentary and digital representation of the show in such a way that he is an outsider operating on the inside.

Television's Public Intellectual

In 1996, Michael Ignatief delivered a series of public lectures called *The Illuminati* on a BBC series that he later updated for broadcast on the CBC.[3] For the rebroadcast in the year 2000, Ignatief (2001) provided an interview and commentary that focused on three points. He first argued that great thinkers of the twentieth century featured in the show were in some sense defined by being outside of the system; as such, they were generalists who, in Edward Said's

---

tion that we must return to something that we have lost. For my purposes, I am only interested in Ignatief's brand of liberalism and its commitment to a form of pluralism that I believe is used as a very effective marketing tool on *The West Wing*.

2. Jay David Bolter and Richard Grusin (1999) developed the concept of remediation in their eponymous book. Bolter and Grusin define the term as, "the ways in which new digital media refashion or 'remediate' older visual and verbal forms—for example, how the World Wide Web refashions graphic design, printing, radio, film, and television."

3. For more on this series, see www.radio.cbc.ca/programs/ideas/ideas.html.

terms, "spoke truth to power" (Said 1996, 85–102).[4] Second, he suggested that this group—which began with Voltaire (under the assumed name of Francois Marie Arouet, 1694–1798) and ended with Jean-Paul Sartre (1905–1980)—was gone and had not been replaced. Finally, he asserted that there is a growing desire to see the return of these public intellectuals.

For Ignatief, the public intellectual acts as a check on the given political power structure and brings forward new sets of ideas important to the general population. He describes the function as one that establishes the tone of debate in society. Famous examples are Emile Zola's involvement in the Dreyfus affair and later the position of intellectuals in France during the May 1968 actions.[5] For Ignatief, the leading light in this line of intellectuals was Sartre. With Sartre gone, there is a void in our intellectual and public lives.

Though it is interesting to examine the notion of the public intellectuals that Ignatief presents, it is important to note that his field of vision seems tainted by a predilection toward European thinkers. While it might be hard to imagine one hundred thousand people attending the funeral of Alan Bloom, Noam Chomsky, or bell hooks, as they did for Sartre, it would not be beyond the realm of belief to suggest that these people and others like them may indeed be considered public intellectuals. Ignatief, ever the purveyor of cultural capital,[6] seems to mourn a certain form of the public intellectual in-

4. Said has long been a proponent of a more active role for the intellectual in contemporary politics. Still the best example of his general position on these issues is to be found in the book *Representations of the Intellectual* (1996). That text, which is a collection of lectures, features a fifth section specifically titled "Speaking Truth to Power," which argues for a level of responsibility on the part of academics, who are seen to possess a privileged speaking position.

5. Zola's famed essay *"J'accuse"* charged the Catholic Church and contemporary press with anti-Semitism in the pursuit of Captain Alfred Dreyfus, who was on trial for selling military secrets. Zola's publication led to his own conviction for libel after a much-celebrated courtroom battle. There has been a great deal of writing on the subject; *The Dreyfus Affair: Honour and Politics in the Belle Époque*, by Martin Philip Johnson (1999), is among the best. The May 1968 actions are of similar fame and interest and are addressed in a number of books, one of the best being *The May 1968 Events in France: Reproductions and Interpretations* by Keith Reader and Khursheed Wadia (1993).

6. The notion of cultural capital stems from the ideas first addressed by John Guillory in his 1993 book *Cultural Capital: The Problem of Literary Canon Formation*. In the introduction to

trinsically tied to certain strains of European modernism that connects well with his own brand of left liberalism.

The notion of the public intellectual in these terms involves a position that is distinct from prevailing political discourse. During the period that Ignatief focuses on, the role takes on a quintessentially individualist flavor. The outside voice is contingent upon the ultimate separateness and integrity of the speaker. In the current American context, this means that people like William F. Buckley Jr. and Ralph Nader would not qualify for consideration because of their overt ties to the central field of conversation (Buckley in the media, and Nader in the political sphere).

To qualify as an independent thinker, Ignatief suggests that candidates must follow three rules. They must position themselves outside, they must be hyperinformed, and they must rigorously cultivate an above-average intelligence. This done, the individual earns the right to speak for the masses. The public intellectual then asks questions that the citizenry cannot imagine for themselves. In Ignatief's terms, these "illuminati" have a mandate to exercise a little cognitive hubris: they have a greater right than most to speak and be heard.

For this public intellectual, mediation is key. Ignatief points to the thousands of listeners who tuned in to the BBC in the early part of the twentieth century to listen to complex lectures delivered by logical positivist Isaiah Berlin (1909–1997).[7] He argues that there is a dearth of challenging discourse in our contemporary society leaving us in a deep state of cultural lack. Holding his apparent biases to one side, Ignatief makes an interesting point when he speaks of a desire for critical rather than ideological discussion. By leaving current topics of debate open within the character of *The West Wing*'s president, Aaron Sorkin is able to capitalize on the desire for critical complexity detailed by Ignatief. This complexity, in keeping with Ignatief's

---

that book, Guillory presents what he perceives as an attempt by the academy to drive up the value of its work through an imposed scarcity that results from controlling the means of cultural production.

7. It should be noted that Ignatief was a good friend of Berlin's who wrote his biography in 1998. Berlin is perhaps best remembered now as a political philosopher in the liberal tradition, rather than for his early work with the logical positivists.

modus operandi, is that most standard form, liberal democratic pluralism. In presenting a show that highlights a bipartisanship that governments often espouse but elide, Sorkin provides an uplifting representation of democracy.

In the American cultural context, the manifestation of this desire for complexity exhibits three prominent trends. There is a supposition that audiences do not always want complex issues resolved into categorical absolutes. In specific political terms, there is a link to a desire for nonpartisan debate over key issues. Culturally, there is awareness that any debate in the American context involves a need to deal in some way with historical precedent. The way in which the country began speaks directly to its developing social networks. Thus, a living history must play a role in any new debate. These elements highlight a form of public desire for a different way to address American politics. Finally, it seems clear that there is a fundamentally textual element buried in this quest.

The final aspect relates directly to the writing, signing, interpretation, and emendation of the American Constitution. Not surprisingly, *The West Wing*'s America also operates in a quintessentially philological state, one that is created, legitimated, and continually remade through public acts of textual interpretation. What lies at the heart of America's underaddressed desire for public, political debate is a respect for the country's originary document as officially adopted in 1789 and modified by amendments and Supreme Court interpretations. There is an engagement with the underlying intentions of the authors. An examination of words, texts, and their meanings that are so strongly imbued with historical importance calls for a particular type of study. This blending of form and content set in contextual relief parallels the type of research that is conducted by those engaged in what Randolph Starn describes as "the new erudition." This form of research has also come to be known as "the new philology."[8] Practitioners of this methodology are supposed to make rigorous examination of every aspect of the text that they are studying—from its physical construction to the varying intentions of later editors who contribute to the document's continued exis-

---

8. Starn edited a special edition of the journal *Representations* (famous as the central journal of the "new historicism") devoted to "the new erudition." The edition examines a number of approaches involving various forms of historical and historicist scholarship (1996, 1–15).

tence and growth. Through this research, new trajectories of discourse emerge that are directly influenced by textual heritage. Most important, as long as the documents survive and can be consulted, they ensure the existence of the state. Separating the documents out and making them the purview of the select further solidifies their power as independent entities.

The robust practice of interdisciplinary research highlights one of the reasons for the popularity of *The West Wing* in general and President Bartlet in particular. Whether he is looking for last-minute Christmas gifts in a bookstore ("In Excelsis Deo") or lying in bed attended by his staff ("Mandatory Minimums"), papers and books continually surround this president. He demonstrates his knowledge of classical texts in episodes such as "In Excelsis Deo," where he offers commentary on arcane volumes found in a rare bookshop in Georgetown. This in-depth textual as well as historical knowledge limns a philological president, one well equipped to work with, represent, and stand in for America's central documents.

His classically grounded intellectualism provides him with two of the qualifications to make Ignatief's list. He is hyperinformed and he works diligently to make himself intelligent. That he is also in a sense an outsider is a consistent point of the television series. In the now-famous flashback scenes that began the second season's episodes ("In the Shadow of Two Gunmen"), he is repeatedly described as a nonpartisan, nonpolitical academic—someone untainted by Beltway mentality.

Moving outside the world of the television drama and into the alternately real world of television's coverage of politics, it is important to remember that *The West Wing* began at a time when there was a great deal of talk about a general public disenchantment with politics. Could this disenchantment have stemmed from the public's real need for a more complex dialogue to satisfy an Ignatief-like desire? Perhaps it is not the field of political ideas that lost the attention of the public but the pollsters' and pundits' focus on a swirl of shifting topics when attempting to gauge public opinion. The source of the disenchantment in this scenario is the mediation itself. That is, people may be tired of who is speaking and how they are being addressed. Repackaging or remediation offers one explanation as to why a television drama that presents current events appeals to critics and the public. Thus, Sorkin and his associates are able to play to public interest by returning to the basis of public debate. In philological terms, Sorkin is emphasizing a greater level of access to the arena of debate surrounding the constitution by introducing and examining basic issues—but leaving them fundamentally unresolved. Thus, in what is a distinctly pluralist offering, debate over the document and its issues tends to break across interpretations of meaning and never over the viability of the text qua text.

The Faster Information Gets, the More Sense Bartlet Makes

With the deluge of data that accompanies the information age, there are often calls to find cultural meeting places that provide meaningful contexts for the plethora of messages we receive daily. Very few such textual meeting places offer so much in terms of pedigree as does the founding American document. By borrowing some of the power of its hallowed tradition, Sorkin is able to embed the constitution within his representation of the presidency. In this way, *The West Wing* allows not only for a specific critique of American politics; it offers America a new public intellectual.

To maintain Jed Bartlet as a public intellectual, Sorkin presents a few different perspectives of his character: he is outside of power because he maintains a split position on key issues such as abortion and the death penalty (he is against both in principle, but upholds their application). Thus, he is more an embodiment of the complexity of the issue than an ideologically driven proponent of one political vision. He is an expert on the history and interpretation of documents, as we are continually reminded by his interaction with texts and narrative. Further, he holds a doctorate in economics and is, according to the episode "Post Hoc, Ergo Propter Hoc," a Nobel laureate. In that episode, he plays at classical scholarship when he quizzes the staff on the meaning of the phrase from which the episode gets its name, finally giving his own definition of the famous logical fallacy at the etymological root of the common legal term. Deepening his philological lineage is his suggestion, in an episode entitled "What Kind of Day Has It Been," that his great, great, great grandfather was an original signatory of the *Declaration of Independence*. His continual link with America's textual condition runs throughout his family history. The show's back story informs the audience that the

Bartlets founded New Hampshire, now the site of the country's earliest—and trendsetting—presidential primary.

The contemporary backdrop for the acceptance of Bartlet is as important as its historical counterpart. Much has been made of the loss of faith in, and respect for, public office. Growing lists of "insider" books that attempt to re-establish an interest in political life attest to this fact. Books such as Joseph Lieberman's *In Praise of Public Life* (2000) and David Gergen's *Eye Witness to Power* (2000) are two among many examples.[9] If we accept that political interest and/or faith had fallen before *The West Wing* came to air, how can we explain the nonpartisan draw created by the drama within a simulated White House?

The Constitution of Character

Part of the answer lies in character development. To whatever degree Jed Bartlet is a constructed president, he is by no means a wooden or one-dimensional character. He does not replicate the standard positions of one or another party position. Moreover, he is almost painfully human. Yet, as a character, he also develops in a way that allows him to act as a functional archive for the living records of American political discourse—a development that will reach completion when his term ends and his documentary history finds a home in a presidential library bearing his name. In keeping with this development, he speaks rapturously of his dreams of public debate and great conversations to Leo, his friend and chief of staff: "I'm sleeping better. And when I sleep I dream about a great discussion with experts and ideas and diction and energy and honesty, and when I wake up, I think, 'I can sell that' " ("Mandatory Minimums"). Viewers who recall Aaron Sorkin's earlier foray into political drama in the film *The American President* (1995) will note similarities between this president's connections to the constitution and that of President Shepherd (Michael Douglas) in the earlier project.[10] In that film, the widower president finds himself under attack for his relation-

---

9. Both Lieberman and Gergen are Washington insiders whose books respond to what they see as a need to reengage the American population with their system of government.

10. My thanks to Peter Rollins for his suggestions regarding Sorkin's *American President*.

ship with lobbyist Sydney Ellen Wade (Annette Bening) by Senator Bob Rumson (Richard Dreyfus), who insists on making personal attacks rather than addressing political issues. Throughout the film, Douglas's character resists engaging in this form of "character debate" until, in a climactic press conference, he argues that in his experience being president is "entirely about character." In order to combat the earlier critiques of his foe, the president accuses Rumson of wanting to reject the constitution. Turning the character debate back on his nemesis, President Shepherd asks, "Why would a senator, his party's most powerful spokesman and a candidate for president, choose to reject upholding the constitution?" In formal terms, Sorkin is providing room for identification, for a linkage between character and document. In the philological sense, he shows someone ideally suited to historical stewardship. It is important to note that neither *The West Wing* nor *The American President* promotes notions of a utopian resolution of the two-party system into a joyful synthesis. Instead, these dramas provide a representation of the pressing political issues of the day that have at heart feelings of nostalgia for a lost sense of decency in American democracy. In each case, the resolution is found in a president who accepts the role of the public intellectual, who specializes in the textual analysis of America's founding documents.

Again, the issues are not resolved into ideological positions but are guaranteed by the character. Two of the best examples of this type of unresolved complexity in *The West Wing*'s president are his aforementioned positions on the death penalty and on abortion, both of which are prohibited by his Catholic faith—a faith that we are told he actively practices (interestingly, Sheen calls himself a "radical Catholic" and is known for his offscreen participation in public protests related to nuclear power and environmentalism). Even the characters around the president offer examples of this malleability, perhaps the most compelling being chief of staff Leo McGarry, a recovering alcoholic and substance abuser, who is spearheading drug legislation. Bartlet and his crew stand out from messages related to political disenchantment and instead give form to the complexity of issues that are at the heart of American political debate.

The nature of the unresolved complexity in Bartlet tends to highlight issues that cut across party lines. Clearly, the series is not without its own obvious biases. What Sorkin taps into in order to sell his show is a desire in a certain sector of the public to be treated as active thinkers. This reaction forms a direct rebellion against absolutist sound bites. *The West Wing*, then, offers a public intellectual who counterpoises the representation of the actual or real president. Jed Bartlet as president preserves the complexity of the issues, a respect for intelligent debate, and a commitment to the U.S. Constitution. Thus, Bartlet as public intellectual operates in a manner that allows him to qualify as one of Ignatief's "outsiders." That Bartlet's position is from within the genre of television drama creates parallels with and distinctions from his public intellectual forbearers. Sartre made many of his political comments in the popular press and in novel form. Still, some might be troubled by the different states of reality inhabited by the flesh-and-blood Sartre and by Sorkin's telegenic avatar.

The West Wing and Textual Community

Any current discussion involving different kinds of texts necessarily involves considerations of the hypertextual or marked-up forms of text made ready for Internet presentation through a series of links. Before conducting an examination of the use of hypertextuality, the textual and philological aspects of power that sustain President Bartlet require scrutiny. In Brian Stock's *The Implications of Literacy* (1983), he examines the growth of a society, in this case early English society, around its documents. Citizens, Stock argues, structure their lives around their documents. The American constitution acts as a central document in what Stock calls a textual community (88–240). Although many of the people in the community have never seen the actual document, it exists as a reference point for their lives. In the American context, the Constitution stands as a democratic meeting place for the opinions of its citizenry. In watching *The West Wing*, in such numbers and with such devoted regularity, viewers seem to be attempting to return to the promises of their documentary past.

We must ask, how could Americans not identify with a document that gives them their natural identity? Whether by inclusion or exclusion, the Constitution has helped to shape the citizenry in American history. A philological president understands this situation because he knows the document, knows its interpretation, its history, and its cultural impact. Inside the mise-en-scène of *The West Wing*, Jed Bartlet is this type of president. Outside it, he is a public intellectual speaking "truth to power" in a manner that serves Sorkin's Hollywood-liberal mentality.

The president lives a life that is immanent history, a life that is inscribed in both the past and the future. So, when William Jefferson Clinton (1993–2001) emphasized his middle name, it was out of recognition of history, but it also reminded listeners of the future that Thomas Jefferson (1801–1809) was able to shape. A similar example of immanent history occurs on *The West Wing* when the staff and president read the one-hundred-year history book that compares changes over the past century ("Let Bartlet Be Bartlet"). In that episode, Josh's assistant Donna reminds him (after he upbraids her for a report containing a text by James Madison that he says resembles a "social studies paper") that it is the text from James Madison, more than current research, that will help him with his legislative agenda. In these contexts, history is less a field of commentary on a series of past events than a living and growing archive that influences both current politics and future development.

As Jacques Derrida argues, archives are as much about the future as the past (1995, esp. 33–39). The presidential archive, whether in the living body of the sitting president or in the history of his time in office, is an active corpus linked to originary documents. The textual nature of this archive secures those documents. It is then reinforced by the creation of presidential libraries, which become material reminders of the essentially philological nature of the office.

The documents and their greater archive involve a developing history of the American presidency and a designated meeting place of the American people. Though these aspects often go unarticulated, they are what allow the constitution to be a locus for debate on issues ranging from slavery to abortion and capital punishment. Though the document reads in many ways, its sociohistorical position entails an underlying guarantee of some form of permanence. It is from the power of this permanence that Aaron Sorkin borrows to define his president. Thus, Bartlet comes to embody the personalization of politics. What makes President Bartlet a peculiarly philological president is the equal balance of history and textuality in his composition. This balance offers a blend of the ideological underpinnings of constitutional debate as discussed by Bernard Bailyn in *The Ideological Origins of the American Revolution* (1992), where he argues that the political divide surrounding the revolution involved a distinction between the colonials' perception of a "constitution" as a specific document, and the British belief in constitution as the accrued lessons, legislation, and practices of natural history.[11] In Sorkin's philological representation of the documentary history of America, the specific document and its historic essence coexist.

Clearly, part of what attracts viewers to *The West Wing* is its offer of a new space for political discussion. Add to this a media avatar who moves beyond the electronic and into the visceral by speaking truth to mediated power, and by directly addressing an insufficiently addressed desire for complex debate, and the result is some very powerful television. Bartlet then is a public intellectual in digital form. By maintaining the undecidedness of political debate within his character, he represents a form of democracy that respects the right of citizens to decide issues on their own. Sorkin achieves the effect through the presentation of an embodiment of the appreciation of text, context, and access. In the end, Josiah Bartlet speaks truth to power by revivifying America's textual past. (That this space only exists for most of us along thin lines of coaxial cable only really matters during the commercial break.)

The West Wing, Hypertext, and Space

Space is used in very specific ways on the show. Specifically, the approach *The West Wing* uses reinforces what can be called *hypertextual television*: a form of televisual display that uses a spatial rhetoric to create (or at least aggravate) and then manipulate a particular form of desire in viewers.

Ted Nelson, who invented the term, defines hypertext as, "a body of written or pictorial material interconnected in such a complex way that it could not conveniently be presented or represented on paper" (Nelson 2001).[12] Nelson's 1965 definition is simple and direct. What it does not capture is the affective quality that the word *hypertext* has since accrued. Propo-

11. I am grateful to Peter Rollins for pointing me toward Bailyn's work in this area.
12. For more information see Nelson's home page: www.sfc.keio.ac.jp/~ted/.

nents of digital technology have increasingly come to equate the hypertextual with notions of the atemporal and nonspatial, as if hypertextual somehow meant hyperreal. Atemporal because hypertext denotes a mode of information that involves not only Nelson's complex interconnections, but also an implementation of perceptual simultaneity. These technocultural gestures suggest a pace of life that is increasing with alarming rapidity and asserts that the population is under stress as a result. The hypertextual organization of previously textual space offers a direct challenge to textually based thinking inherent in Aaron Sorkin's public intellectual.

The concept of hypertextual television evokes the related concept of remediation, as defined by Bolter and Grusin (1999). They describe remediation as relating "the ways in which new digital media refashion or remediate older visual and verbal forms" (3–15). Aaron Sorkin uses this remediation to create tension by overlapping texts, television, and hypertext (or hypermedia). Bolter and Grusin argue that remediation can take place either from older to newer or the reverse (5–9). Sorkin uses both of these aspects. He brings textual influence forward into television at the same time that he brings hypertextual influence back to television and text. Current popular examples of these types of overlap are found in the variety of rolling stock tickers, weather updates, and bulleted information lists on news broadcasts such as CNN, CNBC, and (the appropriately titled) CTV News Net.

These programs present a worldview in which viewers must multitask in order to keep up with an ever-increasing stream of information. Further, it is not enough to be able to work on a variety of projects in close proximity, to replicate the complexity of Nelson's hypertext; rather, we must participate in a simultaneity of representation. The nature of information consumption is usefully encapsulated in Frederic Jameson's "intentionally paradoxical" formulation that in the postmodern, "difference relates" (1997, 31). Jameson offers as examples the work of installation artist Nam June Paik, featuring stacked televisions, each demanding attention, and David Bowie's character Thomas Jerome Newton, who watches fifty-seven televisions at once in the film *The Man Who Fell to Earth* (1976). Hypertextual television attempts to capture some of this stress on one screen.

The West Wing offers an example of one way in which this new form of hypertextual television operates in contemporary culture. Sorkin's version recalls Jameson's work but stops short of requiring the theorist's Marxist critique of societal stress. This is a direct result of the show's use of a two-tiered release involving a stabilizing form of technology and a reassuring father figure, which combine to pull the audience back from the full tension at the heart of the chaotic world presented in *The West Wing*.

Following the tradition of shows like *Law and Order* and *ER*, *The West Wing* capitalizes on the public's fascination with its own response to an ever-quickening world. Using ripped-from-the-headlines themes, these shows are able to build upon America's obsession with real-time representations of itself. Entailed in the production is a new form of critique that plays off valences of power at work in the social spaces represented.

From an Althusserian perspective, these shows are ideological state apparatuses that glamourize repressive state apparatuses.[13] That is, they are mainstream institutional shows that provide a message that officials are working hard and that in the end—while they may make the occasional mistake—they have our best interests at heart. Moreover, they pose an argument that what is really needed is more money and more support for the programs of big government—more money to fight the threat of disease, more money to fund the New York City police force, and more money to support whatever the American government decides is in the global interest. Finally, in the series there is a mood of capitulation developed as the show's key characters settle for small changes and minimal triumphs against the backdrop of a hopelessly complicated world. This strategy takes place in a number of ways on *The West Wing*; of primary importance is the show's rhetorical use of physical space.

The West Wing in Motion

Perhaps *The West Wing*'s most famous formal aspect is its use of the "walk-and-talk" (also now known as the "peda-conference"). In this hypertextual

---

13. Althusser's well-known work on ideological and repressive state apparatuses is found in the book *Lenin and Philosophy, and Other Essays* (2001). Briefly, ideological state apparatuses (ISAs) are cultural machinations that placate a population and persuade it to believe in the existing power structures. Repressive state apparatuses (RSAs) are the physical means of control

dance, individuals walk through the halls of the West Wing, sometimes three and four abreast, briskly speaking about crucial issues in domestic and foreign policy, sprinkling their conversations with essential narrative elements and office gossip. Participants join and leave the walk-and-talk staying only long enough to emit highly polished sound bites. The camera—poised on a steadicam unit strapped to the camera operator—shows them breaking off and joining new groups while continuing the smooth, breakneck pace of governance. In the backdrop, we see televisions tuned to CSPAN—and CNN-like stations. Every desktop has a flat screen computer open and powered up. Notably, there is rarely a screensaver; a marker that would indicate a workstation that would have to have stopped interfacing for what would be an obscene fifteen-minute period (the average time it takes for the default screen savers to start). The walk-and-talk is complemented by quick scene changes that maintain a number of subplots. One key effect is an emphasis on the speed at which the government works and to accentuate the notion of simultaneity. The message is that those who do not move quickly will be left behind in Jed Bartlet's West Wing.

There is an implicit question here—who could move this quickly or this well? These characters are witty, attractive, and hyperintelligent. Moreover, they have purpose; they believe strongly in *something*. This all-pervasive belief helps address the tension the show builds around technology and politics. As such, it is central to what makes the show appealing to its audience.

The show uses an elaborately designed, three-dimensional West Wing that is in fact a good deal more spacious and better equipped (at least on the surface) than its real-life counterpart. The actual West Wing, with its cramped hallways and antiquated technology, could not support the same technocultural motif that Aaron Sorkin's virtual wing does.

Once set in motion, action is captured on a steadicam. This device is a wearable camera equipped with a counterweight that allows the operator to

---

that the state uses, such as the police, military, and hospitals. For my purposes, it is not necessary to follow all aspects of the structural Marxist position that Althusser developed, but rather to point out and query the cultural and political environment that has given rise to a flood of television shows that are in essence ISAs that use RSAs as subject matters. A few examples are *ER*, *Law and Order*, *The Agency*, *Third Watch*, *Boston Public*, and of course *The West Wing*.

be mobile while the view from the lens remains perfectly still. This counter-weight stands in for what is perhaps most marketable about the show. This small piece of equalizing technology reaches out to the viewing public and says everything is okay. The office may be moving fast, and the political issues may be complicated, but you are stable. (This in direct contrast with the shaky, handheld camera used on such shows as *NYPD Blue* in order to heighten tension through a set of visual cues.) On *The West Wing*, this calming mechanical counterweight has a cultural complement of equal if not greater force.

Father Knows Best in *The West Wing*'s Pilot Episode

The show's domestic force is perhaps best illustrated in the "Pilot" episode, which aired on September 22, 1999. The story begins by presenting a series of scenes that introduce the main characters. These are uber-Democrat and chief of staff Leo McGarry (John Spencer); C. J. Cregg (White House press secretary, played by Allison Janney); Toby Zeigler (communications director and New York intellectual extraordinaire, played by Richard Schiff); and Josh Lyman (the Fulbright scholar and deputy chief of staff, played by Bradley Whitford). In one of the early shots in the first act, Josh is asleep at his desk. The story unfolds, revealing that he misspoke the day before on the talk show *Capital Beat*. While on air he called fellow panelist (and religious right-winger) Mary Marsh a worshipper of a "corrupt God that is currently under investigation for tax fraud." Such a statement said much for Josh's cutting wit, but provided Bartlet's enemies with a powerful weapon.

Finally, the camera comes to Sam Seaborn (Rob Lowe) the clean-cut Princeton man with a name and persona that somehow manage to be whiter than Theodore Cleaver. Sam is in bed with a call girl who is smoking pot. Though he does not yet know she is a prostitute, he will respond to that news in the same way he does to her offer of the joint—by immediately distancing himself while insisting that he makes no judgment in doing so.

The device by which all of these introductions occur is a series of simultaneous pager messages announcing, "POTUS has been in a bicycle accident." This strange word is heard in each sequence until Sam's companion remarks on his friend's "strange name." Sam informs her, "he's not my friend, he's my boss, and it's not his name, it's his title—President of the United States." Cue theme music and a shot of a rippling American flag veiling the White House.

Afterwards, through numerous walk-and-talks and information updates, the show builds tension around a perception of a busily working White House. The story culminates in a meeting between Mary Marsh and the Christian right on one side of a room with Toby, C. J., and Josh on the other. The camera occupies the space between. This meeting has been arranged to allow Josh to apologize. It quickly goes sour when Toby accuses Marsh of anti-Semitism. In an attempt to salvage the meeting, one of the members of the evangelic group brings up a point his group is interested in lobbying. In so doing, he references the First Commandment, which he incorrectly gives (surprising for a minister) as honor thy mother and father. When Toby challenges him the irate minister screams, "Well, what is the First Commandment then?"

"I am the Lord your God. Thou shall worship no other god before me." Uttering this line, President Bartlet enters the room, the first episode, and the series. From this point forward, it is apparent that the greatest counterweight to the commotion in the White House is this scholarly—yet decisive—president.

There is no mistaking the form of domestic calm that is effected by this entrance. The characters' responses to Josh's misbehavior resolve into a "wait till your father gets home" motif that Bartlet is quick to satisfy. He kicks the religious lobbyists out of the building and lovingly chastises the staffers who head to their offices. On his way out, the ill-behaved Josh is called back and told firmly "don't ever do it again." Sorkin's virtual president finds his grounding in an old-style liberal character type: the Ivy League father figure who has all the answers. The problem is that Sorkin's new version of this old form carries with it many of the same problems from which it has continually suffered. These difficulties are by now so apparent that they are, in a later episode, voiced by one of the characters, Toby Ziegler, who accuses the president of "eastern, Ivy League isolation" that causes him to forget the actual suffering of ordinary people ("The Two Bartlets"). As it turns out, this is the beginning of a character twist for Bartlet, where he is shown to have two sides to his public personality (hence the episode's title): the first side is Bartlet's intellectual acuity, which Toby connects to the classic tenets of American liberalism; the other is the part of Bartlet's character that causes him to move away from the left and into the center in order not to offend. Tellingly, the episode's climactic scene and the following installment develop the idea that his move to the center is part of a pathology for which he needs help. Described as a desire on the part of the president to find love from his father, this move offers Sorkin an interesting way to contrast different segments of the Democratic Party in terms of the sick Bartlet and the healthy Bartlet, which follows more closely a certain form of Hollywood liberalism. It is interesting that this is not Sorkin's first foray into armchair psychoanalysis. In a move that cries out for Freudian analysis, the second season introduced the beautiful, blonde, Southern, Republican lawyer Ainsley Hayes (Emily Proctor), who is kept in the basement of the West Wing in the "heat exchange room." Hayes gets and maintains her job by "whupping" Sam ("In This White House") or by demonstrating her "lipstick feminism" in order to put left-wing feminists in their place ("Night Five"). What is the audience to make of the Democrat Sorkin's desire to lock a young female Republican in the basement?

The air of domesticity linked to textual mastery and interpretation that Bartlet brings to the White House develops in subsequent episodes. One example is provided in the episode "Mandatory Minimums." The president is shown late at night, propped up in the family bed and surrounded by books and papers, listening to what each of his staffers has accomplished that day. The characters line up at the foot of his bed, waiting their turns to share what they have done that day. He compliments them on a job well done, imparts some wise advice, and bids them goodnight. This imposed domestic space offers a form of calm against the unsettling aspects of political life.

Watching *The West Wing*

So, who watches *The West Wing* and to whom does this textual domesticity appeal? Ratings show that the U.S. audience splits evenly across Republican and Democratic lines. The unifying factor seems to be the audience's income. *The West Wing* is the number one show in households making more than

$100,000 a year.[14] There are many potential explanations; one must be the show's glorification of a tier-one university mindset. After all, the president, however saccharine, is a Nobel-laureate economist who quotes Latin and classic literature. Further, characters continually discuss where they went to school, how long they were there, and what awards and grades they achieved.

Also important is a form of pluralism embodied in Sorkin's commander in chief. He stays on the fence for important issues: he is antiabortion but will not legislate against it; he feels strange having dinner alone with a man but is not opposed to same-sex marriage; he is a free-market economist but is not averse to quoting Chairman Mao. It seems that Bartlet acts as a repository for the desire for meaning, any meaning, in order to hold out against a perceived relativism in the sociopolitical sphere. The result seems to be that, whether donkeys or elephants, any patriarch will do in a storm.

If Bartlet is a dominant force in the mediated world of *The West Wing*, his power does not stop there. During the 2000 presidential election, the cast appeared in-character lobbying for the Gore/Lieberman ticket. On the *Tonight Show*, guest Martin Sheen (who plays Bartlet) was shown in a backstage scene receiving the script for *The West Wing* from (the real) Al Gore who handed over the document, saying, "here, it's ready" (October 31, 2000). While the Leno show may be known for its hyperbolic representations of political issues, a valid point about the series was made.

The height of this form of campaigning came when Sheen gave a speech at a California treatment center saying that George W. Bush was a "white knuckled-drunk" who could fall apart at a crucial moment because he had never sought proper treatment for alcoholism.[15] In this powerful message, Sheen seems to blur his special Hollywood knowledge of the twelve steps with his cultural experience as television's favourite president.

The ties between the White House and the show are particularly close. The program has advisors from both the Democratic and Republican parties (though the latter came on board later). Clinton *wunderkind* George

---

14. For details on show demographics, see *Hollywood Reporter* 2000.

15. Sheen said this in a speech in a California treatment center. The story was picked up and reported by the Associated Press on November 13, 2000.

Stephanopoulos did a morning news broadcast from the set, reporting first on architectural similarities and then moving on to contemporary political issues (*Good Morning America,* March 1, 2001). As further testimony to the legitimacy of the show, a number of U.S. schools now use taped episodes when teaching civics classes.

More recently, Sorkin's comments in the *New Yorker* (which were subsequently picked up by CNN ["*West Wing* Creator Criticizes Brokaw Special" 2002]) regarding the media's treatment of President Bush in the wake of the events of September 11, 2001, caused a real-world stir (March 4, 2002). In that piece, Sorkin attacked news anchor Tom Brokaw for hosting a show entitled "The Bush White House: Inside the Real West Wing" (January 23, 2002), which aired just before *The West Wing* on the same network. While *The West Wing*'s creator argued that he was in full support of President Bush, he felt that the media had not done its best to be objective, saying that their coverage was like a "valentine" to the president. In the same piece, Sorkin described his desire to rework the history of the 2000 election by staging a new election between the intellectual Bartlett and a Republican candidate who is "not the sharpest knife in the drawer." The recasting involved the plotline established in "The Two Bartlets" episode, where a demonstrably intellectual president is encouraged to show off his particular form of intelligence in order to best a Republican candidate; one wonders if Al Gore's script urged this direction for the program.

The Message Is Medium

Given that *The West Wing*'s political message is so successful, it may be worthwhile to ask just what the message is. Part of the show's motive seems to involve an attempt to define a new political mythology. This tension surrounding the preservation of America's hereditary, chartered sense of self comes at a time when the country is particularly obsessed with its own potential for decay. The Clinton scandals—and impeachment proceedings— left behind classic symptoms of moral decay that left many of Sorkin's ilk in dismay. Further factors in this decay arrive in the form of a threat of diffusion brought on by the data glut entailed in globalization, and more recently by the strains of the "War on Terrorism." The message offers a matrix of beliefs that ensure that the American identity is still firmly in place and can move onward and outward without risking dissolution. It is telling that in the wake of the events of 9/11 *The West Wing*'s message has remained essentially the same. With the exception of a hastily crafted response episode that gained the nickname "Terrorism 101" (the third season's "Isaac and Ishmael"), *The West Wing* has maintained its format. The show's challenges seem now to lie in a need to develop characters that are emerging from the glow of early success and will need to find depth in order to continue. So, while the audience may be changing as a result of current politics, the celebratory nature of Sorkin's take on American democracy remains attractive to viewers—for now.

◆   ◆   ◆

Marshaled to Sorkin's cause is an implied shift in the way contemporary culture thinks about the organization of knowledge. This epistemological shift occurs between a population trained to focus on texts with sequential linear constructions and a new digitally aware group capable of running many processes at once. Here Sorkin calls to mind the anxiety-causing views found in the art of Nam June Paik and David Bowie as examined by Frederic Jameson. It is not necessary to assume that this shift is in any sense real in terms of the operations of viewers' synapses. Rather we may regard this epistemological shift as a cultural perception of a rivalry between the focused mind of grand mal modernism and a new postmodern brain capable of monitoring the NASDAQ, the weather, and the Summit of the Americas simultaneously.

The West Wing maximizes the tension between modern and postmodern epistemologies by collapsing the worries of information overload into the complications of current political issues. Thus, both form and content join in what Jameson calls an "overt stress of decentring" (1997, 15). But rather than being left in this state of befuddlement, the audience is quickly reoriented by the combination of the steadicam gaze and steadying voice of a president who imposes an ideal domestic space in the White House. Within this space, the *grand familia* is capable of interpreting all incoming information and resolving the issues into what amounts to a Rawlsian view of American politics—that is, one founded upon notions of tolerance, fiscal responsibility through fairness, and a distinct notion of social justice.[16]

The resolution of this tension capitalizes on a manipulated frenzy at the nexus of the global and the hypertextual, and on their concomitant challenges to our notions of space; it offers a form of nonresolution based on a supposition of the freedom of exchange of discourse. Sorkin makes his message more palatable by employing the language and images of the aforementioned ideal American domestic space. Using the notion of remediation as discussed by Jay David Bolter and Richard Grusin (1999), *The West Wing* further develops this split between the frenetic world of multimedia communications and the more focused thought of the textually defined characters Jed, Leo, and Toby by continually portraying them holding material examples of documents. The effect then is to impart a message to the concerned viewer that the old answers are still the best answers (though you should probably buy a new laptop as well).

The excess of information used to define the new media marketplace in which the show trades portrays a hypertextual substrata carrying a message of the loss of meaning delivered at blistering speed. Here, the show counterpoises an overt textuality embodied in a liberal democratic brand of domestic life. The inherent textuality involved in this process develops an essentially philological American president, who embodies the constitution, offers historical interaction with his forbearers, and finally realizes an architectonic apotheosis as presidential library.

The message the show imparts is of particular interest in terms of its audience. *The West Wing*'s demographic is highly educated. Viewers are also the target audience for the news channels whose programming features the new multitasking approach to media. They are the fastest growing group of Internet users and may be particularly receptive to the show's message because of high-tech product marketing focused directly on them. This power carries over to the political in that this group lobbies and votes in greater

16. Rawls's particular version of "justice as fairness" was perhaps the most influential argument in American liberalism during the 1970s, 1980s, and 1990s. He first developed the ideas in *A Theory of Justice*, published in 1971. He continued to defend the ideas until his death in 2002; see for example *Political Liberalism* (1996), first published in 1993.

numbers, and that, when they vote, more of their votes are declared valid by election officials.

To say that the show appeals only to a targeted nostalgia though would be too simple. There are clear indications that *The West Wing* is trying to offer something new. The show has discussed gay rights, race reparations, policy on Cuba, soft money, Puerto Rican statehood, and the fact that the real drug problem, like the media problem the show foregrounds, is in a large part an American creation. Moreover, it features a president who can actually speak, who reads and knows Latin. A little bourgeois perhaps, but this audience seems to prefer a politician who can do a *West Wing* walk-and-talk to one caught in the all too human realities of *real politick,* where the meticulous eye of the media searches for and exploits any sign of weakness in a politician's life.

Yet, if *The West Wing* gains from the remediation of a textually grounded liberalism, it also incurs some of the same costs that this way of thinking always entails. It is at heart a show that promises that the Ivy League will save us. Everyone other than that group of elites is clearly subservient and is treated with the special condescension that certain elitist factions of the center-left have honed to a fine art.

Shows like *Law and Order* and *The West Wing* allow viewers to believe they have a firm grasp of the complexities in their world—or at least of America's world. But, is the democracy of these shows the democracy of real America? Whatever its relation to the actual, the show seems to posit a new ideal. Whether or not these ideals themselves are dangerous, we should ask if *The West Wing*'s particular form of idealism is useful. In our current context, it seems that a strong element in the American population has an unaddressed desire to believe in something politically positive. It is the path marked by popular books like Joe Lieberman's *In Praise of Public Life* and David Gergen's *Eyewitness to Power.* In an attempt at a post-ideological pluralism (which bears some relation to what some refer to as the "New Way," as espoused by Anthony Giddens, friend and advisor to Tony Blair and director of the London School of Economics[17]), the audience is sold complex-

---

17. For more on Giddens, see his London School of Economics home page at www.lse.ac.uk/Giddens/.

ity as a motivation both for action and for complicity. In this formulation, the public is shown a form of political exchange that prides itself on capitulation to an unseen and relentless chaos. What this perhaps elides is the actual nature of contemporary conflict resolution. As the United States increases its reliance on contract law and the judiciary both at home and abroad, it may be misguided to commit too much energy to glorified notions of participatory democracy. Nevertheless, *The West Wing*'s particular brand of democratic idealism is an extremely efficient way to market the United States' number one global export: a normative form of democratic rule based on individual property rights.

This product, when packaged for *The West Wing*, first heightens, and then offers a remedy for, the symptoms of postmodern political stress. Through its interaction with America's founding documents, and through the repackaging of current political issues, this transcendent form of media reaches beyond coaxial cable and into the everyday lives of Americans. It offers a new public space for debate, presided over by a new kind of virtual public intellectual. In the end, it may just be believing in believing, but that is a hell of a lot more comforting than what is on CNN.

7 | The Left Takes Back the Flag

*The Steadicam, the Snippet, and the Song
in* The West Wing's *"In Excelsis Deo"*

GREG M. SMITH

A good episode of a prime-time serial ensemble drama has to accomplish many difficult tasks. The makers of the series have to juggle several plotlines in parallel action to keep key cast members in front of their audience and to provide dramatic payoffs for them. In addition, a serial drama must invoke the past histories of its characters to take full advantage of an audience's long-term relationship with those beloved individuals. The temptation is to rely on talk, talk, talk, but the reigning television wisdom says that static talking heads are visually deadening. How, on the one hand, does a series like *The West Wing* pack all the required action and information into an episode without bogging the audience down in dialogue? And how, on the other hand, does it avoid taking on too frenetic a pace, overloading the audience with a blur of information? Producers could string together a rapid series of short scenes to cover the many separate pieces of required plot information, but the overall effect would be disjointed. An episode needs some unifying element to bring together the disparate plot strands into a cohesive, satisfying whole.

Close attention to a particular episode's aesthetic strategies can provide a grounded explanation of how *The West Wing* manages its narrational juggling act. How does the episode balance the need for multiple plotlines with the need to create a cohesive whole? Using the first-season episode "In Excelsis Deo," this chapter shows how *The West Wing*'s aesthetic strategy depends on the coordination of key visual and verbal techniques. "In Excelsis Deo," which won an Emmy for Outstanding Writing in a Dramatic Series in 2000, exemplifies how the series uses conversational snippets and steadicam tracking shots to accomplish its dramatic tasks. Along the way to its lyrically musical coda, the episode also displays one of *The West Wing*'s most innovative strategies: its activation of rousing, traditional, patriotic imagery in the service of left-wing politics.

Sound Bites

As the title indicates, "In Excelsis Deo" (the Latin translation of the proclamation of the angels to the shepherds at Jesus' birth: "Glory to God in the highest") is a Christmas-themed episode, full of bustling to prepare the White House for the holidays. Mandy (Moira Kelly) is making arrangements for a special Christmas reception, and Donna (Janel Maloney) pesters Josh (Bradley Whitford) about getting her a present. Press secretary C. J. (Allison Janney) and reporter Danny (Timothy Busfield) continue to dance around the conflict between their attraction and their official roles. More serious matters arise when the White House staff realizes that Leo (John Spencer) will soon be lambasted by a zealous Republican congressman who wants to expose Leo's history of drug use. In spite of Leo's admonition to remain calm, Josh convinces Sam (Rob Lowe) that they should take action, interrogating Sam's prostitute friend, Laurie (Lisa Edelstein), for incriminating information about possible Republican sexual indiscretions. In another dramatic plotline, the White House follows the unfolding story of a gay high school student (modeled on the real-life Matthew Shepard case in Wyoming) who was beaten and murdered, thus sparking a policy debate on hate crimes. Through a chance connection, Toby (Richard Schiff) gets involved in the final affairs of a homeless veteran found frozen to death near the war memorials on the National Mall. Toby begins to understand the aggravating bureaucracy that a man of his high status normally bypasses, and he blasts through protocol on behalf of the departed to arrange for a military funeral in the episode's closing moments.

The vast majority of conversations in this episode are conveyed through simple shot-reverse shot editing. All television dramas rely on shot-reverse shot conversations as their basic material, but different dramas choose additional visual techniques to tell their stories. The television genre that has worked the longest at juggling multiple plotlines is, of course, the soap opera. Mainstream prime-time serial drama tends to reject many of soap opera's more marked devices for conveying information. Verbal asides, flashbacks, voiceovers, and dream sequences are considered a bit heavy handed.

The prime-time serial drama tends to use devices that are not so "tainted" with their association to soap opera. *ER* (1994–), for instance, avoids an overreliance on static shots of talking heads by alternating its fairly standard conversational scenes with elaborate, kinetic, steadicam camera movements during emergency incidents. This technique traces its lineage to the more highly valued feature film practice of the sequence shot, used in films from *Touch of Evil* (1958) to *The Player* (1992). *Homicide*'s (1993–99) much ballyhooed televisual style used flashy jump cuts and other continuity violations to add pep to its character interactions, although it did tend to rely on more standard editing for most of its dramatic interchanges.

Series also use a range of techniques to unify an episode's plotlines and to provide a satisfying sense of closure. The courtroom drama is perhaps best prepared to offer such tight closure because a lawyer's final arguments provide a natural forum for making connections and drawing conclusions. *Northern Exposure* (1990–1995) turned to disc jockey Chris Stevens (John Corbett) to provide a running philosophical commentary on the characters' activities, using the forum of a radio show to provide voice-over narration. *Oz* (1997–), the show that manages to juggle the largest number of plotlines and principal characters, steps out of the diegesis to provide a unifying element. Wheelchair-bound Augustus Hill (Harold Perrineau) directly addresses the camera with literate musings about the fates of the characters. All of these shows recognize that a successful prime-time ensemble drama must find its own set of aesthetic techniques to unify the episodes of a series into a cohesive whole that expresses a consistent viewpoint.

Any discussion of *The West Wing*'s aesthetics should begin with Aaron Sorkin's dialogue. Sorkin alternates rat-a-tat interchanges with florid speechmaking to create a distinctive voice for the show. One of the ways that Sorkin and, in this episode, writing partner Rick Cleveland accomplish so much business in so short a period of time is through the use of *mini-scenes*. Historically, dramas devoted an entire scene to communicating a single new plot development, and thus the show moved forward one step at time, one scene at a time. Giving a whole scene to every significant character interchange would make it almost impossible for *The West Wing* to do multiple plotlines. Therefore Sorkin and Cleveland choose to break single scenes into separate dramatic mini-scenes that are unrelated to each other narratively but which share the same time and space. Characters come and go in pairs, each couple intent on its own conversation but each occupying center stage for only a brief moment.

For instance, in "In Excelsis Deo" President Bartlet (Martin Sheen) visits a rare bookstore in Georgetown with members of his staff, all of whom seem uninterested in the historic texts. The camera tracks with Charlie (Dulé Hill) and then settles on Bartlet as he discourses about a book of animal fables in iambic pentameter to a bored Leo. When Mandy passes in front of them, the camera follows her as she and Josh bemoan their fates in this bookstore. Then Bartlet and Leo cross behind them, and the camera follows their conversation. They begin by discussing Leo's plans for the holidays but soon move to a more serious discussion of the scandal brewing around Leo's former excessive use of prescription drugs. Charlie interrupts their conversation, and the camera follows Bartlet as he briskly starts to exit the store. The camera lingers for one more conversation in the store—Leo urges Josh not to act rashly on his behalf. The brief conversations might as well be separate scenes as far as the actors' dramatic objectives are concerned, but they are efficiently conveyed and effectively unified by including them in a single movement-filled scene in a closed environment.

While this reliance on mini-scenes is characteristic of *The West Wing*, it is not unique to the series. John Wells's *ER*, for instance, also uses mini-scenes to break up the business of an individual scene into separate conversations. However, Sorkin's dialogue in *The West Wing* and in his other show *Sports Night* (1998–2000) is distinctive in that it breaks up single conversation between two characters into multiple topics, thereby conveying information quickly while mirroring the complexity of the *West Wing* world.

Sorkin's characters tend to switch from one topic to another at a moment's notice, sometimes devoting only a single line to a subject. Just as he fractures scenes into mini-scenes, he also divides individual conversations into *snippets,* extraordinarily brief dramatic units that together comprise a complete conversational interchange. For example, in "In Excelsis Deo" C. J. and Sam begin a hallway conversation about the pros and cons of "hate crime" legislation. Sam is hesitant to legislate against what people are thinking and is satisfied to let laws against violent action punish the perpetrators. C. J., disturbed by the news of the attack on the gay high school senior, feels that society should punish these cases more heavily. The discussion is political, philosophical, and passionate. Suddenly, without transition, C. J. turns to a discussion of their Secret Service code names. She is worried about what her code name ("Flamingo") implies about her. In the spirit of snippets, Sam picks up the new topic without question and without missing a beat.

Similarly, C. J. asks Danny for his opinion on hate crimes, and when his answer displeases her, she asks him to dinner so that he can convince her of his position. This conversation (in which C. J. partially backs down from her invitation, claiming it is not a date) ends with this set of snippets:

C. J.. This is a business dinner. In fact, bring your notebook.
DANNY. OK.
C. J.. My secret service name is "Flamingo."
DANNY. That's nice.
C. J.. I have to feed my fish.

The shot continues, revealing a brief interchange between Danny and Josh ("Hey Danny." "Hey Josh." "How's it going?" "Hard to tell." "OK." "OK."). Still within the same shot, the next scene begins (in which Josh gives Donna a Christmas gift).

These brief conversational snippets have several functions. They provide the pleasure of witty, rhythmic banter. They also can tersely incorporate the previous history of the show into the current moment. In order to get the humor of Danny and C. J.'s little haiku, one has to know not only that C. J. is obsessing about her Secret Service code name but also that lovestruck Danny gave her a live goldfish, not understanding that she actually likes the Pepperidge Farm Goldfish snack crackers. Evoking the characters' past history is a central technique of the serial drama, and conversational snippets can do this both effectively and playfully.

Turning the conversation on a dime also helps to convey how busy the lives of these characters are: their jobs are so important that they do not have time to make conversational transitions, and so they all naturally understand that dialogue must lurch from one topic to the other. This conversational tactic has added benefits for the actor. Actors often search their lines for subtext, for the meaning hidden under the lines spoken. Sorkin tends to build this subtext explicitly into the structure of the conversation. Actor Allison Janney knows that while C. J. is engaging in a passionate debate about the morality of hate crime legislation with Sam, her character is still bothered that the code name "Flamingo" makes her appear ridiculous. Janney knows this because C. J. turns the conversation to this inane subject without any outside provocation. Placing one conversational snippet after another gives the actors valuable clues about their characters' sensibility.

Breaking conversations into these smaller units allows *The West Wing* to contrast the high seriousness of these characters' jobs with moments of low silliness, which humanizes the *West Wing* staffers. Citizens hope that the White House staff is comprised of intelligent people who argue political questions with moral fervor, but they also want these politicos to be ordinary people, people human enough to obsess about a nickname.

The most dramatic contrasting moment in "In Excelsis Deo" occurs during a bit of presidential window dressing, a photo opportunity in which President Bartlet hams it up with a group of schoolchildren with well-rehearsed questions. Bartlet keeps pretending that he does not know what country he is the president of, and the delighted children keep shouting their reminder. The silliness of this moment halts when Charlie calls the president aside to tell him that the battered gay high school student has just died. After a solemn moment, the president immediately returns to his duty as First Jester, joking with the children. One can imagine that the president's day is filled with moments that alternate between the ludicrous and the earthshaking; Sorkin and Cleveland use brief conversational snippets to reveal these contradictions. In an era in which political messages need to be packaged into sound bites, the conversational snippet in drama condenses a great deal of information about the daily lives of characters, maximizing dialogue efficiency with a syncopated variation on the telegraphic style of network and cable news programs.

Dashing Through the Halls

The problem with depending on the snippet is that it creates a choppy rhythm. As Sorkin and Cleveland demonstrate, it can efficiently accomplish a great many tasks, but the technique requires a balancing force to smooth over the disjunctures. A good series episode needs a unifying device that can guide the program toward a satisfying conclusion.

Steadicam tracking shots in *The West Wing* give coherence to the various bits of dialogue. As in *ER*, these shots create visual interest, which is probably more needed to energize the representation of politics (a much more abstract practice than emergency medicine). But the steadicam serves a larger purpose in *The West Wing*. The series uses these tracking shots to provide a visual unity that counterbalances the verbally fractured snippets, making it possible for the show to make longer eloquent statements.

The tracking shot in *The West Wing* often begins by focusing on a small action, often by a bit player (e.g., carrying a gift basket) or on an object (a wall decoration). The camera almost immediately picks up one or two of the central characters moving through the White House office space. The camera follows as a couple of principal players march quickly through the hallways, discussing one or more topics. Then one of the characters forks off and is almost immediately replaced by another principal, who initiates another discussion. Several exchanges of characters can occur during one long continuous shot. The camera need not follow the same character throughout the shot as long as one holdover from the last conversational duo is still in the frame. Often these shots end as they began, with the camera focusing on a bit player (e.g., a Secret Service man) with the primary couple walking offscreen. In this way the camera stages a series of pas de deux, with partners pairing off and then cutting in in one prolonged dance. This steadicam of interchanging couples is the defining visual trademark of *The West Wing* and wordlessly communicates the dynamism of the dedicated people who work there.

For example, consider the previously mentioned hallway steadicam sequence that follows C. J. and Sam as they discuss first hate crimes and then her Secret Service code name. After C. J. leaves the frame, the camera follows Sam as he talks about his imminent departure for Bermuda with the secretaries. Josh now enters the frame as Sam continues to discuss his vacation; the camera then follows them into the office, where a conventionally filmed scene begins between Josh and Sam.

This particular episode begins with another example of these elaborate tracking shots. After initially following a bouquet being delivered, the camera picks up Mandy and C. J. discussing the details of preparations for the White House Christmas holiday celebration. As Toby and Sam enter the conversation, the camera arcs around them, showing a full 360-degree view of the gaily decorated lobby (while Sam interjects trivial snippets about weatherman Al Roker and about the sales figures for the song "Feliz Navidad"). One of Sam's snippets about the coming of the new millennium triggers an argument between Sam and Toby about the millennium's exact date, and this argument propels all four characters (and the steadicam) down a hallway. This first tracking shot is elegantly matched to the subsequent tracking shot by a natural wipe (an object that moves across the screen, giving the appearance of and serving the function of a "wiping" transition). In this particular instance, the edge of a wall creates the natural wipe, producing an apparently natural continuity between two steadicam shots. (*The West Wing* frequently uses the edges of the set walls or characters crossing in front of the principals to create fluid and visually interesting edits.)

When such a smoothly gliding visual style becomes a norm for the series, then variations from that norm can bear aesthetic force and narrative meaning. While Toby and Sam debate about the millennium, a secretary comes behind them with a phone message for Toby. All is business as usual until the secretary says that the message is from the D.C. police, who want to speak to Toby. Then the steadicam shot stops, cutting to a static shot of the characters turning around in silent amazement. The actors pausing a beat and the abrupt halt of the steadicam mark this as a dramatic turn of events. After this moment has passed, the characters disburse, except for Sam and C. J., who walk and continue the millennium conversation (now followed by the camera). At the first mention of C. J. as "Flamingo," Sam pulls her offscreen, ending the shot with a final image: the same floral arrangement that started this steadicam sequence, providing an elegant formal closure.

"In Excelsis Deo" also reveals how the tracking shot can be used not just for aesthetic purposes but also to make social commentary. The episode tells how Toby becomes involved in the world of the Washington homeless when an impoverished veteran, Walter Hufnagle, is found dead, wearing a coat that Toby had donated to charity. Toby is outraged at the negligent treatment that this U.S. Marine Korean War veteran's body receives, and he intervenes personally. At night he ventures into the urban demimonde for the homeless, and the camera follows him in long shot as the well-dressed Toby Ziegler walks through an alien environment. This tracking shot cannot help but evoke the earlier tracking shots through the lavish world of the White House, and the contrast is striking. In this particular episode, director Alex Graves uses the tracking shot to comment on the differences between America's haves and have-nots.

A primary function of these tracking shots, however, is to smooth over the herky-jerky energy of the fractured conversations. The steadicam track down the hall is not the most frequent shot in the series, but it is the most dominant consistent pattern of technique, used to distinguish the particular look and ambiance of *The West Wing*. It is this aesthetic technique that unifies the various scattered arguments about several different topics into a cohesive political statement that is forcefully voiced in the episode's coda.

In the End, a Song

The combination of the steadicam and the snippet allow *The West Wing* to accomplish one of its most distinctive purposes: to connect the personal with the political. The series presents the compelling fantasy that the White House is inhabited with articulate people who are wholeheartedly devoted to their political beliefs and who also are full of human foibles. It shows characters who can be so moved by the plight of a particular forgotten veteran that they violate protocol and arrange for a Marine honor guard funeral. It depicts persons who are outraged at the violence perpetrated on a young man solely because of his sexual orientation, and yet that high moral outrage does not make them into stuffy caricatures. This political fervor does not exclude them from the pettiness and the petulance, the merriment and the mistakes, that characterize everyday interactions among normal human beings. *The West Wing* presents both dimensions of its characters, slammed side by side through its juxtaposing technique.

The end result can be a coda of considerable power. *The West Wing* does not have a standard way of closing its episodes, like a courtroom drama's summary arguments or Chris Stevens's radio wrap-up in *Northern Exposure*. An episode may end with one of Sorkin's lyrical speeches or with a long story. But the closing device attempts to provide a denouement that unifies the various plot threads into a formal whole.

"In Excelsis Deo" uses a song to create a particularly lyrically coordinated finale. Much in the way that *Homicide* often did, the series here uses a highly foregrounded piece of music to anchor a montage connecting its disparate threads. In the White House, a boys' choir performs the carol "The Little Drummer Boy." Earlier Mrs. Landingham (the president's secretary, played by Kathryn Joosten) reveals that her twin sons Chris and Simon were killed near DaNang, Vietnam, on Christmas Eve 1970. She accompanies Toby and the dead veteran's brother George—also homeless—to a full honor guard funeral for the former Marine.

The montage is jam-packed with gloriously patriotic brief shots (the visual equivalent of the verbal snippet) of the veteran's interment at Arlington National Cemetery. The young voices sing in harmony back at the White House, serving as a reminder of a similarly orchestrated effort of young manhood during wartime. Director Alex Graves intercuts the precision honor guard reverently folding an American flag with a shot of the West Wing staff falling into line formation to listen to the carolers. The intercutting makes the formal point that both groups are soldiers serving the same higher good: the nation.

There are fine character details in this montage, as well, giving insight into the persons involved, not just the politics. Toby, an inexpert mourner, has to be reminded (by the driver's example) to salute the flag-draped coffin. The camera shows that Toby, the veteran, and Mrs. Landingham, the mother, both flinch involuntarily at the loud discharge of the honor guard's rifle salute.

This is powerful patriotic iconography, but the thing that is most unusual about this imagery is that it is used in service of left wing politics. In the last several decades, the Left has tended to shy away from flag-waving because it is all-too aware that what the flag stands for is not all positive. The flag has been used as a symbol both to unite people against tyranny and to encourage young people to die for arguably political policies. The New Left is often unsure about what it is saluting when it salutes the flag, and so a good leftie like Toby needs to be reminded of this formality. Except in wartime, the New Left tends to avoid wrapping itself in the flag, leaving that imagery available for almost exclusive peacetime use by others.

The West Wing, like the left wing under William Jefferson Clinton, has begun to recognize the power of such patriotic symbols. By leaving that imagery to the Right, the Left sacrifices a strong unifying element. The politics of this episode could not be more clearly leftist. It tells the story of a young man killed by antihomosexual bigotry today and two young men killed during a tragic war thirty years ago. This is America. And yet the lyrical coda salutes the notion of national service, that people who sacrifice for the nation—in the military or in government—are engaged in a noble endeavor. In making that point, the Left does not need to stop being the Left. I am glad that Toby and Mrs. Landingham wince when the rifles blast. It reminds us that wars have human costs, and the Left should always flinch at that. Toby's and Mrs. Landingham's presence show that their personally scarred histories can find encouragement in the collective rituals of patriotism. In "In Excelsis Deo," the song finishes what the steadicam and the snippet have begun. *The West Wing* links the personal with the political, and it drapes the flag around both.

8 | From *The American President* to *The West Wing*

A Scriptwriter's Perspective

JASON P. VEST

F or Aaron Sorkin, the White House is an arena for the opposition, in-
tersection, and—perhaps most important—dramatic exploration of
personal and political life. As the screenwriter of Castle Rock Entertainment's 1995 film *The American President* and the primary scriptwriter of
NBC's weekly one-hour television series *The West Wing,* Sorkin's fascination
with the executive branch allows him to explore the contentious inner workings of the White House as well as the private lives of the staff members responsible for helping chart the political destiny of the United States. This
unprecedented theatrical examination (to date, no screenwriter has devoted
so much attention to the presidency as Sorkin's seventy-three credits [1]) entails
a shift in Sorkin's vision of the presidency mandated by the differences be-

---

1. Sorkin's seventy-three script credits count *The American President*'s two-hour screenplay, as well as Sorkin's credited writing status as author of seventy-two *West Wing* episodes
through the November 13, 2002, broadcast of "Process Stories." (This number will continue to
grow as the series progresses; assuming that *The West Wing* survives through the end of its fifth
season, Sorkin could write as many as forty-four additional teleplays. More likely, Sorkin will
allow *The West Wing*'s writing staff to author more scripts as time passes to provide greater diversity within the series' dramatic voice while lessening his workload so that he can pursue other
projects.) Since the authorship of television episodes can be complex, a single credit is assigned
to Sorkin for teleplays for which he receives onscreen credit as the episode's sole writer, teleplays
that he writes singlehandedly based on storylines proposed by (an)other writer(s), and teleplays

tween cinema's and television's narrative structures. While Sorkin has been roundly criticized for depicting presidential administrations that are too slick, too leftist,[2] and too good to be true, examining a few intricacies of screenplay and teleplay[3] format will demonstrate that his presidential representation becomes more openly political, institutional, and complex as he moves from *The American President*'s primary focus on the president's personal life to *The West Wing*'s broader concern with issues, policies, behind-the-scenes details, and the personalities of the White House staff.

The Same, Yet Different

Even a cursory examination of Sorkin's progression from *The American President* to *The West Wing* allows the casual observer to note many similarities. In both, the president is a Democrat who supports leftist proposals: *The American President*'s Andrew Shepherd (Michael Douglas) eventually endorses an energy bill that reduces automobile emissions by 20 percent over ten years and promises to deal with crime by banning assault weapons, while

---

that he authors in conjunction with other writer(s). The last two categories are collaborative, indicating that Sorkin did not write every page. However, since I have not been able to examine every *West Wing* script (many are not publicly available), I award Sorkin a single credit even for scripts that he did not solely write. This approximation should not be taken as an attempt to dismiss or to diminish the work that *The West Wing*'s writing staff accomplishes in producing the series.

2. I use the term "leftist" advisedly to indicate that Bartlet's political beliefs place him left of center despite the centrist Democratic image that he cultivates and that comes under fire in the episode "Let Bartlet Be Bartlet." I have chosen to avoid the terms "liberal" and "conservative" because I believe that, in the partisan political climate that became increasingly rancorous after Ronald Reagan's election and which has, to date, not abated, these terms have been evacuated of all but superficial meaning. In my opinion, "liberal" and "conservative" are more often used as demonizing labels than as useful political descriptors, so resuscitating the appellations "leftist" and "rightist" seems less contentious, if equally abstract.

3. Technically, a screenplay is a script written for a cinematic, two-hour format, while a teleplay is a script written for a television format of varying lengths. In Hollywood, a screenwriter produces scripts for the movies, whereas a telewriter creates scripts for television. This subtle distinction causes me to use the term "scriptwriter" to describe both screen- and telewriters.

The West Wing's President Josiah "Jed" Bartlet (Martin Sheen) considers proposals to reform the campaign finance system, to integrate gays and lesbians into the military, and to decriminalize narcotics while emphasizing drug treatment.

Shepherd struggles with the public perception of his role as a father and as a single adult pursuing romance with *The American President*'s female protagonist, Sydney Ellen Wade (Annette Bening), causing his popularity rating to fall from 63 to 41 percent before Shepherd eventually defends both Sydney and his American Civil Liberties Union membership at an impromptu press conference. After one year in office, Barlet's approval rating hovers between 48 and 42 percent, lowering his staff's morale. This theme culminates in the episode "Let Bartlet Be Bartlet," in which the president so tires of censoring his actual views in order to appear as a moderate, centrist leader that speaking his mind becomes more important than winning a second term in office.

Shepherd has a daughter, Lucy (Shawna Waldron); Bartlet has more than one child, but only his daughter Zoe (Elizabeth Moss) plays a recurring role in *The West Wing*'s first season. Both Shepherd and Barlet have similar staffs: female press secretaries (Robin McCall [Anna Deavere Smith] and C. J. Cregg [Allison Janney], respectively); wry, world-weary, middle-aged personal secretaries (Mrs. Chapil [Anne Haney] and Mrs. Landingham [Kathryn Joosten]); and a young, Stephanopoulos-like advisor unafraid to offer passionate personal opinions (Lewis Rothschild [Michael J. Fox] and Sam Seaborn [Rob Lowe]). In both *The American President* and *The West Wing,* the president's chief of staff is a close personal friend, a grizzled political veteran who not only provides policy advice, but also takes credit for getting the administration elected, and a man of either Scottish or Irish descent: A. J. MacInerney (Martin Sheen) in Shepherd's case, and Leo McGarry (John Spencer) in Bartlet's. Perhaps the most obvious connection is that Martin Sheen is a prominent member of both the cast of *The American President* and *The West Wing.*

With so many similarities, it might seem that Sorkin merely recycled *The American President*'s major characters, concerns, and dramatic conceits when creating *The West Wing.* Indeed, this criticism has some merit. According to Matthew Miller (2000), Sorkin pitched *The West Wing* series concept to executive producer John Wells as nothing more than "senior staffers in the White House," without having prepared any scripts, story outlines, or character sketches. More important, Shari Sylvester (2000) reports that Sorkin had numerous unused ideas from his initial 385-page screenplay draft of *The American President*. Since a typical screenplay runs approximately 120 pages, Sorkin's fertile imagination had obviously provided him with more ideas than the film's two-hour running time would allow.

This temporal limitation exposes important clues to the manner by which *The West Wing*'s series format has allowed Sorkin to create a more nuanced institutional portrait of the presidency. While some observers assume that a television episode is simply a shorter form of cinematic representation, the conflation of these two media forms ignores the differences between the individual status of a film and the serialized nature of a television series.

It's the Economizing, Stupid

In *TV: The Most Popular Art* (1974), Horace Newcomb addresses the differences between cinema and television by identifying three crucial elements of "the television aesthetic." They are "intimacy, continuity, and history" (1974, 245). Although the medium's visual nature invites comparisons with film, Newcomb believes that television can provide far more personal drama: "[Its] presence brings people into the viewer's home to act out dramas. . . . Television is at its best when it offers faces, reactions, explorations of emotions registered by human beings. The importance is not placed on the action, though that is certainly vital as stimulus. Rather, it is on the reaction to the action, to the human response" (245–46).

Careful readers might observe that the only portion of Newcomb's aesthetic endemic to television is its presence in the home. Although cinemagoers must travel to a theater for the communal experience of watching a movie, films can and do offer faces, reactions, and emotional exploration. Further, nothing precludes a movie from concentrating on the human intimacy that Newcomb values or from subordinating plot to character. Much of the critical success of many films in the popular press, whether *Gone with the Wind* or *Monster's Ball,* depends upon how close a connection the audience feels with the characters and how believable a character's human response is.

Still, the final two elements of Newcomb's aesthetic illuminate *The West Wing*'s structural differences from *The American President*. Dramatic television's serial nature provides for extensive continuities of character, plot, and theme, allowing faithful television viewers to develop an ongoing, ever-developing history with a series that a film cannot equal.[4] Therefore, *The West Wing* offers far more opportunities to encounter its characters, narrative, and symbolism—to see how they build, cohere, and even contradict themselves—than does *The American President*.

A literary metaphor can also explain these differences: a film is a short story, while a television series is a novel. Barring sequels, a film is a single event that must narrate a story in two to three hours. However, episodes of a television series, even though they are half as long as a traditional film, are similar to a the chapters of a novel by allowing the writer to develop characters over a longer period of time and through more distinct situations than a film. With twenty-two episodes in a standard network season, a television series has greater opportunities than any movie to revisit themes, characters, and plotlines in screen time roughly equivalent to eleven feature films. Since *The West Wing* has been renewed through the end of its fourth season, Sorkin and his writing staff have at least eighty-eight one-hour stories to tell (or the equivalent screen time of forty-four films).[5]

4. Longer running film series—including James Bond, *Star Wars, Star Trek* (which, of course, is based on Gene Roddenberry's five-series television franchise), and Michael Apted's *7-Up* documentaries—are obvious exceptions to this observation. However, even the Bond films, which reached a milestone with the 2002 release of the series' twentieth installment, have taken forty years to produce the same amount of entertainment (roughly forty-four hours) that *The West Wing* accomplished in two seasons. This fact emphasizes how much more quickly a television series is produced than a film, indicating the sometimes enormous logistical difficulties in creating a weekly series.

5. Although I fully expect *The West Wing* to run more than five seasons, NBC has only renewed the series through the conclusion of its fourth year. A network makes the decision to renew a series based on a variety of economic factors, including the cast's salary demands, marketing initiatives, the revenue generated by ancillary merchandise, the production's overall ex-

While this analogy might seem obvious, it creates different opportunities for and demands on scriptwriters. A film's writer must introduce the story's protagonists quickly, develop them during a central plot that may include numerous subplots, and resolve the situation in 120 to 180 pages. As Syd Field writes in *Screenplay: The Foundations of Screenwriting* (1982), which has become a Hollywood bible for screenplay format,[6] "[a] motion picture is a visual medium that dramatizes a basic story line. And like all stories, there is a definite *beginning, middle,* and *end.* All screenplays contain [a] basic linear structure [that] is a model, a pattern, a conceptual scheme" (7, emphasis in original). This paradigm consists of three continuous acts. Act 1 lasts for thirty pages, sets up the characters, and introduces the basic dramatic situation; act 2 comprises the screenplay's middle sixty pages, deepens the protagonists' conflicts, and creates dramatic tension by providing obstacles to

---

pense, the cost of the network's licensing agreements with the studio (in this case, Warner Bros.) and production companies that own the series, and, especially, the potential revenue when the series is offered for syndication rights. If *The West Wing* becomes unprofitable or NBC projects that costs will overrun profits, the network will not hesitate to cancel the series. However, all reports show that, in its third year, *The West Wing* made more profit than any other returning program of its freshman 1999–2000 season. In addition, if *ER* (in its ninth season during fall 2002), *NYPD Blue* (in its tenth season during fall 2002), *The X-Files* (which ran nine seasons), and *Law and Order* (having been renewed through the end of its fifteenth season and with two spinoffs currently in production) are any indication, *The West Wing* occupies the enviable position of an hour-long drama that has not only captured a loyal audience, but also has the ability to attract new viewers. Therefore, the series may well run beyond five years, providing Sorkin and the series' present and future producers with ample opportunity to create drama.

6. Field's book has been the bestselling screenwriter's guide for many years, so much so that he is often referred to as a "dean of Hollywood screenwriting." However, in recent times, other writers have advocated breaking many of Field's traditional scriptwriting rules, particularly by extending act 1's length, providing unexpected dramatic plot points, and not resolving the story. Although Field declares in the expanded Edition of *Screenplay* that "[t]he days of ambiguous endings are over" (10), increasing numbers of screen- and telewriters—I am thinking particularly of Darin Aronofsky's *Pi* and the writing staff of Chris Carter's now-defunct *Millennium* television series—are breaking Field's rigid injunctions about form. This is not to say that these writers do not structure their screen- and teleplays into acts, or that the stories do not conclude, but that greater experimentation with form and a willingness to end stories ambivalently became more prevalent during the 1990s.

surmount; act 3 uses the screenplay's final thirty pages to resolve the conflict while providing a sense of closure for the characters.

The American President's screenplay follows this format precisely. Sorkin (1995) introduces Shepherd on page 1 (corresponding to the film's first minute [7]), quickly focusing on the president's personal life. Within the script's first thirty pages, we learn that Shepherd is a widower and single father, that his wry sense of humor enables him to bear the burdens of office, and that his past as a history professor predisposes him to take a long-term view of issues. He meets Sydney Ellen Wade, the film's female protagonist, on page 17. Their interaction ends on page 25, followed by Shepherd asking Sydney to accompany him to a state dinner honoring France's new president on page 30. At this point, we know for certain that *The American President* will focus on their romance, rather than strictly political issues, although public concerns are the context in which the romance grows.

Pages 31–90 of the screenplay chart how Shepherd's and Wade's relationship becomes personally stronger even as it negatively affects his presidency. Sorkin alternates the action between scenes of each character's occupation (Wade is an environmental lobbyist working to pass the aforementioned energy bill, even though Shepherd places more importance on an omnibus crime initiative) and quiet moments together before Shepherd's refusal to respond to character attacks made by a Republican senator-turned-presidential candidate, Bob Rumson (Richard Dreyfuss), on top of his

---

7. As Field asserts in *Screenplay* (1982) and Madeline DiMaggio comments in *How to Write for Television* (1990), conventional wisdom holds that one page of script equals one minute of screentime. Therefore, a two-hour film has 120 pages, while a standard teleplay contains sixty pages. This figure does not hold for scripts that have a tremendous amount of fast-paced dialogue, in which characters engage in the type of accelerated verbal exchange that characterizes *The West Wing* (*Moonlighting*, for example, often used eighty—to ninety-page shooting scripts for a one-hour episode because of the snappy banter between its two protagonists). The difference can clearly be seen in Sorkin's fifty-seven-page script for the pilot episode as compared to his seventy-two-page script for "Lies, Damn Lies, and Statistics." Both episodes are approximately forty-eight minutes long, so the pacing of the dialogue, scenes, and sequences occurs more quickly in the latter case. In addition, post-production, especially the editing process, often removes scenes written into a teleplay so that these scripts, even final drafts and shooting scripts, are not totally accurate documents of the televised episode.

refusal to support the energy bill, alienate Wade. *The American President*'s final thirty pages find a beleaguered Shepherd pushed by his staff, particularly MacInerney, to defend his character, his policies, and his relationship with Wade before the nation. The film ends with the couple reunited as Shepherd prepares to deliver the State of the Union address.

While Sorkin skillfully weaves Shepherd's private and political life into *The American President*'s screenplay, the predominant theme is that the president's occupation should not interfere with his personal affairs.[8] Shepherd explicitly argues this point to MacInerney while playing billiards: "I'm talking about something that in no way is at conflict with my oath of office. I'm a single adult and I met a woman that I'd like to see again socially. . . . I don't want to check a polling sample to see if this is okay, like I'm asking permission to stay out an hour past curfew. This isn't the business of the American people" (Sorkin 1995). As MacInerney points out, the situation is not so simple, but the screenplay's readers and the film's audience cannot ignore

8. This theme also characterized much of Bill Clinton's eight years in the White House, providing an intriguing historical relationship between real and fictional presidents. Although Shepherd is not accused of marital infidelity, his affair with Wade is seen as a sexual impropriety, even by some members of the Democratic Party who refuse to support Shepherd's legislative proposals for fear of being associated with an unpopular chief executive. Shepherd finds the attention paid to his personal life objectionable, invasive, and disruptive—and similar to Clinton's, who disliked the excessive public interest that accompanied his alleged extramarital affairs during both terms in office. The scandal surrounding Clinton's involvement with White House intern Monica Lewinsky, the resulting investigation by independent counsel Kenneth Starr, and the subsequent impeachment proceedings had not yet occurred when Sorkin wrote *The American President,* but the parallels between Shepherd's and Clinton's personal lives intruding upon their public roles are unmistakable. The Lewinsky scandal—particularly Clinton's false statements to a grand jury—have a resonance in *The West Wing.* During the series' second season, Bartlet's multiple sclerosis becomes a legal issue when Toby Ziegler and White House counsel Oliver Babbish (Oliver Platt) believe that concealing this condition from the public constitutes an abuse of executive power. The second season's finale, "Two Cathedrals," sees Bartlet disclose his condition publicly, while several third-season episodes, beginning with the two-part premiere "Manchester," find the White House staff testifying before congressional committees investigating the scandal. The situation resolves itself in "100,000 Airplanes," in which the audience learns that Barlet accepted congressional censure just weeks before. This plotline, while less salacious than the Lewinsky scandal, echoes the general outlines of Clinton's second-term troubles.

how Sorkin uses politics as the backdrop, rather than the hub, of the Shepherd-Wade relationship. *The American President*'s restructuring of the traditional American film romance is refreshingly entertaining because it places the notion of romance in the nation's highest office so that the tension between private and public life becomes manifest. In 124 pages, Sorkin focuses primarily on Shepherd and Wade's lives (and life together) to illuminate this tension and to make them fully rounded characters. McCall, Rothschild, and MacInerney receive little independent development, but rather function as shields and sounding boards for Shepherd. Wade's colleagues and her sister Beth (Nina Siemaszko) receive even less attention because Sorkin, as an experienced screenwriter, knows that he must economize. He simply cannot devote equal, or even approximate, attention to the minor players, all of whom remain relatively flat characters. Sorkin's and *The American President*'s focus becomes the personality of the president rather than the institutional character of the presidency.

Time Enough at Last

By contrast, *The West Wing*'s four-act pilot episode defers Bartlet's introduction until its final act, preferring to focus on the personalities, the duties, and the interactions of his senior staff (the denizens of the West Wing). With twenty-one additional first-season episodes in which to define, to build, and to refine Bartlet's character, Sorkin need not rush the president onstage. The pilot episode creates dramatic tension by consistently referring to Bartlet's personality through the dialogue of the principal characters before the president appears. While vacationing, Bartlet has ridden his bicycle into a tree, prompting chief of staff McGarry to call him "a clutz . . . a spaz." Deputy chief of staff Josh Lyman (Bradley Whitford) fears that his appearance on *Capitol Beat,* a Sunday-morning political program on which Lyman insults the female leader of a conservative Christian coalition, has so angered Bartlet that the president will fire him. In fact, only McGarry's intervention and Lyman's agreement to attend a meeting with several conservative religious leaders prevents the latter from losing his job. Sorkin is able to inform the audience that Bartlet is both an accident-prone, fallible, perhaps comical human being and a leader who not only is concerned (in appearance, if not in fact) about the opinions of those who disagree with his politics, but is also capable of passionate feelings and adroit command decisions.

The pilot episode, however, spends its first three acts delineating the personalities of the senior staff while establishing plotlines that will continue throughout the first season. Sam Seaborn (Rob Lowe) spends the night with Laurie (Lisa Edelstein), a Georgetown University law student who also works as a high-priced call girl to pay her tuition. This subplot plays into future episodes, reaching a climax in the first season's penultimate episode, "Lies, Damn Lies, and Statistics." Lyman gets reacquainted with Mandy Hampton (Moira Kelly), his former lover as well as a former advisor to Bartlet, now working for Democratic senator Lloyd Russell (a man opposed to many of Bartlet's policies). Hampton eventually joins Bartlet's staff, although a memo she writes for Russell before leaving him for her White House position both attacks Bartlet's administration and causes tremendous concern in "Let Bartlet Be Bartlet." Neither situation receives more than seven pages (or seven minutes of screentime) during the pilot, for Sorkin knows he need not examine either of the plotlines in depth or resolve them by the episode's conclusion (having ample opportunity in future installments to deal with the ramifications of the storylines he initiates here).

Sorkin's narrative pace in the pilot, as in most episodes, is extraordinarily rapid. He moves from subplot to subplot with a speed that requires great authorial dexterity. In addition to the Seaborn-Laurie, Lyman-Hampton, *Capitol Beat,* and presidential accident storylines noted above, the pilot episode includes subplots about a group of Cuban refugees riding rafts toward Miami, communications director Toby Ziegler's (Richard Schiff) efforts to preserve Lyman's job, and Seaborn's disastrous attempt to relate the White House's history to a touring fourth-grade class taught by McGarry's daughter. Sorkin must intersperse these subplots throughout the story while weaving them into a coherent narrative that culminates in act 4's introduction of Bartlet.[9] Indeed, this sometimes blinding narrative pace accounts for

---

9. This introduction gives a brief, yet memorable, idea of Bartlet's personality, while Sorkin's staging emphasizes Bartlet's total command of the situation. Lyman, Ziegler, and Cregg disagree with three leaders of the Christian movement—Al Caldwell (F. William Parker), Mary Marsh (Annie Corley), and John Van Dyke (David Sage)—about the proper order of the biblical

much of *The West Wing*'s exciting, engaging tone. Viewers must actively attend to every episode's details if they wish to understand the story.[10]

The numerous short scenes that Sorkin piles on top of each other in every *West Wing* episode produce an impressionistic experience. The audi-

---

commandments. Perhaps unbelievably, Mary Marsh asks, "Then what's the first?" Sorkin's script reads:

> And from the doorway, a MAN, standing with the help of a cane, speaks . . .
> MAN. I am the Lord your God. Thou shalt worship no God before me.
> And the MAN, of course, is PRESIDENT JOSIAH (JED) BARTLET, Democrat of New
> Hampshire, and a descendant of one of the original signers of the Declaration.
> Looking every bit the country lawyer, you wouldn't immediately guess that he's
> brilliant, which he is. While the left hand is lulling you with folksy charm, you don't
> even hear the right hook coming.

Bartlet not only has the privilege of speaking the First Commandment in the first person, but also enters the scene as the episode's most powerful figure. Sorkin immediately links Bartlet, who up to this point has been discussed as a doddering, accident-prone individual, to the highest possible status, namely godhead. Bartlet's seemingly contradictory personality, with an avuncular ease on one side and a predatory aspect on the other, is not confined to scene description. Bartlet tells a number of folksy stories about his family before throwing Caldwell, Marsh, and Van Dyke out of the White House for not denouncing a fundamentalist Christian group that has mailed Bartlet's granddaughter a Raggedy Ann doll with a knife in its throat to protest the young woman's prochoice beliefs. Bartlet then narrates another family story before ordering his staff back to work. While he is undoubtedly a charming man, the script's characterization and dialogue make clear that Bartlet is not a person with whom to trifle.

10. While this analysis credits Sorkin's writing as suitably complex in terms of plot, some critics find *The West Wing* to be a slick, superficial program that deals with so many issues and character arcs that no depth emerges from them. John Podhoretz condemned the series' primary characters in a March 2000 *Weekly Standard* cover story (reprinted here as chap. 14): "Human beings? These characters aren't human beings—they're noble soldiers in a noble cause, and they have been washed clean of every impurity because of it" (see chap. 14, 223). Caryn James (1999), the *New York Times*' chief television critic, finds the series "wildly uneven," portraying nuanced situations before shifting to "scenes of Martin Sheen making the right moral decision with the music swelling in the background." I do not have space to conduct a literary analysis of *The West Wing*'s dramatic merits or of its political philosophy. I will say that Podhoretz's comment ignores a great deal of character development during the first season, although his analysis can be more reasonably applied to "Isaac and Ishmael," the rushed-into-production episode

ence receives few extended portraits of a character or an issue, but must allow a more complex accretion of details to build. While every episode has an identifiable beginning, middle, and end, so many plotlines continue into future episodes that faithful viewers receive a more complicated picture of the president, his staff, and the presidency's internal functioning than *The American President* supplies. Sorkin and his writing staff structure *The West Wing* in story arcs: extended plotlines that last for multiple episodes, that unexpectedly re-erupt to force both characters and viewers to rely upon their knowledge of previous events, and that allow Sorkin to broaden his focus from a single overriding plot (such as *The American President*'s Shepherd-Wade romance) with only two major characters and several minor players to multiple storylines concerned with a multiperson ensemble (in the first season, Bartlet, McGarry, Cregg, Ziegler, Lyman, Hampton, Seaborn, and Charlie Young [Dulé Hill], Bartlet's personal aide[11]).

This argument does not imply that *The West Wing*'s television format is artistically superior to *The American President*'s cinematic imperatives, but merely observes that *The West Wing* affords a more extensive, complicated vision of the presidency. Rather than restricting itself to Bartlet's personal life or to a single plotline, *The West Wing* deals with a variety of political issues and character storylines. Just as a novel provides its author with a broader narrative canvas than a short story does, *The West Wing*'s episodic, serialized format allows Sorkin and his writing staff to reveal the presidency's larger institutional concerns: domestic policy debates, foreign policy deci-

---

that responded to the September 11, 2001, attacks on New York City and Washington, D.C. Preceding the third season's premiere, this self-described "play" sees Cregg, Lyman, Seaborn, and Ziegler passionately (and often naïvely) preaching the values of tolerance, diversity, and liberalism to a group of presidential scholarship high-school students. James's arguable criticism is a matter of narrative style that should be considered when assessing *The West Wing*'s literary strengths. While I do not fully agree with her cynical dismissal, I also feel that she has proposed an intriguing, problematic assessment of the series' narrative success.

11. Moira Kelly and her character, Mandy Hampton, departed *The West Wing*'s cast at the conclusion of its first season. Janel Moloney, previously credited as a recurring player for her role as Lyman's efficient, quirky assistant, Donnatella Moss, became a full cast member as of the second season's premiere episode, "In the Shadow of Two Gunmen." At the beginning of the third season, Stockard Channing, portraying First Lady Abigail Bartlet, became a primary cast member.

sions, military crises, Supreme Court nominations, an ambitious and contro-versial drug decriminalization proposal, personality conflicts, private tri-umphs and defeats, as well as—perhaps unavoidably—the senior staff's familial status. This broader canvas is the television scriptwriter's privilege, providing the potential for complex, nuanced, and thoughtful storytelling.

Public Personae, Private Lives

To illustrate the sometimes subtle, yet crucial, differences between film and television narratives—or, more precisely, between Sorkin's responsibilities as a screenwriter and telewriter—an analysis of two apparently identical scenes from *The American President* and *The West Wing* will crystallize the dramatic potential of each medium. The first involves Shepherd and MacInerney playing billiards after Shepherd's refusal to support the energy bill causes Sydney to lose her position with an environmental lobby, to end their relationship, and to announce her intention to move to Hartford, Connecticut.

> MACINERNEY. Hartford? What's in Hartford?
> SHEPHERD. Richard Reynolds' district office . . . she's thinking of run-ning his campaign. Twelve in the corner . . . (Shepherd *gets down over the ball.*) Hartford . . . insurance capital of the world. Have a good time, Syd. (Shepherd *smacks the ball into the correct pocket.*)
> MACINERNEY. Listen, I'm gonna have Janie clear your schedule for the weekend. You need to get some rest.
> SHEPHERD. You handling me, A. J.?
> MACINERNEY. No, sir.
> SHEPHERD. Good
> MACINERNEY. But I will if you don't start taking your head out of your ass.
> SHEPHERD. Excuse me?
> MACINERNEY. Lewis is right. Go after this guy [Rumson].
> SHEPHERD. Has he lied?
> MACINERNEY. What?
> SHEPHERD. Has Rumson lied in the past seven weeks?
> MACINERNEY. Has he lied?

SHEPHERD. Other than not knowing the difference between Harvard and Stanford, has he said something that isn't true? Am I not a Commander-in-Chief who's never served in the military? Am I not opposed to a Constitutional amendment banning flag burning? Am I not an unmarried father who shared a bed with a liberal lobbyist down the hall from his twelve-year-old daughter?

MACINERNEY. And you think you're wrong?

SHEPHERD. I don't think you win elections by telling 59 percent of the people that they are.

MACINERNEY. We fight the fights we can win.

SHEPHERD. Oh don't—

MACINERNEY. You fight the fights that need fighting!

SHEPHERD. Is the view pretty good from the cheap seats, A. J.?

MACINERNEY. I beg your pardon?

SHEPHERD. Because it occurs to me that in twenty-five years I've never seen your name on a ballot. Now why is that? Why are you always one step behind me?

MACINERNEY. Because if I wasn't, you'd be the most popular history professor at the University of Wisconsin.

SHEPHERD. (*Throws down his cue stick.*) Fuck you. (*Shepherd heads toward the door.*) Have Lewis put the final draft of the State of the Union on my desk in the morning.

MACINERNEY. Yes, sir.

SHEPHERD. (*Reaches the doorway*) If Mary hadn't died, would we have won three years ago?

MACINERNEY. Would we have won?

SHEPHERD. If we had to go through a character debate three years ago, would we have won?

MACINERNEY. I don't know. But I would've liked that campaign. If my friend Andy Shepherd had shown up, I would have liked that campaign.

SHEPHERD. (*He nods absently.*) Yeah. (Sorkin 1995)

This scene, which uses two minutes and twenty-four seconds of screen time, is important within *The American President*'s overall context. Sorkin offers the film's only glimpse of Shepherd's and MacInerney's past, as well as the sole instance of serious disagreement between them. MacInerney ceases playing Shepherd's loyal servant for one moment, responding to the president's charge of political cowardice by taking credit for Shepherd's public success. This rejoinder prods Shepherd into a final, poignant self-realization that his wife's death may be truly responsible for his presidency.

Sorkin indicates depths of character and a shared history through indirection and innuendo. He does not have time to provide more than a cursory sense of Shepherd and MacInerney's friendship or the conflicts that characterize this relationship, so his dialogue, while referring to the political sphere, remains intensely personal. The scene's subtext bristles with a long-simmering, unresolved tension between the two friends, which actors Michael Douglas and Martin Sheen nicely portray.

Dramatically, this scene serves as a segue to Shepherd's impassioned defense of his principles, his administration, and his relationship with Wade. Shepherd's decision to justify his values proceeds out of this disagreement with MacInerney, finally focusing on the president's status as a widower rather than as a politician. Rank drops away as the scene concludes. Rather than a president seeking his chief of staff's opinion, Shepherd is now a man wondering how his private life has influenced his political success. MacInerney's response is telling: "If my friend Andy Shepherd had shown up, I would have liked that campaign." This simple, quiet, almost elegant reply gives Shepherd the confidence to assert his moral authority as president, yet this decision remains personal.

As the next scene opens, Shepherd begins his speech without announcing it to his staff. MacInerney's words have obviously resonated with Shepherd, causing him to stake a political position (pro-environment, pro-gun control, anticrime) from within his status as a man in love with Wade. Sorkin resolves Shepherd and Wade's ruptured relationship by integrating the president's political and private lives, yet emphasizing the personal dimension. The film's final scenes, which occur as Shepherd walks toward the House of Representatives chamber to deliver his State of the Union address, find Shepherd and Wade bantering easily, much as an engaged couple does. This denouement brings *The American President* to an emotionally satisfying resolution. While we have little doubt that Shepherd will prevail politically, his love for Wade predominates.

Politics as Unusual

By contrast, a seemingly identical scene from *The West Wing*'s first-season episode "Let Bartlet Be Bartlet" illustrates Sorkin's fascination with the presidency's institutional character. Barlet's low approval rating has the staff feeling depressed. Lyman attempts to get Bartlet's Federal Election Commission nominees, both of whom support campaign-finance reform, confirmed while Seaborn meets with military advisors and congressional representatives to discuss fully integrating homosexuals into the military. The senior staff members implicitly understand, however, that Bartlet's centrist proclivities prevent them from advocating their heartfelt, leftist, "liberal" positions for fear of alienating a moderate electorate. This situation becomes combustible when Hampton reveals that a memo she wrote while working for Lloyd Russell's office—which not only harshly criticizes Bartlet's middle-of-the-road policies, but also portrays his administration as demoralized, listless, and politically vulnerable—has been leaked to the *New York Times*. Bartlet summons McGarry to the Oval Office to discuss the situation.

As Charlie Young watches, McGarry admits that the memo's content upsets him. Bartlet tells his chief of staff that all criticisms of McGarry as a man who pushes the president toward a safer, more centrist political position are old news and, moreover, untrue. McGarry surprises everyone by saying that he knows such accusations are false because Bartlet, and not McGarry, drives the administration toward the political center. "We're stuck in neutral because that's where you tell me to stay," McGarry says, implicitly accusing Bartlet of political cowardice.

The discussion becomes more heated when Bartlet recalls that he did not originate the idea of campaigning for president. Rather, McGarry convinced Barlet to run so that Bartlet could speak his mind on important issues. When McGarry comments that the many cameras and microphones at the White House give Bartlet a public platform from which to speak his mind at any time, the president complains that McGarry has continually restrained his legislative agenda on a variety of issues, including teacher pay, campaign-finance reform, relations with China, and gun control.

MCGARRY. Brought you in from where? You've never been out there on guns, you've never been out there on teachers. You dangle your feet and I'm the hall monitor around here. It's my job to make sure nobody runs too fast or goes off too far. I tell Josh to go to the Hill on campaign finance, he knows nothing's going to come of it.

BARTLET. That's crap.

MCGARRY. Sam can't get real on "Don't Ask, Don't Tell" because you're not going to be there and every guy sitting across the table from him knows that.

BARTLET. Leo, if I ever told you to get aggressive on campaign finance or gays in the military, you would tell me, "Don't run too fast or go too far."

MCGARRY. You never told me to get aggressive about anything, I'd say "I serve at the pleasure of the President." But we'll never know, sir, because I don't think you're ever gonna say it.

BARTLET. I have said it and nothing's ever happened.

MCGARRY. You want to see me orchestrate this right now? You want to see me mobilize these people? These people who would walk into fire if you told them to. These people who showed up to lead. These people who showed up to fight. (*Points to Young*) That guy gets death threats because he's black and he dates your daughter. He was warned: "Do not show up at this place, your life will be in danger." He said, "To hell with that. I'm going anyway." You said, "No." Prudent or not prudent, this twenty-one-year-old at six hundred dollars a week said, "I'm going where I want to" because a man stands up. Everyone's waiting for you. I don't know how much longer.

BARTLET. I don't want to feel like this anymore.

MCGARRY. You don't have to.

BARTLET. I don't want to go to sleep like this.

MCGARRY. You don't have to.

BARTLET. I want to speak.

MCGARRY. Say it out loud. Say it to me.

BARTLET. This is more important than re-election. I want to speak now.

MCGARRY. Say it again.

BARTLET. This is more important than re-election. I want to speak now.

MCGARRY. Now we're in business. (*He moves to a nearby table, fetching a yellow legal pad.*)

BARTLET. What's happening?

MCGARRY. We got our asses kicked in the first quarter, but it's time to get up off the mat.

BARTLET. Yes.

MCGARRY. Say it.

BARTLET. This is more important than re-election. I want to speak now.

MCGARRY. I'm gonna talk to the staff. I'm gonna take them off the leash.

BARTLET. *(As McGarry writes on the legal pad)* You have a strategy for all this?

MCGARRY. I have the beginnings of one.

BARTLET. What is it?

MCGARRY. *(Places the legal pad on Bartlet's desk. The words "Let Bartlet Be Bartlet" are written on it.)* I'm gonna try that for a little while. *(He exits as Barlet looks on half-skeptically, half-approvingly.)*

Apart from showcasing the considerable acting talents of John Spencer and Martin Sheen, this scene (four minutes, eight seconds of screen time) contains similar themes to the aforementioned and quoted *American President* scene. The chief of staff takes the president to task for not speaking his mind. The president objects to this characterization, suggesting that, since the chief of staff remains in the shadows, he does not understand the burdens of being commander in chief. The close personal friendship between the two underscores their disagreement, while their past history forms the locus of the entire scene: the chief of staff is no simple yes-man, but rather the only advisor who can use his friendship with the president to press an emotional, rhetorical, and political advantage.

However, this scene's tenor departs markedly from *The American President*. The subtext of a repressed, festering *lack* of communication that must find voice in an interpersonal argument becomes far more apparent. McGarry (who only refers to Bartlet by title, never name) refuses to make his portion of the argument explicitly private until the president plays upon McGarry's feelings of friendship by reminding the chief of staff of his role in convincing Bartlet to run for the White House in the first place. Even here, McGarry utilizes personal concerns (Young's relationship with Zoe and the senior staff's loyalty to the president) to demonstrate how Barlet's centrism has been mistaken for political cowardice, to illustrate how Bartlet's employees find themselves in pointless endeavors, and to emphasize how Bartlet's presidency is in dire institutional peril.

McGarry's intimate knowledge of Bartlet's personality allows him to manipulate the president's intellectual, moral, and ethical pride, as well as Bartlet's beleaguered emotional state, to force the president into a crucial realization: speaking his mind is not simply an act of private conviction, but also of political, public necessity. Although not manifestly mentioned, Mc-Garry pushes Bartlet to reclaim the bully pulpit that the presidency affords him. Bartlet's hobbies, private passions, and familial relationships do not prevail. Rather, Sorkin uses this scene to establish a new direction for his protagonist and *The West Wing* as a series. The administration must refocus its primary mission from accommodating majority opinion to leading the American people in a direction in which they may not wish to travel. While Ziegler, Cregg, Lyman, and Seaborn approve of Bartlet's decision, validating their private political opinions and providing "Let Bartlet Be Bartlet" with an upbeat emotional resolution, the final shot of Bartlet looking into McGarry's office with a skeptically satisfied smile reminds viewers that these events will affect the personal and professional lives of the staff in future episodes. Sorkin need not resolve all the issues in this outing, but he can allow *The West Wing*'s broader narrative scope to mutate by accommodating the alterations that he makes here.

Let Sorkin Be Sorkin

To Sorkin's credit, the first season's final three episodes all depict Bartlet and a presidency with renewed vigor, offering an aggressive drug decriminalization proposal before an assassination attempt furnishes Sorkin with the occasion to fuse the political and personal even further. The second season's two-part premiere, "In the Shadow of Two Gunmen," alternates the senior staff's private pain in dealing with Lyman's severe gunshot wounds with flashbacks that establish how the characters came together during Bartlet's hard-fought presidential campaign. The presidency's institutional origin proceeds from the passions, conflicts, and commitments of its senior staff, retroactively stressing the importance of personal interests in building political power while bringing *The West Wing* full circle. Sorkin reveals the complex interweaving of the personal and the political, the private and the public, the individual and the communal that circumscribes Bartlet's administration. As a scriptwriter, he synthesizes these tensions not only to entertain, but also (consciously or unconsciously) to disclose the ability of *The West Wing*'s serialized layout to complicate *The American President*'s relatively straightforward, romantic, personal, and understatedly political plot. This extensive reworking of Sorkin's previous cinematic themes becomes possible because series television affords him and his creative staff greater time, a larger dramatic scope, and more opportunities to linger with *The West Wing*'s core characters. By recognizing the differences between film and television, then exploiting them to good effect, Sorkin is able to write scripts appropriate to each medium. More important, he is able to extend, to examine, and to explore *The West Wing*'s characters and the presidency's institutional composition in ways that *The American President* does not (and, because of film's temporal limitations, cannot).

As such, Aaron Sorkin adroitly moves from *The American President*'s single screenplay to *The West Wing*'s numerous teleplays to probe the nature, limits, and possibilities of executive power. While they may be unapologetically unctuous, brazenly leftist, and irritatingly idealistic, Sorkin's scripts utilize memorable images, witty dialogue, idiosyncratic characterization, and Byzantine plotting to narrate compelling stories that viewers find difficult to ignore no matter how much they finally dislike or distrust Sorkin's vision. His appreciation for the distinct dramatic possibilities afforded by film and television allow Sorkin to offer different—and sometimes competing—portraits of the presidency. While *The American President* focuses mainly on the president's personal life, *The West Wing* permits a greater integration of the president's private experience with his political, public responsibilities. The resulting complexities produce a detailed dramatic landscape for *The West Wing* to explore, finally achieving a closeness to characters, issues, and themes that *The American President* suggests by economy, subtext, and indirection. Although a film's larger budget is often thought to provide its screenwriter with a broader storytelling vista, Sorkin's movement from the big to small screen suggests precisely the opposite. *The American President* seems more contained than *The West Wing*, giving its audience a more concentrated emotional and intellectual viewing experience, while loyal television watchers receive a more intricate and, finally, more complete, understanding of *The West Wing*'s personal and political scope. Neither form of scriptwriting is better than the other, but Sorkin's television work gives him more dramatic room to maneuver, which finally produces a more comprehensive and satisfying portrait of the American presidency.

THE WEST WING

PERCEPTIONS OF *THE WEST WING*

---

9 | The Sincere Sorkin White House, or, the Importance of Seeming Earnest

PAMELA EZELL

The *West Wing*, created by television writer and producer Aaron Sorkin, may embody the nicest, most congenial, most harmonious presidential administration in the history of the institution. President Josiah "Jed" Bartlet, as played by Martin Sheen, is a plain-speaking Democrat, a Nobel Prize-winning economics professor who still maintains his link to the people, and a man of faith (Roman Catholic) and tolerance. Bartlet is that rare president who manages to take decisive military action and still maintain his liberal base of support. In private moments, we see him grapple with issues of morality and justice.

Ironically, *The West Wing* debuted in the fall of 1999, an era of dubious executive morality that followed President Bill Clinton's historical impeachment in 1998 on grounds of perjury, obstruction of justice, and abuse of power. Presidential misconduct actually derailed *The West Wing*'s earlier attempt to earn a berth on the NBC schedule in 1997. Executive producer John Wells told *USA Today* that the Bill Clinton-Monica Lewinsky scandal caused the network to get "cold feet" about the commercial viability of *The West Wing*. "They said they couldn't take it to the advertisers in that climate" (Graham 1999, 3).

A straight line of cynicism about politicians can be drawn from the 1974 resignation of Richard Nixon in the wake of the Watergate scandal to Clinton's granting of 140 "fire sale" pardons during his last hours as president in 2001. Yet Sorkin's program is anything but cynical; it is earnest. Arriving on the air during the moral disappointments of the Clinton presidency, Bartlet and his cadre of loyal, idealistic aides seemed the perfect antidote for a nation weary of human frailty in its ultimate leader. In exchange for the convoluted ethics and "pork belly" partisanship endemic in real politics, *The West Wing* provided a softer, gentler version of the highest office in the land. Bartlet and the members of his administration are noble: they serve with the zeal of missionaries, the kindness of campus counselors, and the ethical fiber of Sunday school teachers.

The superiority of Sorkin's version of the White House is by design. Sorkin has said, "[*The West Wing*] imitates just enough the sounds and appearance of reality" (de Jonge 2001, 42). In September 2000, when Terence Smith interviewed Sorkin on the PBS series *The NewsHour,* he asked how important it is to "be faithful to the facts" while writing the show. Sorkin answered, "The appearance of reality is more important than reality" (Sorkin 2000).

Despite his well-publicized drug problems, including an arrest at the Burbank airport in April 2001 for possession of cocaine, marijuana, and hallucinogenic mushrooms, at heart Aaron Sorkin is himself a classic Hollywood version of an idealist. He volunteered to work for the George McGovern campaign at the age of eleven. Actor Richard Schiff, who won an Emmy for his portrayal of Toby Ziegler during the series' first year, said in *George* magazine, "We're more like a White House world that he'd like to see" (Waxman review reprinted in this volume, see chap. 12). According to an inside informant quoted in this same *George* cover story, although Sorkin voted for Bill Clinton twice, he did not really like him as president (chap. 12, 209). Sorkin has not confirmed or denied that rumor, but it is easy to see how such a true believer—and a man who struggles with his own addictions—might wish to invent a White House devoid of human weakness.

The West Wing is Sorkin's second significant work on the theme of the presidency. His first venture was a feature film, *The American President* (1995), directed by Rob Reiner and starring Michael Douglas as President Andrew Shepherd. Shepherd, a widower with a preteen daughter, falls in love with a lobbyist, Sidney Ellen Wade (Annette Bening). In spite of Shepherd's refusal to allow his staff to "spin" his love story in a way that will not jeopardize his upcoming bid for reelection, Shepherd and Wade find themselves at the center of a media firestorm. They become the subject of tabloid headlines and pundit scrutiny. Meanwhile, Shepherd's approval ratings plummet and he is forced to compromise on a key initiative Sidney represents—a deal he promised her early in their relationship. (This plot line echoes events that occur in the third season finale of *The West Wing*, "Posse Comitatus," when Josh Lyman [Emmy-winner Bradley Whitford] politics for welfare reform legislation that will cause his activist girlfriend Amy [Mary-Louise Parker] to get fired.) Ultimately, in *The American President*, Shepherd is able to reassert his principles, reaffirm his love for Sidney, and recommit himself to the presidency. In *The American President*, as in *The West Wing*, the preference is for truth, not artifice. In both cases, the president is committed to justice, not politics.

Based on the research he had done while writing *The American President*, Sorkin believed the White House could be the source of endless drama. Sorkin saw that the backstage stories and personalities of the White House could "be as gripping as the palace intrigues that inspired dramatists from Sophocles to Shakespeare" (Miller 2000, 89).

Because of common subject matter and similar sentiments, Sorkin is sometimes compared to the Italian-American filmmaker Frank Capra, whose name has become synonymous with patriotism and old-fashioned American idealism. Capra's many films include *Mr. Deeds Goes to Town* (1936), *Mr. Smith Goes to Washington* (1939), and *Meet John Doe* (1941). Sorkin himself invites comparison to Capra with frequent references to Capra's films in his own scripts. In *The American President*, for example, when Sidney Ellen Wade arrives at the White House for her first visit, she introduces herself to the guard with her full name and state of origin, Virginia. Her companion, a more cynical—and perhaps more typical—Washington lobbyist, urges Sidney to hurry up, saying of the guard, "He doesn't need to know that." Sidney answers, "Forgive me. This is my first time at the White House. I'm trying to savor the Capraesque quality."

"He doesn't know what Capraesque means," her colleague says.

"Yeah, I do," counters the guard. "Frank Capra. Great American director. *It's A Wonderful Life*, *Mr. Smith Goes to Washington*. Sidney Ellen Wade of Virginia, knock 'em dead."

In the "Game On" episode from the fourth season, when Sam Seaborn

(Rob Lowe) is about to be introduced to a character named Will Bailey (Joshua Malina), he does an imitation of Jimmy Stewart as *George* Bailey from Capra's *It's a Wonderful Life* (1946): "Merry Christmas, you old Building and Loan!" he bellows.

Sorkin's *West Wing* demonstrates a Capraesque notion of honesty as the best policy, and celebrates the common man for his wisdom and tolerance, while turning away from the establishment elite. During the third season, in "H.Con-172," after the secret of President Bartlet's multiple sclerosis has been revealed, Bartlet is offered an opportunity to resolve the situation by accepting a censure in the form of a congressional resolution. After debating the issue with Leo, Bartlet agrees to accept the censure, saying, "I was wrong." Over Leo's objections, he continues:

> Lots of times we don't know what right and wrong is, but lots of time we do. And come on, this is one. I may not have had sinister intent at the outset, but there were plenty of opportunities for me to make it right. No one in government takes responsibility for anything anymore. We foster, we obfuscate, we rationalize. "Everybody does it." That's what we say. So we come to occupy a moral safe house where everyone's to blame so no one's guilty. I'm to blame. I was wrong.

Bartlet seems to know that the American public will forgive this lapse of judgment, and as the stunning triumph of "Election Night" in the fourth season proves, he is right.

In *The West Wing*, regardless of how exalted the heroes become, they remain accessible to average, "little" people. The leading characters take on responsibilities most of us avoid, and actual politicians only seem to when the cameras are rolling. For example, Simon Donovan (Mark Harmon), a Secret Service agent from the third season, is a big brother to an African American youth, a legacy passed on to Charlie (Dulé Hill) in the fourth season episode "20 Hours in America." In an episode from the first season, "In Excelsis Deo," Toby attends the funeral of a homeless veteran he never knew, simply because the man died wearing an old coat Toby had given to the Goodwill. In the Thanksgiving 2000 episode, "Shibboleth," the leader of the free world, like millions of other rookies cooking their first turkeys, makes an anonymous call to the Butterball help line. Moments like these add to President Bartlet's sincerity and accessibility.

Still, President Bartlet and his staff are so much more than just good people and plain folks. As the opening episodes of the second season revealed ("In the Shadow of Two Gunmen, Parts I and II"), each staff member has left a high profile, lucrative—if somewhat unfulfilling—career to assist Bartlet's underdog campaign. His wife (Stockard Channing) is a physician. The entire West Wing team is exceptionally well educated and articulate.

Writing about *The West Wing* for the *New York Times* shortly after the terrorist attacks on America in September 2001, Peter de Jonge said:

> For the first two years of its life, the show's depiction of an executive branch truly populated by the best and brightest was a balm to the millions of viewers weary of the endless frustrations and scandals of the Clinton era. The political operatives that Sorkin summoned from his imagination were so smart and scrupulous and impassioned that they were irresistible in a moment when real-life politics seemed trivial. (44)

In numerous interviews, Sorkin has admitted that his characters are "heroic" versions of their real life public service counterparts, and that "the show is kind of a valentine to public service" (Sorkin 2000). Often, he claims, "Government people are portrayed either as dolts or as Machiavellian somehow. The characters in this show are neither" (Sorkin 2000). Sorkin has a commitment to create idealized role models. "It isn't enough for me to write something that people will like," he told the *New York Times*. "I think the young men in my scripts have to be in some shape or form the husbands and boyfriends that women want. I think the fathers have to be the fathers that sons and daughters want. I think the bosses have to be the bosses employees want" (de Jonge 2001, 44).

Sorkin's commitment to creating an idealized White House hit its zenith with the introduction in the second season of a new recurring character, Republican Ainsley Hayes, played by Emily Proctor. In the first scene of her first episode, "In This White House," Ainsley, representing the conservative point of view, "wipes the floor" with Sam on a Sunday morning talk show. Impressed by her performance, Bartlet, determined to bring the best and the brightest into his administration regardless of their party affiliation, offers her a job. Of course, Ainsley won't take it. She has no desire to work "in this White House." But then she visits the West Wing and sees the team responding to an African coup with dispatch and compassion. Later, when she meets two of her Republican friends for drinks, Ainsley remains transfixed by the glow of power and civic purpose she observed. Her friends make fun of Bartlet and his staff. Ainsley jumps to their defense. "They're righteous, they're patriots," she says, "and I'm their lawyer." Just like that, Ainsley is converted.

Storylines like this one seem to support Sorkin's claim that his drama is an original fiction, based on no particular White House. Although *The West Wing* has employed several writers with White House credentials, such as Clinton press secretary Dee Dee Myers and Reagan speechwriter Peggy Noonan, Sorkin says the writing staff "functions as a think tank and a research group with me writing a script every week" (Littleton 2001a, 1). These consultants provide possible storylines and details, so that Sorkin, who has no professional political experience, can write plausible scripts. "I'll make it emotional or funny," he says. "I'll make it the difference between C-SPAN and watching television" (Miller 2000, 93). As a rule, the scripts avoid references to any president since Eisenhower (de Jonge 2001, 42). For the most part, Sorkin says, he will not "compete with actual events. . . . I still don't like to grab yesterday's headlines and make them next week's episode" (Endrst 2000, 10).

Despite plot lines that deal with serious subjects (a military dispute between India and Pakistan or the process of securing a Supreme Court nomination) and educational topics (the intricacies of the census or estate taxes), Sorkin often reminds journalists that he is "a fiction writer" whose job is to entertain, not to teach (see chap. 12, 204). When interviewed by Matthew Miller for *Brill's Content*, Sorkin said *The West Wing* is "not meant to be good for you" (2000, 95). Dee Dee Myers added, "There's a great opportunity . . . through the lives of these characters to explain issues that are sometimes too complex or too obscure-feeling for the press to make interesting and accessible" (95). Miller observes that it often feels as if Sorkin is saying, "Give me the most boring issue you can think of and I'll make a gripping drama out of it" (95).

From the beginning, *The West Wing* has enjoyed a consistent audience of several million viewers, so it would appear that Sorkin's confidence in his talent as a dramatist is justified. *The West Wing* has occupied a unique niche as a political show with a popular following. Earlier programs with political themes have a dismal track record. In 1992, television pioneer Norman Lear (*All in the Family*) produced *The Powers That Be,* starring John Forsythe as Senator William Powers. The show lasted twenty-one episodes. That same year, Steven Bochco (*Hill Street Blues, N.Y.P.D. Blue*), produced *Capitol Critters,* an animated prime time series about rodents and insects in the White House, which was exterminated after just seven episodes. In 1995, after their success with *Designing Women,* Linda Bloodworth-Thomason and Harry Thomason—longtime friends and campaign associates of Bill and Hillary Clinton—moved the character of Suzanne Sugarbaker (Delta Burke) to Washington as a U.S. representative. *Women of the House* ran for an unlucky thirteen episodes.

The West Wing, however, overcame this political jinx. John Wells explained his rationale for the show's success in the November 2000 issue of *George* magazine:

> Every three or four years, a show hits a pop sensibility . . . and that's what happened when *The West Wing* came on. We'd reached a point in the culture where we assumed that people who want to choose public service have the basest of motives of self-aggrandizement and financial gain. . . . [Yet] the public wants to believe in the political process, wants to believe in politicians. Wants to believe that the people who are leading us are doing so— even if there are ideological differences—to make the country better. (See chap. 12, 206–7)

The West Wing is successful precisely because it depends on an idealized version of the White House that does not and cannot exist anywhere but the Warner Bros. backlot. It is as if the program has excised all the messy, offending parts of its characters, like the Nixon tapes with the missing minutes and all the expletives deleted.

In Sorkin's world, the characters may be flawed, but only slightly, and they must be working to overcome any personal problems. Members of the

White House staff, including the president, have on occasion sought the professional help of therapists and the religious guidance of the clergy. Every member of the inner sanctum, from POTUS—the catchy acronym for president of the United States—on down, is remarkably vulnerable to and accepting of each other. Were the West Wing walls ever privy to more sincere conversations? Has there ever been a group of political appointees more in touch with their feelings? Even their light-hearted remarks are sensitive. Only on *The West Wing* could the White House's annual tradition of "pardoning" one of two turkeys take on the solemnity of Solomon. (In the "Shibboleth" Thanksgiving episode, press secretary C. J. Cregg [two-time Emmy winner Allison Janney] convinces President Bartlet to spare *both* birds!)

The sincerity and self-actualization of the Bartlet staff soar in the episode from the first season when chief of staff Leo McGarry (John Spencer) is publicly revealed to be a recovering alcoholic and Valium addict. Like many *West Wing* episodes, this one has a title with a scriptural ring: "He Shall, from Time to Time." The biblical tone is appropriate in this instance because the story culminates in a redemptive moment of forgiveness between President Bartlet and his closest friend, Leo.

Initially, Leo is stunned when he learns that the president suffers from a mild form of multiple sclerosis, something he and the first lady, in a rare act of deception, have kept hidden from everyone.

> LEO. Jed, of all the things you could've kept from me . . .
>
> BARTLET. You haven't called me "Jed" since I was elected.
>
> LEO. (*Sits.*) Why didn't you tell me?
>
> BARTLET. 'Cause I wanted to be the president.
>
> LEO. That wouldn't have stopped me from getting you here. And I could've been a friend.
>
> BARTLET. You've been a friend.
>
> LEO. But when it was time to really—
>
> BARTLET. I know.
>
> LEO. When I was lying on my face in the motel parking lot, you were the one I called.
>
> BARTLET. When you stood up there today [at the press conference], I was so proud. I wanted to be with you.

Bartlet concludes the scene by saying, "I'm so sorry, Leo. I really am."

In her review of *The West Wing*, Lesley Smith cites this episode and criticizes Sorkin for sacrificing drama that "should grab the audience by the throat" for "idealized visions" where "nothing of value is at stake." Smith writes:

> Leo offers to resign. The president refuses to consider it. *Pro forma* response, except that he sticks to it. Episodes of intense (all male) *têtes à têtes* . . . ensue, all ending in declarations of support for the beleaguered chief of staff. But didn't anyone want his job? Where was the self-interested jockeying for position, the rivalry between the young ambitious heirs apparent, and the president's serious search for a possible replacement just in case Leo went down? (2000, 2)

Apparently, in Sorkin's vision of the White House, staff members are selfless; their dedication to their own achievement is second to their commitment to a common cause.

In fact, on *The West Wing*, the highest office in the land is remarkably free of office politics. Bartlet's sunny White House contradicts the accounts of several former staffers from various administrations who have reported in their memoirs incidents of treachery, backstabbing, manipulation, and duplicity in the White House.

One recent first-hand account of life inside the West Wing comes from former Clinton aide and current ABC commentator George Stephanopoulos, whose book, *All Too Human: A Political Education,* paints a view of the West Wing in sharp contrast to Sorkin's. Like his television counterparts, Stephanopoulos brought a religious conviction to his career in public service—he comes from a long line of Greek Orthodox priests and approached his professional life as one would a religious vocation—but he had other qualities, human character traits most of us recognize. Stephanopoulos admits that, at times, he let "ambition, insecurity, and immaturity get the best of him" (1999, 6). He confesses to enjoying meting out "revenge" on Republicans (23). He cites several conversations when President Clinton used profanity, including once when U.S. soldiers had been killed in Mogadishu.

Stephanopoulos writes that the president said, "We're not inflicting pain on these fuckers. When people kill us, they should be killed in greater numbers. I believe in killing people who try to hurt you, and I can't believe we're being pushed around by these two-bit pricks" (214). This is hardly the sort of modulated, peacekeeping conversation one was used to hearing from the "official" President Clinton.

Would Jed Bartlet talk like that? There are network censors, of course, but even if *The West Wing* were on cable television, it is difficult to imagine that he would. Compare this incident to the scenes from the season three finale, "Posse Comitatus," where Bartlet agonizes over the decision to assassinate even one proven terrorist mastermind, a defense minister from a fictional Middle Eastern sultanate. Bartlet and Leo discuss the situation during a Broadway benefit performance of Shakespeare's War of the Roses plays, while the company sings, "And victorious in war shall be made glorious in peace." Bartlet resists making the decision, saying, "It's just wrong." Leo urges him to authorize the assassination. "Why?" Bartlet asks. "Because you won," Leo answers. Poor Stephanopoulos did not work for the likes of Jed Bartlet and Leo McGarry. If he had, perhaps he would not have felt so compromised by his years inside Bill Clinton's White House.

By far, the events Stephanopoulos relates concerning Clinton advisor Dick Morris would be the most difficult to reconcile with the Bartlet administration. Stephanopoulos reports that for two years, Clinton "engaged [Morris] to run a covert operation against his own White House," and that, during this time, "no single person more influenced the president of the United States than Dick Morris." At the same time, "Harold [Ickes] and Erskine [Bowles] let [Stephanopoulos] know that Dick was constantly undermining [Stephanopoulos] with the president, telling him I was too liberal and too much of a leaker to be part of the team" (Stephanopoulos 1999, 329–31). Whether Morris's allegations about Stephanopoulos were true is unclear, but eventually Morris and Stephanopoulos met for dinner, threatened each other, and then came to a standoff. President Bartlet has brought in political consultants (Bruno Gianelli, played by Ron Silver) and pollsters (Joey Lucas, played by Marlee Matlin) to help him lay the groundwork for his reelection, but these outsiders have not disrupted the natural rhythm and professional harmony of the West Wing. There is a sense that President Bartlet and Leo McGarry would not stand for such secret meetings and undermining alliances among their staff.

Aspects from episodes of the second and third season cover territory that might be more familiar to Stephanopoulos and other former White House staffers, such as the storyline concerning the "cover up" of President Bartlet's multiple sclerosis and the resulting investigation. In *All Too Human,* Stephanopoulos describes his preparation for an appearance before the grand jury during the Whitewater hearings. He calls hiring an attorney a Washington "rite of initiation" (Stephanopoulos 1999, 249). At one time or another during *The West Wing*'s third season, President Bartlet, the first lady, and various members of the administration have been coached, questioned, deposed, and defended by attorneys. They have appeared before congressional committees and medical ethics boards. All the while, they have maintained their high ideals. (In many ways, this ethical dilemma served to make these characters more real, more human, than they were during the program's first two seasons.)

A large part of the credit for the success of *The West Wing* belongs to its ensemble cast, who are able to make these larger-than-life characters believable and likable. Not only are they a group of seasoned professionals, but several of them—most notably the actor who plays the president—are politically active in real life. Even though he is a self-described pacifist, and given his high profile as a left-wing activist, the casting of Martin Sheen as Jed Bartlet is especially apt. Sheen is a devout Roman Catholic and has protested against nuclear testing, on behalf of migrant workers, and in favor of gun control. He told the *Cincinnati Enquirer* that his contract on *The West Wing* includes time off for protest rallies and poverty marches. "I make my living as an actor, but this is what I do to stay alive," he said. "My faith demands it. I love my country enough to risk its wrath" (Kiesewetter 1999, 2). In fact, New York's *Daily News* reports that Sheen has engendered the wrath of various law enforcement agencies on numerous occasions, having been arrested an estimated seventy times since 1986 for various acts of civil disobedience (Rush and Molloy 2001, 18).

Bartlet is not Sheen's first role of presidential proportions. He was cast as President Kennedy in the mini-series *Kennedy* (1983), and he has acted in other films set in the White House, including playing chief of staff in Aaron

Sorkin's feature film debut, *The American President*. But in his role as Jed Bartlet, Sheen has captured the imagination of American viewers and, presumably, voters. During the election campaign of 2000, when candidates Al Gore and George W. Bush had the lowest prime-time ratings ever for presidential debates, one poll reported in the *Calgary Herald* that if Josiah Bartlet had been running, "he would have swept the country with 75 percent of the vote" (Berens 2001, 6). Sheen has laughed off any suggestion that he should parlay his success as a television president into a career in politics, saying: "I don't have a personal interest in politics, per se. I have a great interest in the issues that are publicly debated but I have a far greater interest in social justice and peace. I could never be free to explore that if I was bound to a constituency. If I was bound to a constituency, I would have to foreclose my principles" (Behrens 2001, 6). Sheen's role as Bartlet gives him a weekly television constituency of several million viewers and brings increased visibility to his causes without forcing him to modify his opinions as so many politicians must do to maintain their posts.

President Bartlet's popularity may be due in part to an optimal mix of characteristics drawn from several recent presidents. In episodes that bring Bartlet into direct contact with voters, such as the "flashback" scenes in the two-part fall 2000 season opener, "In the Shadow of Two Gunmen," he demonstrates a no-nonsense ability to communicate with average citizens. Julie Hinds noted that this attribute is reminiscent of Harry S Truman's "plain speaking" approach to public appearances and Ronald Reagan's profile as "the Great Communicator" (2000a, 1). In another instance, Bartlet seems to possess the most ineffable of presidential qualities, a charisma to equal Reagan's "Teflon-coating" and Bill Clinton's "bounce." Time after time, the pundits predicted that the people would turn on Reagan or Clinton following a perceived gaffe or misstep, but it did not happen. In an episode titled "Let Bartlet Be Bartlet," when Bartlet ignores advice from his handlers to withhold potentially unpopular opinions on certain issues and takes his case straight to the American people, his approval ratings soar. Yet, in spite of his feeling for the common man, Bartlet is one of the leading minds in Sorkin's version of America. Prior to holding public office, his career as an economist and an academic resulted in an often-mentioned Nobel Prize.

Bartlett is also an American blue blood. One of his ancestors signed the

Declaration of Independence as a representative to the Continental Congress from New Hampshire. Still, his family was not rich; he attended private prep school on a tuition waiver because, as viewers learned in the episode "Two Cathedrals," his distant and disapproving father was the head master. Perhaps it is this troubled relationship that informs Bartlet's FDR-like commitment to a government dedicated to taking care of its least fortunate citizens. Maybe it also fuels Bartlet's need to prove himself on the world stage. Like Bill Clinton, Bartlet exudes a workaholic's love for the job of president and the art of politics. Unfortunately, his irrepressible need to shake hands and reach out to the public at the rope line culminates in an assassination attempt at the end of the first season.

Bartlet also strikes a balance between two extremes in recent presidential politics: he is both a Washington insider, with three terms as a congressman from New Hampshire, and a Washington outsider, with his university professorship and two terms as the governor of the New Hampshire. On the series, Bartlet brings fresh ideas to the challenges of the presidency, and he has the political savvy—most of the time—to make those ideas work.

Lawrence O'Donnell, a former producer of *The West Wing* with a long career as political aide and national affairs columnist, has observed that Bartlet is "the president we'd like to have." O'Donnell believes, "We used to have more people in public office in the Bartlet mold. . . . The newer generation of politicians are a win-at-all-costs group. Winning isn't the only thing that matters" (Hinds 2000b, 1). Just before the November 2000 presidential election, commentator Bill Press, cohost of CNN's *Crossfire,* explained Bartlet's popularity when he said, "Americans still want to love their president, and Martin Sheen's character is more lovable than Al Gore or George Bush" (Hinds 2000b, 1).

Apparently, the producers and stars of *The West Wing* are enjoying their political cachet. They take frequent trips to Washington, D.C., to shoot part of the series on location. Rob Owen of the *Pittsburgh Post-Gazette* reported that throughout the Clinton years, the series' producers enjoyed a "phenomenally friendly" relationship with the White House (2000, 1). According to executive producer and director Thomas Schlamme, "When we've gone to Washington, we've had access to things" (Owen 2000, 1). Apparently, this access continued beyond the change in administrations. In April 2001, Bush staffers hosted cast members and producers on a tour of the White House. (Notably absent from the tour were both Martin Sheen and President Bush; Sheen had publicly called Bush "a moron" a few weeks earlier, and Bush was busy with other unnamed guests.) While in Washington, cast members also attended the White House correspondents' annual dinner (Lindlaw 2001, 1). At least one high-profile politician has inquired about appearing in a cameo role. The *Bergen County Record* reported that during the 2000 presidential campaign, someone from Bush's organization called to see if Bush could appear on the show in a small part, something like a pizza deliveryman. "We don't do that kind of thing," Sorkin said (Shister 2001, 2). Behind the scenes, former political aides and bureaucrats with Washington experience submit their résumés in hopes of being selected as a series consultant, a post that pays a reported thirty thousand dollars per season (Fiore 2001, 2). Members of both parties admit to watching the show. Donna Shalala, former secretary of health and human services in the Clinton administration, told reporter Gail Shister that she builds her schedule around it and "would do a *West Wing* guest shot 'in a minute.' " Shalala also revealed that she'd like to take the place of consultant Dee Dee Myers, saying, "I'm more experienced than she is" (Shister 2000, 8).

However, in spite of all the critical accolades and widespread popularity of *The West Wing* during its first two years, even before the terrorist events of September 11, 2001, and the war that followed in Afghanistan, there were some who felt the series might be losing its grip on the nation's psyche. In May 2001 Tim Goodman wrote, "Without a revamping of the show in some significant fashion, it runs the risk of losing its importance, dropping its political cachet and looking for all the world like a fine, if not sterling, bit of Hollywood fictional fluffery. . . . Either the show changes, or it . . . ends up irrelevant in the dustbin of history" (60). Two months later, Sharon Waxman observed: "One minute *The West Wing* is riding the crest of a cultural wave, sweeping up Emmy and Peabody awards, adorning glossy magazine covers, making a star of its creator, Aaron Sorkin. . . . The next minute, there's blood in the water and discontent in the air. . . . The cycle of success in Hollywood almost always includes a moment when an ugly underside is revealed" (Waxman 2001, 1). The "ugly underside" to which Waxman refers included well-publicized contract disputes between the supporting cast members and the producers, and between the writing staff members and the producers. In general, the actors and writers sought to share in the spoils of the series' success through salary increases. There were also squabbles about Sorkin's tendency to dismiss the contributions of all other staff writers as "research," and to insist that he is responsible for the quality of each episode (Waxman 2001, 1–2).

It was around the same time that Sorkin was arrested at the Burbank airport for drug possession. As the series third season was about to begin, the once-sterling reputation of the idealized *The West Wing* seemed tarnished, and Sorkin's role as an arbiter of American morality seemed diminished.

After September 11, NBC allowed Aaron Sorkin to write a new "stand alone" season-opener in response to the terrorist attacks. Although the resulting episode, "Isaac and Ishmael," drew more than twenty-five million viewers—a record number according to the *Hollywood Reporter*—critically, it failed (Littleton 2001b, 11). The bulk of the episode was a "chalk talk" between West Wing staffers and several students who are stuck in the White House during a security breach. Numerous critics panned the episode, none more vociferously than Tom Shales, the television writer for *The Washington Post*. Shales labeled the episode "pretentious and pietistic hubris" and complained that "instead of a drama, [Sorkin] offered up a lecture, a sermon, a seminar" (Shales 2001a, 1). A few weeks later, Shales again criticized "Isaac and Ishmael":

> The producers of . . . [this] fatuous series . . . threw together a special post-terrorism edition that basically preached at viewers not to hate their Arab neighbors for what extreme Islamic extremists had wrought. *The West Wing* tried to make the matter all tidy and manageable and even tried to make it seem over, as if this token gesture from Hollywood in prime time freed us all to go back to our beloved frivolous diversions and unreal realities. (Shales 2001b, 2)

In January 2002, *Electronic Media* reported that *The West Wing*, the winner of numerous awards and multiple Emmys, had lost its critics' award for best series to a new show with a decidedly different view of presidential politics, Fox's *24 (*Freeman 2002, 24). Waxman warns, "Part of the dizzying euphoria of being on top in Hollywood is the certain knowledge that it probably won't last. For Sorkin, how long it all lasts may be in his own hands" (2001, 2).

Undeniably, Aaron Sorkin is a fiercely talented writer, with a particular gift for the big speech and the memorable turn of phrase, as he demonstrated when he wrote the line, "You can't handle the truth," for Jack Nicholson's character in *A Few Good Men* (1992). Sorkin's flair for speechifying and his commitment to an idealized version of the White House mean that he is un-afraid to broach the big issues—universal health care, abortion, nuclear waste. And as long as he continues to find a balanced way to tell the human stories behind these issues, *The West Wing* will resonate with viewers. It is probably just as well for *The West Wing* that Sorkin's intention is to create his own version of the presidency instead of dramatizing reality. There is no way that even the most imaginative of Hollywood writers could have dreamed up a series of events more difficult to believe than the hijackings of four airliners on September 11, 2001, and the collapse of New York's World Trade Center. Perhaps there is still room in the hearts and minds of television audiences for a White House series with a smart, principled, and compas-sionate president and his loyal, ethical, and sincere staff. Only time will tell if such idealism can remain relevant in the face of a changing world.

10 | *The West Wing* as a Pedagogical Tool

Using Drama to Examine American Politics
and Media Perceptions of Our Political System

STACI BEAVERS

When so many eligible adults fail to vote in presidential elections, why would the American viewing public want to occupy its entertainment hours with presidential politics? It would seem that a sharply written, intelligent political drama could never succeed in the face of modern political cynicism. Yet, since its debut in 1999, *The West Wing* has provided both provocative political dialogue and strong ratings. *The West Wing* finished in thirteenth place in the Nielsen ratings in its second season, and it stood in seventh place in the fall of 2001 ("Television's Top Fifty" 2001; Snierson and Kepnes 2002, 7). The series has also garnered such critical accolades as back-to-back Peabody Awards and seventeen Emmys.

Series creator, coproducer, and lead writer Aaron Sorkin serves as the driving force behind *The West Wing*. Sorkin, who created ABC's critically praised but short-lived *Sports Night* (1998–2000) and who wrote *A Few Good Men* (1992), has created here a cast of smart, engaging characters led by President Josiah Bartlet (Martin Sheen), a liberal Democrat hailing from New Hampshire. Bartlet appears to share most of Bill Clinton's ideological sympathies, but his stable family life saves him from the embarrassments of Bill Clinton's personal baggage. His senior aides share his principles and a determination to work as a team to achieve Bartlet's progressive agenda.

For those who study and teach politics or history for a living, *The West Wing* unsheathes a double-edged sword: a great strength of the series is its

175

ability to put a human face on engaging political discussions, demonstrating that politics can be accessible and enjoyable; but this fictional White House also presents potential dangers. As good dramatic television should, the program deliberately plays the emotions of viewers through such techniques as the sophisticated use of cameras, editing, and music. If the Bartlet White House serves as a popular measure of what presidential politics should be, however, no doubt reality will frequently fall short of creator Sorkin's vision. When oversimplifications or inaccuracies prevail on screen in the name of drama, will viewers build their perspectives and actions on flawed criteria? Could even greater cynicism result?

Careful use of clips from the television series can illustrate particular concepts and stimulate classroom discussion and analysis of various topics. Attention to the series, however, should also be structured to help students develop the critical viewing skills necessary to engage in independent evaluations not only of television drama, but also of such visual media as films, documentaries, and TV news reports.

The Pedagogical Potential of *The West Wing*

No single television or film representation of the presidency can accurately capture the essence or the complexity of the presidency. Actor Martin Sheen (who plays President Bartlet) has admitted, with respect to *The West Wing*, that "[i]t's not possible to have any clue what it's like to be president" and that "the only thing we can get into are [*sic*] the relationships that happen behind and away from public view—the personal moments, and [our conception of] the effects of policy and personalities on the staff" (Kiesewetter 2000, E1). *The West Wing* becomes valuable as a pedagogical tool by providing both engaging discussions of contemporary policy debates and intriguing explorations of underlying political power relationships.

Whether created as fiction or nonfiction, film and television programs may illustrate key points and spur students to pursue further information and insights for themselves. In our era of sound-bite politics, *The West Wing* addresses many contemporary domestic and foreign policies at least as sensibly as do many government officials. Former Drug Enforcement Administration (DEA) official Robert Stutman has echoed this sentiment, stating, "The most intelligent discussion I've heard among politicians concerning the drug issue happened to be on TV about six weeks ago. Unfortunately, it was on *The West Wing* and it was President Josiah Bartlet" (Sepinwall 2000, E7). Clips of such deliberations, with their fast-paced and focused dialogue, may help students to jump-start their own examinations of contemporary issues ranging from the methodology and import of presidential approval polling to slavery reparations for present-day African Americans (discussed respectively in the episodes "Lies, Damn Lies, and Statistics" and "Six Meetings Before Lunch").

The American people cynically realize that real-life candidates giving speeches and interviews have been carefully prepared and scripted for their own "performances," particularly when these candidates repeatedly parrot the same lines, as in recent presidential campaigns. Unfortunately, *The West Wing* often presents the audience with a more human face than contemporary real-life leaders frequently present. For example, in the episode "The Short List," in which President Bartlet selects his first nominee to the Supreme Court, the characters discuss the right to privacy and drug testing with more apparent passion than do real-life political leaders. The episodes "Mandatory Minimums" and "Ellie" also present discussions of the nation's drug policies that would likely make many real-life government officials nervous.

The series moves beyond contemporary policy debates to explore more fundamental concepts of political power and relationships. The presidency came to dominate American politics and policy agendas in the twentieth century thanks in no small part to television news coverage focusing on individual presidents. *The West Wing* helps demonstrate that "the presidency" is not only about the single individual often represented on television; it is also about a vast institution. The White House teems with advisors and assistants who handle issues on the president's behalf—and sometimes even handle the president himself. In the show's pilot episode, President Bartlet appears on screen only in the last few minutes, illustrating that much of the presidency's weight never even reaches his shoulders; many matters are addressed by the denizens of his West Wing. The various staff characters and the extras trailing through the hallways provide a view of the presidency as an institution supported by the efforts of many individuals.

The show's explorations of various political relationships could also provide opportunities for classroom analysis. For example, the edgy rapport between White House press secretary C. J. Cregg (Allison Janney) and journalist Danny Concannon (Timothy Busfield) in the show's first two seasons provides an interesting perspective on the relationship between politicians and members of the press. The tensions between the two characters are particularly interesting because they are based loosely on the real-life romance and eventual marriage of Dee Dee Myers, Bill Clinton's first press secretary, and *New York Times* reporter Todd Purdham. Political commentator (and one-time political operative) Christopher Matthews (1999) insists that, for political figures, "the press is the enemy"; however, both the politicians and the members of the press desperately need each other for mutual survival (183). In such episodes as "Enemies" and "The Short List," staffer C. J. struggles to resist the advances of the charming investigative reporter Danny, whom she fears may want information from her as much as he wants to date her. In short, C. J. must constantly be on her guard with a character with whom she shares much screen time and considerable chemistry.

Many commentators have also attested to the truthfulness of depicting White House advisors (including pollsters and party operatives) as combatants "battling for the president's soul" in the crafting of proposals and priorities (Feinberg 1999, 85). As the Bartlet White House lurches toward taking a stand on any given issue, the president must grapple not only with questions of good and right, but also with the more practical question, what is politically feasible?

In doing so, he must face the conflicting agendas brewing among his top aides. In "The Short List," the president must choose a Supreme Court nominee. On the one hand, communications director Toby Ziegler (Richard Schiff) argues for the safe choice, "a guaranteed confirmation," in spite of the candidate's conservative views on the right to privacy. On the other hand, deputy communications director Sam Seaborn (Rob Lowe) is fighting for a candidate so ideally liberal he is guaranteed only to stir up controversy. Sam's idealism wins on this day, but only after much collective soul-searching and preparation for a confirmation battle. As a point of comparison, Clinton Secretary of Labor Robert Reich has written of his struggle to draw Bill Clinton toward his own progressive liberal agenda, a particularly tough battle after the disastrous 1994 midterm elections drove Clinton back into the arms of pollster Dick Morris, who pushed Clinton toward a more conservative, politically marketable agenda. Reich (1997) describes Morris as representing everything he "detest[ed] in American politics" (280); the real-life Reich, however, was less successful in his battle than was the fictional Seaborn.

In short, the series focuses attention on a variety of provocative topics that instructors and students may explore in some detail. However, an instructor using *The West Wing* in the classroom should ensure that students view the program as engaging fictional TV drama rather than as a weekly civics lesson.

Viewing Drama with the Goal of Political Independence

Political analyst and commentator Curtis Gans has proclaimed television to be the "enemy" of the political process, "the technological innovation which [has] had the most deleterious effect on citizen involvement" (Gans 1993, 26). Some scholars have worked to link television's emphasis on individualism to both the waning of the political parties and drops in voter turnout rates. Building upon Daniel J. Elazar's (1984) conceptualization of American political culture, Allan McBride and Robert K. Toburen (1996) argue that American television programming promotes an individualistic culture that places little value on the public good or civic involvement. They argue that the waning of partisanship in particular, and connections to groups overall as well, "coincided with the widespread availability of commercial television in the United States."

Both film and television manipulate the emotions, which no doubt frequently helps to influence political and social viewpoints. Storylines are developed and cameras and music are deliberately employed for maximum impact. Allan McBride (1998) sees entertainment programming as potentially exerting especially strong influences on attitudes, since "the critical faculties of viewers are likely to be lowered" when they watch for leisure or recreation (549). Such effects are most objectionable if the emotional or ideological cues are themselves built on oversimplifications, inaccuracies, or even distortions. Charges of deliberate inaccuracies have been raised against many politically oriented dramas, including such critically acclaimed productions as *Roots* (Fishbein 1983, 293–97). Although the series was hugely successful in inspiring a national discussion on slavery in America, part of that discussion was built on faulty information. Undoing the effects of such inaccuracies is no easy task.

No evidence is available yet regarding whether *The West Wing* has had any measurable impact on the American viewing public's political opinions, for good or for ill. Certainly one of the program's strengths is its sophisticated use of dramatic techniques to stir emotions. Many viewers no doubt feel a small thrill at the program's opening credits. They are filled with powerful music and contemplative black-and-white shots of President Bartlet and his closest advisors interspersed with images of the White House, Marine One, and a waving American flag. Likewise, viewers get a "feel" for the hustle-and-bustle at the top echelons of political power when the lead characters frequently "walk-and-talk" through the White House's elegant hallways, which are constantly teeming with busy staffers. Interestingly, this aspect of mise-en-scène is made possible through some distortion regarding the West Wing as a workplace: set designer Ken Hardy has admitted that, although Jed Bartlet's Oval Office looks stunningly like Bill Clinton's, the rest of the actual West Wing is less elegant and imposing than the show's set (Weintraub 2000, 1E). Some former White House employees have also pointed out that the actual West Wing is too cramped to accommodate the fast-paced "walk-and-talks" so crucial to the frantic tempo of the Bartlet White House ("TV's 'West Wing' Is Not a Good Replica of the Real Thing" 1999, E5). Others have noted that many of the employees shown bustling through the hallways (and thus intensifying the impact of the "walk-and-talks") should by rights be bustling instead through the wider hallways of the nearby Old Executive Office Building (Anderson 2000, O5).

In spite of the challenges television presents for the development of independent thought, teaching critical viewing skills has at best been a low priority among scholars and educators (O'Connor 1987, 13–14). Political science, for example, gives only limited attention to the study of entertainment film and television in its journals and conferences. Though available film-related books by political scientists are of high caliber (see Gianos 1998 or Giglio 2000), they are few in number.

Given the amount of time many students likely already spend in front of their television sets, many educators would prefer to reduce—rather than increase—classroom attention to the medium. But Patricia-Ann Lee (1990) states the matter particularly well:

> The question is not therefore whether film [and, no doubt, television] is going to appear in the classroom: it may do so directly; it will certainly do so indirectly through the experience and attitudes as well as the intellectual baggage students bring with them. Given these facts we have an obligation to help students learn to deal with this omnipresent and omnicompetent entity, and to encourage them to apply the same critical and discriminating judgment to the study of film that we expect them to use in evaluating more traditional sources (96).

Lee's encouragement becomes even more pointed when one considers how television campaign ads influence emotions and perceptions through many of the same rhetorical techniques that come into play in dramatic productions for television and film. American democracy itself may be hanging in the balance of whether viewers (i.e., voters) can learn to view film and television critically.

Putting *The West Wing* to Use in the Classroom

The obvious task for any instructional use of film or video clips is to move students beyond the typical passivity of viewing and instead put the clips to work as interactive learning techniques that encourage critical thought while also conveying information (Frantzich 1998, 1). One simple way to begin addressing *The West Wing* in the classroom may be to knock away any impressions that the series depicts the final "truth" about the presidency. For example, some simple fallacies regarding the White House as a workplace could be easily pointed out by viewing a hallway "walk-and-talk" scene, then discussing various news/magazine interviews with actual White House employees who downplay the accuracy of the program's mise-en-scène. As Lee points out with respect to film, "in some cases, even defects can become positive resources for teaching" (1990, 104). Here, pointing out such seemingly minor inaccuracies may spur students to question what the show has to say about bigger issues, whether specific policy debates or the underlying power relationships in Washington.

When clips are used to jump-start policy discussions in the classroom, students quickly learn that, in Jed Bartlet's White House, the more liberal arguments usually carry the day. The work of the liberals is made easier by the fact that most characters espousing conservative views are less than sympathetic, to say the least. For example, characters representing the Christian right are often portrayed as ignorant, self-serving bigots who know less Scripture than President Bartlet. In the pilot episode, a leader of the Christian Right (Annie Corley) is quickly revealed as anti-Semitic; in "The Midterms," President Bartlet humiliates a socially conservative radio personality (Claire Yarlett) by mocking attempts to condemn homosexuality on the basis of literal biblical interpretations.

Although the series has been criticized for its left-leaning tendencies, its patterns of character representations and development may provide ideal opportunities for student analysis. What is the dramatic effect of consistently having conservative viewpoints espoused by unsympathetic characters? Even Democratic characters promoting conservative viewpoints are often set up for ignominy. In "Twenty Hours in L.A.," Democratic pollster Al Kiefer (John DeLancie) suggests an issue position that he can "sell" to the electorate and thus (in his view) guarantee President Bartlet's re-election. His suggestion is for President Bartlet to promote a constitutional amendment that would prohibit the burning of the American flag. Kiefer's character is undermined before the viewers even meet him by the clear disdain with which the key staffers discuss him, by the insults they speak directly to him, and finally by his being positioned as a potential romantic rival to deputy chief of staff Josh Lyman (Bradley Whitford). Most conservative characters on the series have the deck stacked against them by such dramatic techniques. Students should ask themselves, how does this affect the outcomes of conflicts between liberals and conservatives?

It is worth noting that one of the few exceptions to this pattern is the character of Ainsley Hayes (Emily Procter), an associate White House counsel who manages to be both conservative and likable. She provides a particularly good foil for Sam Seaborn, who seems to be drawn to her in spite of himself. The Hayes character provides some ideological balance within the

Bartlet White House, but her status within the administration may be best represented by the location of her office—she toils away in the steam pipe distribution venue in the basement ("And It's Surely to Their Credit"). She oftens wins her arguments with Sam, but could her office be a stand-in for the fires of hell awaiting those who hold conservative points of view?

Other potentially useful clips address relations among top officials. The episode "Enemies" depicts a rare Bartlet cabinet meeting in which President Bartlet expresses his distaste for both cabinet meetings and his vice president, John Hoynes (Tim Matheson). Vice President Hoynes, who as a senator from Texas was added to the Bartlet ticket to balance Bartlet's New Hampshire pedigree, is clearly *not* a key player in the Bartlet White House. This interpretation is confirmed as the relationship between these two characters develops over subsequent episodes, such as in "Twenty Hours in L.A." What, if anything, might the relationship between the Bartlet and Hoynes characters suggest about opinions on the vice presidency itself? As will often be the case, determining the "accuracy" of the scene's representation is a complex matter. Here, such a determination requires a broader discussion of the precarious nature of the vice president's job description, a historically powerless office whose role in any modern administration depends almost entirely on the disposition of the president and his relationship with the vice president. The very brief but tense interaction between the Bartlet and Hoynes characters in this episode could be compared to written accounts of the vice presidencies of Lyndon Johnson and Al Gore, who had very different experiences in the office as a result of the very different relationships they shared with their respective bosses.

Several episodes could provide excellent fodder for independent research projects. The episode "He Shall, from Time to Time" reveals that President Bartlet suffers from multiple sclerosis. The episode raises crucial questions regarding a president's ability to withhold key medical information from the American public. At first glance the episode seems too implausible to imagine; after all, the president's physical health is now frequently discussed on television, and presidential candidates frequently disclose their medical records during their campaigns. Even President George W. Bush's embarrassing pretzel-and-fainting incident in 2002, witnessed only by his two dogs, was made public and discussed in the news for days! Further reflection, though, may lead to a different take on the matter. For example, three days after becoming vice president in 1965, Hubert H. Humphrey was kept almost totally in the dark about President Lyndon Johnson's condition after Johnson was rushed to Bethesda Naval Hospital with what at first appeared to be a heart attack (Humphrey 1976, 314). Here, on Johnson's own orders, the nation's second highest officer was kept ignorant. More recently, it is now widely believed that President Ronald Reagan came much closer to death in John Hinckley Jr.'s 1981 assassination attempt than the public was told at the time. Finally, it is worth noting that President Bill Clinton left office in 2001 without having ever provided a full disclosure of his own medical records. The episode's suggestion that a president might keep such an important secret could make for intriguing student research projects into both the ethical and practical considerations of a zone of privacy for presidents. The extent to which the public has historically been kept in the dark regarding the health of our presidents, including President Franklin Roosevelt's paralysis and declining health during World War II, may indeed surprise many students who have grown up watching television clips of their presidents strolling across the White House lawn.

Developing Critical Viewing Skills to Foster Political Independence

Correcting specific misconceptions and encouraging students to put the series into a broader perspective still provides only an incomplete approach to working with television or film clips in the classroom. Historian John E. O'-Connor asserts, "Teachers should be less concerned with identifying factual mistakes on the screen and more with alerting students to the characteristic ways popular film and television productions often manipulate and trivialize historical [and political] issues" (1987, 4). O'Connor argues that instructors should invest some classroom time in "help[ing] keep students aware that the feelings they get from watching a film [or television] are not coincidental" (48). At least some attention to the techniques and terminology of critical viewing, including such concepts as camera angles, lighting, editing, and music, is in order.

As noted above, many political scientists are themselves not particularly well equipped for the charge of teaching students how to translate the language of cinema. However, the goal is not to teach students to become film critics but rather to familiarize them with basic film/television terminology in order to recognize attempts to move them either emotionally or ideologically. The Gianos (1998) and Giglio (2000) books mentioned above would help with this task, as would Nelson and Boynton's *Video Rhetorics* (1997). O'Connor's work in history would prove especially helpful, as would issues of *Film and History,* a journal that O'Connor founded in 1970.

Specific attention to camera work would be crucial to evaluating the program's ability to affect viewers. Our impressions of the heady frenzy of West Wing life are not accidental: the nearly constant motion and fast-paced dialogue require viewers to stay on their toes just to keep up with the numerous plot lines being juggled simultaneously. Even when the characters are still, the camera often arcs around the actors to maintain the impression of constant motion and intrigue, intensifying the discussions. Mike McCurry, former press secretary to President Clinton, has stated, "Ninety percent of what happens at the White House is pure boredom. Believe me" (Miga 1999, 3). One would never know that from the way the cameras of *The West Wing* help build and maintain dramatic intensity where, in reality, there often might be none.

Further, how might students assess their responses to the panoramic shots of official Washington, particularly the powerful establishing shots from outside the White House (frequently shot so that the Washington Monument, signifying the tradition and power of the presidency, as well as its historical roots, is clearly evident)? Certainly the nighttime shots clearly imply that service to president and country never stops. The sense of constant activity is sustained even into the hours when most of the nation is either home watching television or asleep.

High-contrast lighting is also frequently used to good effect. Characters frequently appear with much of their faces in shadow, suggesting conflicting emotions, or perhaps moral ambiguity. Further, it is probably not coincidental that the Oval Office is often fully lighted, in contrast to the much darker offices of several key aides, who handle much of the "dirtier" work of political strategizing. The episode "Six Meetings Before Lunch" makes particularly interesting use of contrasting light patterns in illustrating vastly different meetings taking place simultaneously within the White House. Director Clark Johnson staged a frivolous conversation regarding an attempt to secure a panda bear for the National Zoo in a well-lit room. A much more intense, dramatic debate took place between senior advisor Josh Lyman and Jeff Breckenridge (Carl Lumbly), the president's brilliant but controversial nominee for assistant attorney general for civil rights. The weighty, purely serious debate over slavery reparations to present-day African Americans took place in near darkness, with tight close-ups of the characters intensifying the tenor of the discussion. The contrasting lighting in the two separate discussions effectively enhanced the intensity of the latter discussion.

◆   ◆   ◆

In their guide for classroom teachers, John E. O'Connor and Martin A. Jackson (1974) caution that film and television should be used in the classroom only stringently and only when they help to achieve specific pedagogical goals (48). Unflinching analytical attention to *The West Wing* can spur students both to greater thought about our political system and to critical viewing of politically or historically oriented television and film more generally. Both skills can take students far beyond the passive viewing too frequently associated with dramatic television and toward critical thinking skills so important to lifelong learning.

11 | Victorian Parliamentary Novels, *The West Wing*, and Professionalism

MICHELLE MOUTON

ill Clinton's presidency provoked seemingly endless opportunities for
the American film and TV industry, both exemplifying and contesting
the definition of political merit. *The West Wing* is only one example. Similarly, in the 1860s and 1870s, the British Second Reform Act and its most
prominent Victorian debaters, Benjamin Disraeli and William Gladstone,
prompted a wave of election novels about Parliamentarians—fictional explorations of political possibilities. These works include Margaret
Oliphant's *Miss Marjoribanks* (1864–65), George Eliot's *Felix Holt* (1865),
and Anthony Trollope's *Phineas Finn* (1869) and *Ralph the Heir* (1872). In
both historical instances, political fiction helped to shape popular perceptions of the politician, often through the depiction of elections. Could meritorious politicians win elections while retaining integrity? Having won,
could they effectively lead constituencies? The parallels between *The West
Wing* and nineteenth-century literary experiments are worth exploring for
they highlight a common ideology of the genre: the inefficacy of political involvement except by a small portion of the population.

In a course on Victorian literature and liberalism, parliamentary novels
formed the framework and context for *The West Wing* for a group of students at a small, midwestern, liberal arts college.[1] Students read Oliphant,

---

1. Eight students participated daily in this three-and-a-half week seminar on Victorian
electoral fiction. All were upper-division students between ages eighteen and twenty-two, four

Eliot, and Trollope, and explored the ways political fiction could encourage or discourage democratic participation. Their viewings of several American presidential election movies, including *Bob Roberts* (1992) and *The Contender* (2000), helped students to understand Victorian novels by comparison. Near the close of the term, they viewed and commented upon two election-related episodes of Aaron Sorkin's *West Wing*, "The MidTerms" and "Let Bartlet Be Bartlet." This essay explains the context through which students came to *The West Wing* and examines their responses to it. Student comments suggest that the series reflects class biases that exclude them—regardless of their political leanings—from identifying with political players and full participants in American democracy. The attention in *The West Wing* to what the Victorians would have called the "professional classes" (which included doctors, lawyers, and some politicians) emphasizes rational over passionate discourse, the workplace over domestic or public spaces, and business over personal relationships. Students, because they did not identify with these codes of professionalism, could not envision themselves as the kind of political participants featured by *The West Wing*.

Victorian Novels, Ideal Politicians, and Realism

Victorian political novels of the 1860s and 1870s were spurred by controversy over the benefits and dangers for the upper-middle class of representative democracy. The Second Reform Act (1867) doubled the all-male electorate, enfranchising one in three men and effectively extending the franchise into the lower-middle class. Liberal Victorian parliamentary novels contemporary with the Second Reform Act express largely negative views toward this expanding electorate. Many posit a slippery slope: an eventual working-class majority and resulting mobocracy. To counter or influence this

---

were Democrats, one was a Republican, two did not identify with any political party, and one was a Nader activist. Six of the students were female and two were male. Seven identified themselves as Caucasian, one as Iranian. Only one student had seen *The West Wing* previously, and she had seen only two episodes. I wish to thank all of the students, including Genevieve Gilson, Traci Hanson, Stephanie Hurovitz, Katrina Krupicka, and Stephanie Savage, for their thoughtful participation in this study.

imagined revolutionary majority, novels idealize parliamentarians of "character": men with a liberal arts education; a strong sense of idealism; interest in the general or public good above narrow class interests; a devotion to individualistic conscience above party line; skill in calm, rational discourse in contrast to volatile protestors; and a lack of any private ambition or personal gain accompanying the socially prestigious title of "M.P." (Examples include Plantagenet Palliser of *The Palliser Series*; Mr. Ashburton of *Miss Marjoribanks*; and Phillip Debarry of *Felix Holt*.) These qualities define the man of good judgment who was to be entrusted with decision making for the good of the people, rather than at the pressure of the people.[2] It is not simply coincidental that this meritorious politician—an image still in play today—had all of the attributes and social capital to which upper-middle-class and aristocratic men already had access. That is, the novels endorsed the election of "gentlemen" to Parliament, regardless of a majority working-class electorate. In the event that voting rights were infinitely expanded, fiction and ideology could be used to maintain and increase the cultural, moral, and political authority of the middle class. Narratives could persuade, or attempt to persuade, new voters to trust and elect their social betters.

Furthermore, this ideal politician was constructed through and against a host of impure political figures: overly ambitious and self-interested populist leaders (Turnbull in *Phineas Finn*); politically outspoken women tainted by questionable sexuality (Barbara Lake in *Miss Marjoribanks* and Laura Standish Kennedy in *Phineas Finn*); and opportunistic campaign agents and lawyers who encourage "voting irregularities" (Johnson and Jermyn in *Felix Holt*,). What emerges, then, is a rhetoric in which those most invested in enfranchisement and self-determination—women, the working class, and colonial subjects—appear too self-interested, mercenary, and outside the realm

---

2. John Stuart Mill most clearly elucidated this distinction in *On Representative Government* (1861). Mill (1993) writes: "it is so important that the electors should choose as their representatives wiser men than themselves, and should consent to be governed according to that superior wisdom, while it is impossible that conformity to their own opinions, when they have opinions, should not enter largely into their judgment as to who possesses the wisdom, and how far its presumed possessor has verified the presumption by his conduct" (346). This image of the ideal intellectual politician existed prior to the 1860s, but was more often espoused by Tories than Liberal and Utilitarian leaders during the first half of the century.

of legitimate rational discourse to represent members of their own groups.[3] Students came to *The West Wing* with this construct of the ideal politician, one not unlike Josiah "Jed" Bartlet (Martin Sheen), and with an understanding of the exclusions this ideal entails.

The class also came to the television episodes with a particular understanding of Victorian literary realism. This genre is characterized by an emphasis on the minutiae of the everyday, character development and plausible motive, and an apparent exposure of the darker elements underlying a given society. The aesthetic success of literary realism depends upon the degree to which it can sustain the impression that it reflects real life. Consistency of vision, plausibility, and accumulated descriptive detail aid in a reader's "suspension of disbelief." Commonly, too, these combined elements produce a sense of fatalism about the reality portrayed, about "the way things really are," given the incompatibility of radical resolutions with consistency of vision (Brantlinger 1977, 207). Victorian parliamentary fiction, more specifically, focuses on daily, behind-the-scenes maneuverings of wealth, power, and personal ambition. It typically investigates and claims to reveal a politician's covert motives, ambitions, and deal making rather than, for example, the impact of policy on a population. It is highly topical in its allusions to parliamentary debates on reform, contributing to a sense that only fiction, and not the press or parliamentary speeches, can reveal the "truth" of politics. Realist (as opposed to utopian, polemical, or satirical) political fiction suggests that legislative politics will always be "politics," at its most pejorative. Victorian literary realism, as Patrick Brantlinger argues, advocates political "realism," a political position midway between radical idealism and ultraconservatism, supportive of the status quo (1977, 207). The novels of the 1850s and 1860s, he notes, are filled with "failed reformers and broken or comic idealists" (226).

Thus, even moments of idealism within the genre are subordinated to this overriding fatalism. Victorian politicians who are ideal (i.e., educated, rational, upper-middle-class) and maintain radical, reformist views are depicted as ineffectual in the face of a growing political machinery, a mob of

3. Elaine Hadley's (1995) work demonstrates that in the 1870s, in particular, liberal discourse defined itself against "melodramatic" or feminine forms of public dissent.

uneducated new voters, and the corruption that surrounds and exploits them. These novels thus promote cynicism about even the most ideal politician's ability to improve material and social conditions. Indeed, they suggest that it is the politics of cultural and literary representation—of the novel itself—and not representation in a legislative body that is crucial in effecting change.[4] In this sense, the novels discourage readers from political participation.

What, if anything, does *The West Wing* do differently than this preceding body of political fiction? Does its construct of the ideal politician promote similar exclusions from Congress? Does *The West Wing* encourage or discourage political participation? Asked in positive terms, can realist political fiction ever encourage "radical democracy" as Cornell West, Henry Giroux, and other theorists have defined it—a highly participatory democracy in which all citizens have active voice, and in which citizens work continually to map and intervene in systems of power? Students posed these and related questions regarding two episodes of *The West Wing.*

First, students wrote about their expectations of the series. Some predicted that the show would fall in line with liberal, Victorian novels in its encouragement of political cynicism. As one student wrote, however positively the White House staffers might be depicted, if the show were to focus too narrowly on behind-the-scene political players, *The West Wing* would imply the inefficacy of, or the lack of necessity for, public involvement in government. Another student expected that the show would "portray more of the personal lives of the people involved; [and] focus on . . . drama and intrigue" rather than issues he wished to see. This student went on to articulate his frustration that Victorian novels tend to define political integrity by its opposite, by morally corrupt politicians at worst, or by ineffectual and inelectable idealists at best. He thus expected that *The West Wing* would provide no model of politicians of integrity who could accomplish worthwhile goals from within the system.

Students who were more hopeful about the show expected that its twenty-first-century setting would set it apart from our readings. It could de-

---

4. This shift, which occurred in the middle of the nineteenth century, is the subject of Catherine Gallagher's *Industrial Reformation* (1985).

pict strong and active political women and people of color, all serving in positions of power. Further, they hoped it might depict public opinion as a positive force upon the president's decisions, thereby encouraging political outspokenness. One student went further to specify that the show could "promote political participation [through its portrayal of] aides, younger people helping out in Congress and the White House." Taken together, students wanted a more subversive politics of representation, which in turn might encourage a participatory politics of legislation, than that which they had encountered in Victorian realist fiction: a show that would depict traditionally disenfranchised groups as positive and effective political players, and that would portray popular political involvement and agitation as necessary and meaningful.

"The Midterms"

"The Midterms" is a *West Wing* episode set during congressional elections, midway in Democrat Jed Bartlet's first term as U.S. president. It follows the first season's sensational cliffhanger, in which the president is shot by members of a white-supremacist group. They have taken aim, the White House discovers, not at the president, but at his young, African American assistant Charlie Young (Dulé Hill) for dating the white president's daughter. In the aftermath of the shooting, Charlie lurks in the West Wing corridors while the white White House staffers interact with uncharacteristic, post-trauma edginess. Staffers (as well as the camera) are at times startled by Charlie's entrance and at other times painfully aware of his voiceless presence as they discuss the shooting, debate the legal status of white supremacist groups, and reflect upon their own emotions. Meanwhile, in two subplots concerning race, President Bartlet becomes tempted to involve himself (inappropriately) in a local school board race in order to thwart the election of a bigoted candidate, and the White House endorses a senatorial candidate but withdraws support when it is discovered that he has a history of selecting only white jurors to serve on trials of African American defendants. The episode concludes with reluctant accommodations of idealism to the democratic process: communications director Toby Ziegler (the administration's Jewish, liberal, intellectual conscience, played by Richard Schiff) begrudgingly acknowledges that civil rights laws prevent the targeting of white supremacists for gun seizure, and the president concedes that he must let local constituencies elect whomever they want to represent them. Charlie, having suppressed his emotions about being the target of a racially based assassination attempt, finally experiences catharsis by revealing his role, unsolicited, to an African American computer repairman who has been called in to repair White House computers. The episode's final scene presents the dejected, idealist staffers (minus Charlie) toasting "God Bless America" one by one with a mixed sense of irony and earnestness.

Jed Bartlet's pragmatic politics and the professional activities of his staff are portrayed in a much more positive light, and as more consistent with idealism, than is the case in liberal Victorian political fiction. Bartlet is neither an ineffectual idealist nor a tolerant realist, but navigates between the two poles throughout the series. Two students recognized this distinction. The show differs, one wrote, "by painting a more optimistic/idealistic view of politics and politicians, showing individuals who work hard despite the corruption and bureaucracy and 'politics' of politics." The other acknowledged that there was "less corruption within the government itself" than she had expected.

On the whole, however, the students were disappointed and expressed alienation by the show's cultural politics. It did not provide the radical politics of representation that they had hoped for, and in this sense it seemed not so very different from Victorian political fiction. Students had faint praise, at best, for *The West Wing*'s arguably nuanced and subversive analysis of gender and race. Charlie's silent but watchful presence continually undermines the staff's attempts to resolve emotions through discussions of constitutional issues, through their professional work. Students focused, however, on other aspects of this episode, which fell short of their expectations for a radical politics of representation. One viewer expressed ambivalence at the episode's portrayal of African Americans as an automatic "community"—Charlie's ability to open up to a complete stranger—and its simultaneous individualizing of whites. Although she approved of the show's foregrounded analysis of race, power, and voice, the episode troublingly suggested "whiteness" as a far more individuated and uninterrogated identity than "blackness." Another student pointed out that the show had no clearly working-class or poor characters with the exception of Charlie, who was hired despite his background in urban ghettos. Even Charlie's position at the White House is based largely on luck and therefore seems irreplicable. (In a fortuitous meeting in a previous episode, staffer Josh Lyman, played by Bradley Whitford, has recognized Charlie's merit and ignored his lack of credentials to hire him for the position.) Where, others students asked, were the Asian and Hispanic staff members? Why did most women play subordinate roles as secretaries and assistants, trivialized for humorous effect? This particular episode, in short, did not exhibit the revisionist politics of representation that students wished to see, despite its continual foregrounding of racial and racist politics, and its demonstration of the interconnectedness of political, legal, and personal consequences of racism.

Two moments did come close to meeting the group's call for greater attention to diversity. These were moments with which students could readily identify. First, regardless of each student's political persuasion, they all expressed pleasure at Bartlet's public humiliation of a call-in therapist who fraudulently poses as a psychiatrist (calling herself "Dr.") and justifies bigotry on the basis of biblical verse. They found that the intervention of an authority and father figure in the religious Right was surprising and satisfying, if unrealistic and polemical. They were particularly excited about the fact that they had read similar critiques of Dr. Laura Schlessinger in a magazine for college students, and were thus familiar with the issues. The more fiscally and socially conservative students, too, were able to distance themselves from the Christian Right, positioned by Sorkin as hypocritical, thereby validating their more moderate conservatism. The liberal students found the moment to be a refreshingly polemical one for television drama. This combination of polemical discourse with an issue familiar to the students elicited their strong approval.

The other scene to which students responded positively also involves a father figure's validation of a (socially) liberal stance: an interracial kiss and jokes implying an affectionate sexual relationship between the president's white daughter Zoe and Charlie, whom she is dating. At the beginning of this scene, the camera emphasizes Charlie's tentative approach toward Zoe with a medium-shot, and the dialogue emphasizes their flirtatious distance as Charlie pretends to be happening upon a stranger. The camera then suddenly zooms in to what is nearly a close-up at the moment that Zoe initiates a kiss. The camera work thus underscores the surprising element in Zoe's sexual assertiveness—surprising given her traditional femininity and filial devotion. Leo McGarry (John Spencer) enters and interrupts, asking them to be sure to "take protection." He refers to the Secret Service, but the two assume he means condoms. Through a humorous misunderstanding, the father substitute (Leo is the president's best friend) is mildly embarrassed at his inadvertent reference to sexual protection. This joke about "protection" develops the kiss into a relationship more substantive than its visually sensational effect. Rhetorically, white male supremacists, defended against by the Secret Service, take on the same ominous and threatening attributes as HIV and sexually transmitted infection (STIs). Students found this moment both shocking and impressively bold for prime-time television in its apparent approval of interracial dating and (protected) sex between college students. It spoke to them about issues with which they are intimately familiar, even though they did not all agree with the slant presented.

This moment between Zoe and Charlie did not simply address issues of concern and familiarity to college-age students, but did so using characters with whom they could identify. Despite the fact that students had desired more discussion of political issues than depictions of personal matters in the show, this scene prompted far more discussion than Sorkin's lessons about civil rights laws, education laws, or the structure of a republic. The class discussion returned, then, to the question with which we had begun: could *The West Wing* encourage radical democracy?

On the whole, students felt that the episode raised important issues but did not follow through satisfactorily. While it might prompt discussion of racism, it would not, they argued, suggest solutions. Rather, most viewers could come away feeling as though they thoroughly understood racism and did not need to think about it further. One student proposed that, if the show did not promote legislative changes regarding race and hate crimes, it might at least help to create a sense of class solidarity and cohesion among social progressives regarding race, which could at some point support such legislation. Others agreed that the program might reconfigure boundaries or solidify alliances among viewers. Still, it would likely not prompt activism, or calls for legislation, against racism.

"Let Bartlet Be Bartlet"

The second episode the class viewed, "Let Bartlet Be Bartlet," prompted more polarized views as students discussed the episode's primary concern: the place of political idealism in the nation's capital. Here, President Bartlet decides to "dangle his feet" by airing controversial, unpopular, liberal positions that he has no intention of seeing through. For example, he confronts military leaders with the possibility of removing the military's "don't ask, don't tell" policy regarding the sexual orientation of lesbian and gay members. The president's young and idealistic staff members are becoming disaffected by the apparent meaninglessness of their efforts. In a sentimental and melodramatic interaction, however, chief of staff Leo McGarry reminds the president of his original campaign promises and goals. He persuades Bartlet to push for reforms—for the ideas upon which he was elected—without regard for his popularity or fear of inciting battles. As Bartlet calls in his staff to convey the news (musical swelling, camera lingering, structurally echoing the conclusion to "The Midterms"), they glowingly assert, one-by-one that they "serve at the pleasure of the president," thereby renewing their pledges of idealistic service.

Students were evenly split between those who expressed enthusiasm at this display of idealism and those who regarded it as unrealistic and even dangerously misleading. One "realist" explained that the president's loss of popularity would affect not only himself but also his supporters:

> The prospect of a President going against the system and the way things are done is, I think, unlikely. Risking re-election is fine and dandy when it's just yourself and you get things accomplished. However, disapproval in a President can lead very easily to disapproval in the President's party; not only could the White House be lost, but so too could Congress. The system isn't designed for Cheetah-paced reform, but for painfully slow progress more akin to that of a snail. And even worse than no re-election, if the president backs controversial issues and loses, the consequences on his remaining term could be disastrous; support for all avenues of change dwindles.

The show would mislead viewers into thinking that political integrity is a simple matter, and that political strategy is inherently duplicitous. Another student similarly objected: "what would really happen if a President came forward on some of these issues, even just homosexuals in the military? There would be great public debate, for sure. Unfortunately, our country does not treat men or women who go out on a limb very kindly." In contrast, some students saw it as excitingly unrealistic: "The episode had a considerably more hopeful message than anything we've read. It suggested that . . . action is required of a successful politician. Leaning toward the middle, which has traditionally been necessary [in order] to get and stay elected, has been thrown out of the window in favor of aggressively moving forward without fear of consequences."

The split between students who wanted more realism and those who wanted more idealism, in practice as well as in literature, suggests that disapproval of "The Midterms" does not simply reflect naïve calls for idealism on television. Rather, calls for the show to depict more varied political players, and positive responses to those moments when characters break out of professionalized codes of dispassionate, rational discourse (as do Leo McGarry and President Bartlet), suggest a desire both for more characters with whom the students could comfortably identify and for a broader definition of political action than *The West Wing* provides.

Identification, Professionalism, and Politics

It is important to acknowledge that this class viewed two episodes only, and those out of sequence, and that students were uneasy in their assessments of the series based on so little evidence. Indeed, to theorize about the relationship between serial fiction and legislative politics (or radical democracy) would require multiple viewings and a reconceptualization of the very definition of "politics." In *Novels of Everyday Life* (1999), Laurie Langbauer argues that serial fiction suggests a redefinition of politics as a continual process without closure, and one existing along with—not transcending—the mundane (13–14, 69). Although each episode of *The West Wing* is self-contained, its serial nature means that Bartlet, being Bartlet, will succeed in some of his ideals, fail in others, and trade yet others in deals with members of Congress. Politics in this formulation is an ongoing process and unresolved dialectic between realism (or pragmatism) and idealism, far more hopeful and less cynical about political processes, politicians, and public involvement than Victorian political fiction. Whether this dialectic encourages or discourages democratic participation, and on the part of whom, remains a complex question.

On the one hand, it may be that the series creates the desire for an ideological and not materialist resolution to the problems it raises. Students, certainly, wished to see the show respond to the very problems it analyzes by revising the representations on television of power, race, and gender. On the other hand, if viewer-character identification is a prerequisite of a work's ability to generate interest and involvement in legislative politics, such exclusions matter. Significantly, Charlie and Zoe are not political players in the traditional sense. Rather, the depicted political characters, as well as targeted audience, are already members of the professional class. Hence, the program would likely not encourage the participation in public discourse of those who do not already model professional codes.

The discussions of this class made clear how much *The West Wing* encourages an intellectual politics of critical analysis; but these discussions also suggested that the series legitimates, if sometimes self-consciously, a professional code of behavior as the only one through which political work can effectively occur. The series, too, rewards the cultural capital of the professional class: for all of its often-noted teaching moments about American government, the program rewards those who are already highly politically literate. These students, for example, did not recognize that Bartlet's scrupulous campaign calls from his bed and not the Oval Office alluded to campaign finance laws, as well as to a topical controversy over Al Gore's fund raising. The pleasures of serial fiction largely lie in reader and viewer recognition of allusions to moments in a fictionalized past, anticipation of an ongoing fictional future, and recognition of allusions to a historical "real" embedded within this fictional world.

This analysis does not suggest that *The West Wing* can or should be all things to all viewers, but rather that it is important to recognize what is left out of the program—voters, demonstrators, workers on strike (as opposed to union leaders who negotiate with the president), and politically active young women and men who are on the outside of the professional class and its predominant discourse—as it focuses on players within Washington. As critics acknowledge the show's addictive quality and its many intellectual pleasures, it is important to acknowledge for whom the series is addictive and for whom it holds pleasures. More important, whom does it exclude from the imagined realm of political efficacy, and in whose interests are these exclusions?

During the span of this course, the third 2000 presidential debate was held in town hall format. A professor, who had observed that his students were politically apathetic, asked what the candidates had to say toward their interests and issues. Although political apathy among youth—as well as 1990s political youth movements outside government—are subjects of much recent scholarship (see Giroux 2000, 505–10), neither candidate could respond in a way that was compelling. Gore, in fact, dealt so ineptly with the question that he fell back on one of his frequently repeated sound bites: the future of social security should be important to everyone. Although many college students will join the ranks of the professional class, not all will do so; and critics must ask to what extent moving into fully active political citizenship would necessitate alienation from the students' present-day discourse, concerns, and interests? Just as Victorian novels legitimated the professional, liberal, male politician in order to engender trust in the existing political order, *The West Wing* validates the codes, privileges, and aspirations of the educated, professional class—realist or idealist, Republican or Democrat.

THE WEST WING

CRITICAL RESPONSES:
WEST WING PRESS REVIEWS

12 | Inside *The West Wing*'s New World

SHARON WAXMAN

Election? What Election?

The *West Wing* creator Aaron Sorkin is tipped back in his chair, feet propped on the desk, Merit cigarette in one hand, the other running through the fringe of brown hair that makes him seem—mmmm, what is it? Nervous?

No, cautious. Kind of like a politician.

"If Bush is elected in November, I can't imagine how it would affect the show at all," Sorkin declares with deliberate nonchalance. "It hasn't played in my mind at all."

Of course it hasn't. Why would the fact that there could be radical changes in the political culture in Washington—the backdrop of his popular show—cause Sorkin the smallest moment of concern? Why would the fact that his show is currently embraced by the entire media and political elite as a fantasy version of the Clinton White House—not an Al Gore or a George W. Bush White House—cause him the slightest hiccup of indigestion?

The West Wing has never been more flush. Not only has it brought NBC critical acclaim, plus 13 million literate, upscale viewers every week, but when Sorkin's cast members visit the nation's capital, they are—as he puts it—"more popular than the Beatles." His actors were the stars of the Democratic National Convention in August [2000], and in September they triumphed at the Emmys, where *The West Wing* won nine statues, compared with only one for its rival drama, *The Sopranos*. So the reality that a new administration is about to sweep into Washington—perhaps a conservative GOP administration with a thick Texas drawl—is no cause for concern, right? "It's silly. Ridiculous," Sorkin says, holed up in his office on the Warner Bros. lot, writing episode five of the new season.

Sorkin adds that he's tired of the people who say that his characters are drawn from real life—that fictional deputy chief of staff Josh Lyman (Bradley Whitford) is derivative of former White House aide Paul Begala; that hunky, single speechwriter Sam Seaborn (Rob Lowe) is inspired by single former Clinton aide George Stephanopoulos; or that neurotic press secretary C. J. Cregg (Allison Janney) is somehow related to former Clinton press secretary Dee Dee Myers, one of Sorkin's script consultants.

"Those connections are really nonsense," Sorkin continues. "I'm a fiction writer. I make those people up."

Whew, well, that's a relief.

So Sorkin obviously won't mind if we hear what Martin Sheen, who plays President Josiah Bartlet, has to say about George W., the real-life Republican candidate (Caution: Step back from flying invective): "I think he's a bully. I don't think he has any heart. That scares me," says Sheen heatedly, hunched over some melting frozen yogurt in a mess tent on location in downtown Los Angeles. The show has set up in a parking lot for a shoot at a veterans' hall. It is Sheen's sixtieth birthday and he is wearing a T-shirt that reads, "WHAT'S NEXT?"—the mantra of his television character.

He's not done. "I've seen him. I've watched him—he's like a bad comic working the crowd," Sheen goes on. "He's too angry. He talks too loud. He's acting compassionate—it's not real. It's not there." Pause. "I think he's full of shit, frankly." Sheen is not too hot on Republicans in general. He says: "If a Republican showed me a heart, I'd respond to that heart. I have not seen much heart coming from Republicans."

Sheen is not the only rabidly anti-Republican cast member. Listen to Whitford, who offhandedly describes himself as "a white-bread pinko liberal." Whitford is livid that during one of the primary debates, Bush dared to name Jesus as the political philosopher who has influenced him the most.

"You offer up Jesus Christ in a debate—and then you execute more people than the other governors combined?" Whitford rages, lounging in his trailer between takes.

"Do you really believe that Jesus, who himself was killed because of the death penalty, would be pro-death penalty? I think Bush is a hypocrite, and I think he's proudly uninformed."

If it isn't exactly a revelation that the producers and cast of *The West Wing* are liberals—this is Hollywood, after all—it is still rather curious that no one seems to think that a Bush victory would affect the show in any way. Won't they at least need new parking permits when they go to D.C., or something?

"It will make no difference," affirms Whitford, echoing the sentiments of Sorkin and most others in the cast. "*West Wing* is first and foremost about relationships, about people—the backdrop is politics." And yet, for all the reluctance to admit that a change in administration might matter, *West Wing* has been making moves to the contrary—getting ready for whomever gets elected and whatever the new administration might bring.

If Al Gore wins, the shift in the political culture may be subtle, though even Clinton's heir apparent will bring his own style and tone, not to mention his own staff, to the White House. But if George W. wins, there will be nothing less than a seismic shift in the capital. And in that case, the cast of *The West Wing* may feel less like the Beatles when they visit D.C. and more like . . . the Flintstones.

Maybe it is just pure coincidence, but *The West Wing* has hired two high-profile Republicans as consultants this season: former Reagan and Bush press secretary Marlin Fitzwater and former Reagan speechwriter Peggy Noonan.

Was Fitzwater surprised to get the offer? He was. "They probably wanted a Republican viewpoint," he says.

Not so, says Sorkin: "They're very smart people. They were hired not so much for their Republicanness as much as for their wisdom." Coincidence, too, that there will be a new character introduced to the White House staff—a blond, leggy, in-your-face Republican advisor called Ainsley Hayes (played by Emily Procter). She may remind some of the blond, leggy, in-your-face Republicans like Laura Ingraham and Ann Coulter, who pop up and pop off on the talking-head circuit. Wait a minute. An Ingraham or a Coulter huddled over policy options with a Clinton in the Roosevelt Room? What could Aaron Sorkin be thinking?

"Ainsley Hayes has an extraordinary sense of duty. When her president asks her to serve, she agrees," Sorkin says, grinning in his it's-my-world-get-used-to-it sort of way. "Which makes her perfect for us." Sorkin says he's relishing the upcoming tension between his Republican addition to the White House staff and the Democratic regulars. In fact, he's asked returning consultant Dee Dee Myers for a memo on how the White House staff might torture the new recruit. Myers's answers:

"They could stick her in a horrible office. David Gergen, a Reagan and Nixon consultant who joined the Clinton staff, was put in the old White House barbershop.

"The White House cafeteria might refuse to serve the newcomer. You can't eat there if the proper paperwork hasn't been filled out.

"And it's easy to get lost in the White House if no one guides you."

Political shows have long been considered ratings poison in prime time, and Sorkin took an even greater risk by writing a political drama with a distinct point of view, the Democratic one. Whitford says Sorkin made a good, pragmatic choice: It's better TV. "People respond to progressive Democrats," he says. "It's more heroic to fight for civil rights legislation than a tax cut."

But there's also a more personal angle to the decision.

At age eleven, Sorkin volunteered to help out at George McGovern headquarters, mostly to impress a girl in his class. Incumbent Richard Nixon was on his way to White Plains, New York, for a rally, and the McGovern volunteers were deployed with signs that read "MCGOVERN FOR PRESIDENT." Just as Nixon's motorcade came around the bend, an old lady came up behind Sorkin, grabbed his sign, beaned him with it, and then stomped on it.

Part of him, Sorkin says, has been trying to get back at that lady ever since.

Whatever the motivation, *The West Wing* has become that rarest of rarities on the pop-culture landscape: a zeitgeist show, a reflection of the tenor of our times.

"Every three or four years, a show hits a pop sensibility," says co-executive producer John Wells, who produced another block-buster hit, *ER*. "People forget that *ER* came on in the middle of the Clinton health care debate. When we were on the cover of *Newsweek,* the headline was, 'A health care plan that really works.' That was what we tapped into.

"And that's what happened when *West Wing* came on. We'd reached a point in the culture where we assumed that people who want to choose public service have the basest of motives of self-aggrandizement and financial gain."

However, Wells believes that the public knows intuitively that not all politicians are like that.

He says, "The public wants to believe in the political process, wants to believe in politicians. Wants to believe that the people who are leading us are doing so—even if there are ideological differences—to make the country better."

Slowly, subtly, *The West Wing* has become as much a reflection of the current White House as a reflection upon it. Last winter, Sorkin wrote a moving episode about the death penalty in which a tormented President Bartlet decided not to commute the execution of a federal prisoner. This summer, Clinton went the other way—choosing to postpone the execution of federal prisoner Juan Raul Garca, on whose case the episode was based.

Near the end of last season, *The West Wing* featured a story about campaign finance reform, with Bartlet deciding to buck special interests and appoint reformers to the Federal Election Commission. The *New York Times* then wrote an editorial proclaiming that Washington should imitate *The West Wing*.

The West Wing has detractors, and they consider the show corny. "Human beings? These characters aren't human beings—they're noble soldiers in a noble cause, and they have been washed clean of every impurity because of it," sneered writer John Podhoretz in a cover story in the conservative *Weekly Standard* last March. But most of the press reaction has been glowing. For its admirers, *The West Wing* has become an example of television that can entertain and educate and—in some measure—elevate viewers above the prevailing forces of political cynicism and ennui.

The show is particularly appreciated in Washington these days, where public servants often see themselves as underpaid and underappreciated.

Nowhere was this fan base more in evidence than at the Democratic convention in Los Angeles. *The West Wing* party on the show's Warner Bros. set the Sunday before the convention—ostensibly a thank-you gift from the show to those in the nation's capital who've helped them—was a who's who of Hollywood meets Washington. Everyone—including Clinton chief of staff John Podesta, Chelsea Clinton, Senator Patrick Leahy (D-Vt.), and the editors of *The Washington Post*—were oohing and aahing at the authenticity of the ceilingless Oval Office.

Even Republicans consider *The West Wing* a guilty pleasure. "I was prepared not to like it because it was about my sacred White House," says Fitzwater. "But from the second show on, I've loved it. It very accurately portrays so many elements of presidential life—the frantic urgency about issues and decisions."

Fitzwater acknowledges that the show has detractors in the GOP. " 'Yes, it's liberal-oriented,' I tell all my conservative friends, 'but that's the way the presidency works,' " he says. "And the truth is, my friends all love the show."

Over at Building 146 on the Warner Bros. lot, the signs of a show in its successful second season are everywhere. Outside, a 2000 black Porsche Carrera, top down, is gleaming in Sorkin's reserved parking spot. His office has been transferred from the small, hutch-like suite it was in last year to a sprawling second-floor lair. The design is aggressively masculine—wooden desks, leather sofas, framed maps, and forest-green walls—lots of expensive stuff for a writer who spends most of his life occupied by his Power Mac, gummy bears, and Merits. There is a bar—Art Deco, stacked with unused martini glasses—and an of-the-moment U-Line stainless-steel fridge. There is also a publicist occupying a back corner of the office, yet another nod to the show's newly acquired media heft. The seat-of-the-pants ethos of season one—when a visitor could wander from the set to the writing offices and back again—is long gone.

On the wall closest to Sorkin's desk is a bulletin board with memos about story elements for whatever episode he's writing. The elements come from the writing staff and Sorkin's political strategists, who include, in addition to Fitzwater, Noonan, and Myers, Democratic consultant Pat Caddell and Lawrence O'Donnell, a former aide to Senator Daniel Patrick Moynihan

(D-N.Y.). Sorkin rewrites every line that's given to him, but the staff provides the material that makes up the substance of the show. Sorkin keeps their memos and research papers in a blue binder that he calls, with great feeling, "a book of goodness."

Despite the death penalty show and a few others, Sorkin says he generally tries not to rip ideas from the headlines. "But every once in a while we want to remind you of something in reality," he notes. The driving force of the show is Sorkin's larger message about politics and public service—his deep, and deeply sentimental, sense of patriotism. In July people from *The West Wing* were invited to a Los Angeles Dodgers baseball game, and Richard Schiff caught Sorkin staring, enraptured, at the sight of a row of American flags rippling in the breeze of the stadium.

" 'Look how beautiful that is,' " Schiff recalls Sorkin saying. "It struck me how much that man loves America, loves the Constitution, the Declaration of Independence. If a Republican president comes in, that's not going to change. We're more like a White House world that he'd like to see."

Indeed, one *West Wing* staffer—speaking on condition of anonymity—says, "Aaron Sorkin really doesn't like Clinton. He's very convincing on this subject."

The question is put to Sorkin: Does he despise Clinton? Sorkin laughs, and then he squirms in silence. Finally, he protests weakly: "I like Bill Clinton. I voted for Bill Clinton twice. It would be silly for me to say anything more than that."

Beyond his political sentimentality, it is Sorkin's unerring dramatic instincts that shape the show. Even as a kid growing up in Scarsdale, New York, sneaking into Manhattan to go to the theater, Sorkin found he had an ear for the ebb and flow of dialogue, a knack for sensing the emotional hinge between serious and comic.

He dreamed of being an actor and majored in musical theater at Syracuse University. But then he began to write, starting with *A Few Good Men*, a play about a snotty Navy lawyer who learns the value of public service. It was based on a case he learned about from his sister, a Navy lawyer. The play was on Broadway before being bought for the movies by director Rob Reiner, who cast Tom Cruise as the lawyer and Jack Nicholson as the corrupt colonel. Reiner then commissioned Sorkin to write the romantic comedy *The*

American President, starring Michael Douglas and Annette Bening, which took the writer on research visits to the White House.

That, in turn, propelled Sorkin to write a TV pilot, a behind-the-scenes drama/comedy about the White House, which sat ignored on the desks of network executives for two years. Meanwhile, Sorkin wrote *Sports Night* for ABC, a behind-the-scenes dramedy about a sports news show. After the Monica Lewinsky scandal, with its media frenzy, NBC suddenly thought there might be an audience for politics after all. And *The West Wing* was born.

In last season's cliff-hanger finale, a fusillade of bullets felled the presidential entourage as Bartlet left a speaking engagement. The faces of three teenage skinheads in the crowd were identified as the perpetrators.

"So what's next?" Sorkin is asked during the summer. Who are the survivors? And what about romance? Will Josh date his secretary? Will C. J. get married to reporter Danny Concannon? Will presidential daughter Zoe carry on her interracial romance with presidential gofer Charlie?

And what about President Bartlet's multiple sclerosis?

Sorkin, canny dramatist that he is, says we will have to wait until the end of a two-hour episode to learn how badly the victims were hurt. He also says that Anna Deavere Smith (who played the White House spokeswoman in *The American President*) will join the cast as the new national security advisor. Finally, we will see no more of Moira Kelly as political consultant Mandy (and no, of course she had no connection to real-life Clinton consultant Mandy Grunwald). Other than that, Sorkin says, he doesn't know exactly where the show is going, since he's only up to episode five. He says he writes an episode for eight days at a stretch, and takes about five minutes to pat himself on the back before plunging into the next script. The central conflict of the episode he is working on involves the president and his wife, played by Stockard Channing (who had a memorable showdown with Bartlet in the Oval Office during the first season: "You don't handle me, Jed!"). They are trying to find time in their schedules to have sex.

"The writers came to me and said, 'Here's an idea you're gonna hate. But sleep on it,'" says Sorkin, pulling off his geek-chic horn-rimmed glasses and rocking back in the leather chair behind his desk. The locks that fall across his forehead are brown, but his sideburns have gone gray. He is lean, wearing a green, button-down polo shirt and jeans, and chain-smoking. "They were right. It seemed silly to me." Pause. "And now I'm having the best time writing the story." Does he think it wise to mix the presidency with sex given, y'-know, the Clinton thing? "Well, you think about it," he acknowledges, "but I have faith in the show. . . . I believe that people will see episode five with Martin Sheen trying to have sex with Stockard Channing and not say, 'Well, why doesn't he just grab an intern in the hallway?' " Dee Dee Myers has given Sorkin a memo detailing appointments that might keep a first lady busy (and thus unavailable for sex). Myers has suggested a dedication of a statue, among other things, which Sorkin has seized upon. He plans to have the first lady lecture the president for his offhand put-down of the statue subject, nineteenth-century journalist-adventurer Nellie Bly.

There are other strands in the works: one about military readiness in which press secretary C. J. faces down a general. There's also a story line related to the civil rights activist organization Southern Poverty Law Center, which Sorkin declines to discuss. Could it relate to our skinhead shooters?

The new Republican-era consultants are providing more than political balance. They bring with them behind-the-scenes anecdotes from previous administrations. Fitzwater, for example, who had an extraordinary ten-year run with Reagan and Bush, has already detailed an insider's version of Boris Yeltsin's first visit to the White House. Yeltsin was in Parliament at the time, challenging Soviet leader Mikhail Gorbachev. He wanted to meet President Bush, but the president thought Gorbachev would take offense if he received Yeltsin in the Oval Office.

"Yeltsin refused to come in the building, in effect, unless he could meet the president," Fitzwater recalls. A compromise was struck: Yeltsin agreed to meet Bush in the National Security Advisor's office, "so he could say he met the president and we could say he never got into the Oval Office."

Sorkin loves the anecdote—and says it may show up in an episode. Still, he insists that he has no GOP-inspired contingency themes for after the election. Bartlet is Bartlet, he's a Democrat, he'll stay in power.

"I don't want to overstate our impact," says Caddell. "We're a TV show, after all. But a lot of people in politics and the press watch it intensely. I think its [influence is] more on a subconscious level than a conscious one."

"It's pretty easy to get too big for your britches," Sorkin demurs.

"There's so much praise being heaped on us. It's easy to start believing it." He pauses and plays again with his glasses. "A show that got this much praise this fast is setting itself up for an ass-kicking," he finally offers. "We'd like to not hasten it at all by suggesting that we're good for you: like, 'Thank God we came along to tell you what to think about this—and Barbara Streisand will be out in a minute.' "

The magnitude of *The West Wing*'s influence hit cast members when they were given a tour of the actual *West Wing* on the night of President Clinton's last State of the Union speech. The moment was already surreal enough, and suddenly the president dropped by to chitchat and suggested a story line: something having to do with a journalist and an information leak.

Sheen also sensed the show's power when they were shooting late at night in Georgetown and making a bit too much of a commotion for the neighbors. A middle-aged lady came down to inquire about the noise. And by the way, she said, why the heck doesn't the show have a secretary of state? And it should be a woman, she added. The woman with the complaint was Secretary of State Madeleine Albright.

13 | The Feel-Good Presidency

The Pseudo-Politics of The West Wing

CHRIS LEHMANN

In the heat of Campaign 2000, NBC's publicity department began an ad campaign trumpeting its own version of "a president we can all agree on." The man in question, of course, was Josiah Bartlet, the embattled chief executive played by Martin Sheen in the network's runaway nighttime-serial hit, *The West Wing*. At about the same time, cars in southern California reportedly began sporting bumper stickers that read "BARTLET FOR PRESIDENT." When the Democratic National Committee scheduled a party on the set of the show, in Los Angeles, during the Democratic Convention, more than a few wags commented that the Democrats would be far better off with the charismatic, principled chief executive that television had produced to wide popular acclaim than with the unpersuasive populist crusader who was sopping up bucketloads of Hollywood's political largesse, to dangerously mounting popular indifference.

It's tempting, of course, to write off such goofy talk—much of it the handiwork of publicists—to our pop culture's always dubious engagement with reality. After all, hadn't there been speculation earlier, in the heady, celebrity-ridden primary season, about presidential runs by Warren Beatty and Cybill Shepherd? Isn't it but a turn of the screw to propose an entirely fictional character as a suitable leader of the world's only superpower—much as Pat Paulsen mounted his successive satirical campaigns, and Robert Altman filmed a cult mockumentary around the imaginary candidate Jack Tanner?

But the problem here is that the notion of a Bartlet presidency struck—and continues to strike—many influential observers as a perfectly sound idea. Countless devotees of the show, both in TV journalism and on its many reverent, unofficial fan Web sites, regard the weekly doings on *The West Wing* as anything but satire. The clear critical verdict is that this Wednesday-evening set piece of frenetic Oval Office intrigue presents a far more edifying vision of America's political soul than anything that has wafted out of the Grand Guignol of our scandal-addled, impeachment-scarred, ballot-challenged national government.

In any event, the mere persistence—indeed, the continued, mammoth popularity—of the show signals a curious sort of social contract, ratifying and institutionalizing one of the striking themes of America's post-1960s civitas: the selective (yet ever didactic) liberal retreat into political fantasy. After all, it had long occurred to the show's legions of fans that a Bush victory could revoke a good part of its earnest purchase on topicality. And one leitmotif of press accounts of *The West Wing* over the protracted election of 2000 was to broach the question of how the show—which over its first two seasons has played as a sort of higher-minded, conscience-haunted upgrade of the Clinton White House—might change in the event of a Bush victory. The consensus, as the show's creator and chief writer, Aaron Sorkin, announced, was that no such reality-based revisions would be required: a Bush victory "hasn't played in my mind at all," he said in a lavish cover story on the show in the November 2000 *George*. (See Waxman review, chap. 12 in this volume.) Come December, however, Sorkin did confess to Michael Wolff, in *New York* magazine (2000), that the show couldn't help benefiting from the unsightly overall condition of America's democratic experiment: the time, he said, "is just right for the cavalry to come riding in."

This pair of remarks captures the curious cognitive balancing act *The West Wing* has introduced into our popular culture. On the one hand, it claims no ambitions any grander than those of any other television show—to divert and entertain viewers and (usually in special holiday episodes) to produce agreeably broad and radiant installments in the nation's continuing sentimental education. But on the other hand, it has an overt agenda so breathtaking in its sweep that "ambitious" hardly begins to sum it up: *The West Wing* sets out, week after week, to restore public faith in the institutions of our government, to shore up the bulwarks of American patriotism, and to supply a vision of executive liberalism—at once principled and pragmatic; mandating both estimable political vision and serious personal sacrifice; plying an understanding of the nation's common good that is heroically heedless of focus groups, opposition research, small-bore compromise, and re-election prospects—that exists nowhere else in our recent history.

How, exactly, has this come to be? On the most obvious level, *The West Wing* appeals to liberal viewers as an exercise in wish-fulfillment fantasy, pointing a way out of their post-Clinton predicament. Indeed, the most common theme in the many celebrations of the show's political virtues has been that it gives us a version of Clintonism with both moral gravitas and political backbone, while editing out the more risible parts of the Clinton legacy—an act, commentators say, of "empathy" unthinkable in the normal rounds of political reporting. The former White House aide Matthew Miller wrote, in a wide-eyed appreciation of the show in *Brill's Content* last spring [2000], "By the seemingly innocuous act of portraying politicians with empathy, *The West Wing* has injected into the culture a subversive competitor to the reigning values of political journalism"—which Miller views as rife with "cynicism." This bold subversion turns the weekly melodrama, by Miller's lights, into a sort of pluperfect documentary, redeeming a hopelessly fallen political culture by sheer force of its "humanizing instinct."

It's true that the show eagerly displays its own stirringly "human" themes on its sleeve—as is the case in the nighttime-TV "workplace" serials about hospitals, law firms, and police investigative units on which *The West Wing* is clearly modeled. But since its subject is the nation's politics (and its tacit mission is to revive sagging liberal spirits), *The West Wing* steers wide of the thorny moral conflicts that turn up in those life-or-death TV venues, in which petty personal agendas kick up disasters and catastrophes galore. Instead it offers a pointedly sunny weekly fable about the unassailable motives and all-too-human foibles of the nation's governing class which verges on the Capra-esque.

Reportedly, Sorkin—who developed the show out of material left over from his screenplay for the Rob Reiner feature film *The American President*—had not intended the president to be a central character on *The West Wing*. But here, as in American political life, the president has swollen over time to soak up most of the dramatic interest, even though the formulas that Sorkin favors (previously his most celebrated writing credit was the military-courtroom drama *A Few Good Men*) make Bartlet a two-dimensional glyph of implausible virtue. He is charismatic and quietly omnicompetent, à la Bill Clinton, but viewers are forcefully reminded that he does not share Clinton's (or John F. Kennedy's) priapic weaknesses.

But all this tight moral choreography comes up considerably short of serving as a prescription for even a convincing imaginary liberal revival. In fact, sustained exposure to the logic of the show's plot conventions, the jittery policy patter of its characters, and (perhaps most of all) its sonorous faux nobility inspires a singular distrust. In particular, the way the show strives to dramatize the earnest inner torments of what Christopher Lasch called "the caring class" produces a civic emptiness far hollower than that resounding through either of our major parties.

The show's obsession with feeling also clearly impels its choice of subject matter. The Bartlet administration's key internal conflicts and legislative rallying cries oscillate mainly within the narrow register of lifestyle liberalism, the stealth ideology that fuels Hollywood as it did the Clinton presidency. The heroic outbursts from *The West Wing*'s lead characters are almost always directed at the forces of cultural reaction gathering in the heartland: the religious right, anti-gay moralists, creationists, advocates of antiabortion terror, tough-on-crime yahoos, and shrill defenders of the Second Amendment. Bartlet himself has been a collateral victim of a white supremacist's assassination attempt on his black aide, Charlie Young (Dulé Hill). His White House dotes on hate-crimes legislation and also longs, bizarrely, for a high-profile showdown with the religious right over the currently moot constitutional question of school prayer. These symbolic posturings can only spring from the administration's sense of itself as a missionary outpost in a hostile and benighted culture.

Of course, many of *The West Wing*'s concerns belong on the public agenda, and occasionally they address real threats to civil liberties and social peace. But the dramatically declining membership rolls of the Christian Coalition and the results of polls tracking public opinion on the religious right's pet issues reveal that the specter of a theocratic seizure of the state, rhetorically exaggerated even at the height of the religious right's power, is a rapidly dimming mirage.

Nevertheless, Team Bartlet is constantly consumed by the minutiae of high cultural warfare. Examples are legion, and multiply weekly. In a second-season episode, "The Midterms," there's a high-handed showdown between Bartlet and one Dr. Jenna Jacobs—a moralizing radio talk-show host clearly modeled on Dr. Laura Schlessinger—at a White House reception for various radio eminences. Quizzing her on the biblical injunction against homosexuality as "an abomination," Bartlet takes her on a rapid-fire declamatory tour of the follies of biblical literalism, a punishing performance whose like has not been seen since the climax of *Inherit the Wind*: "I'm interested in selling my youngest daughter into slavery, as sanctioned in Exodus 21:7 . . . what would a good price be?" Now, not only is this stacking the rhetorical deck heavily in Bartlet's favor (even Dr. Laura, bigoted though she can be, does not rest her castigation of homosexuality entirely on biblical literalism). It also provokes a rather enormous question: Why is Bartlet expending such heavy artillery and so much precious time on humiliating a radio talk-show host? And why is he unable to resist a final victory dance over her seated person and prostrated intellect—especially by invoking the majesty of his own presidential eminence over the discredited authority of biblical tradition? ("One last thing," he shouts. "While you may be mistaking this for your monthly meeting of the Ignorant Tight-Ass Club, in this building, when the president stands, nobody sits.") The answer, of course, is that such displays—which occur nearly every week in Bartlet's White House—cost the administration precisely nothing politically while ratcheting up its sense of cultural superiority exponentially.

The West Wing, in other words, plies a resolutely insular, therapeutic vision of presidential politics, one that often renders policymaking indistinguishable from the conduct of an encounter group. Indeed, in the thickets of controversy that crop up in the Bartlet administration, the strongest objection to a policy or a decision to overstep protocol is usually that it doesn't feel right. And when the members of Team Bartlet chart a new policy course, it is because they agree that it suits the perceived national mood or because it springs (in the grand tradition of TV serials) from a profound personal experience. If one of the 1960s' most enduring—if dubious—notions is that the personal is political, *The West Wing* operates from the converse: the political is, above all, personal. In perhaps the most decisive, melodramatic installment of the show—a late-first-season entry called "Let Bartlet Be Bartlet"— the president announces his determination to secure two key reform-minded appointees to the Federal Election Commission. His rationale has little to do with the current political playing field, or even with the prospects for meaningful reform, but turns, rather, on his plaintive appeal to his chief of staff, Leo McGarry (John Spencer): "I don't want to feel like this anymore."

Amid such high drama, it requires a considerable effort of the will to recall that liberals belong to the strain of American political debate that has traditionally prided itself on skepticism about how matters of state power get minted into brute personal agendas. To put things another way, it's hard to imagine any of the show's champions or scriptwriters evincing much concern over, say, Richard Nixon's many funks on the job—let alone endorsing them as a sound basis for executive policymaking. But in furnishing its imaginary, cultural platform for the revival of liberal politics in America, *The West Wing* has also slipped into an uncritical cult of personality—much as the adoration of Bill Clinton has in the real-life house of liberalism. In so doing, *The West Wing* reminds us, down to the smallest details of character and plot resolution, of the very forces that have hollowed out the American liberal faith. In lieu of the majority-forging certainties of the New Deal, the Fair Deal, and the Great Society (and their campaigns against "economic royalists," "isolationists," segregationists, and the like), we find anxious self-examination, second-guessing of the news cycle, and protracted agonizing over the appearance of scandal and conflicts of interest. In place of stirring crusades for equality and justice (about which there is plenty of rhetoric), we see careful chartings and recalibrations of marginal, provisional influence by an executive branch that is unshakably wedded to a view of itself as "under siege, twenty-four hours a day," as Bartlet's chief of staff explains to a recently hired Republican legal aide.

The logic of these morally obtuse but deeply sentimental preenings of high-office holders is disturbing on many levels, but principally because it dramatizes something real: liberals, long sundered from the lineaments of any majoritarian politics, have succumbed to the worship of getting and holding power for its own sake. One saw this not merely in the Gore campaign's diehard (and ultimately self-destructive) scorched-earth efforts to recast the Florida vote in Gore's favor but also, more pivotally, in the dramatic force with which Clinton recast the presidency's reasons of state into reasons of self.

Indeed, the moral calculus of *The West Wing*'s presidency is identical to that perfected by Bill Clinton: all the expenditures of political capital, all the day-to-day trench warfare over Capitol turf, the long-term health of the party and the short-term calendar of the national legislature, were subordinated to the expansion of executive self-regard, to the meaningless conceit of "not feeling like this anymore." Herein resided the stem-winding, therapeutic logic of the year-long national "conversation on race"; the periodic presidential apologies for world-historic wrongs that were usually strategic evasions of actual legislative responsibility; and the fussy feel-good conferences on teen violence and the media. And, needless to say, here sprang the fathomless victimology that choreographed perjury, suborned testimony, concealed evidence, and mounted dubiously timed bombing raids to prolong a grip on executive power that had long atrophied when it came to steering federal policy and national debate toward any meaningful goal beyond the bunker.

As one might expect, Bill Clinton is among *The West Wing*'s biggest fans. He played host to members of the cast at a White House press-corps dinner, and cast members have turned up at DNC fundraisers, providing entertaining photo ops that illuminated the grand yet confused ambitions of both the TV show and the Clinton White House. He reportedly told Rob Lowe (who plays Bartlet's deputy communications director, Sam Seaborn) that the show is "renewing people's faith in public service." It's all a bit curious, since the high-minded Josiah Bartlet would seem to be such a pointed rebuke, in both his person and his policymaking, to Clinton. But in life, as on TV, claims of civic loyalty and reckonings of power, legitimacy, political right, and moral trespass—the stuff of history—provide feeble competition for the blinding power of personality. And it has been a long season of indulgently sentimentalizing the abuse of power. Augurs of the Boomer zeitgeist, from Toni Morrison to Joe Eszterhas to Tina Brown to Greil Marcus, agree that Clinton represents an emanation of a noble American tradition, a Huck-like backwoods avatar of charmingly transgressive appetites. He is half the sybaritic, exoticized, Elvis-style son of the South, tweaking the grim moralists and inquisitors who police the right's DMZ in the nation's cultural combat, and half the aw-shucks poster child of the new global information order, cocking back his head and biting his lip wistfully as he conjures abiding visions of a bridge over the millennium. Before the nation's scandal-weary eyes, Bill Clinton became a pop-cult fable of his own fond imagining, a fantasy figure for liberal partisans who have lost the taste for almost any politics save the full-throated prosecution of meaningless culture wars. It is but a short step from these sorts of reveries to the wholesale invention of a republic ruled by a benevolent great leader, briskly resetting our moral compass and flattering our lifestyle politics in the safety of our living rooms. In this sense, then, it is entirely fitting that Bill Clinton's most immediate legacy should be a TV show that lodges the structure of his personality firmly in our collective unconscious, even while strategically erasing its substance.

Of course, it may seem, with the show's enduring appeal in the dawn of the W. years, that these organizing tropes of the Clinton era are already moldering into harmless TV nostalgia, not unlike the imagineered 1950s of *Happy Days,* or the wide, loud, and burnt-out Ford and Carter caesura of *That '70s Show.* But this casual view of things underestimates the half-life of Clintonism in both reality and pop culture. George W. Bush demonstrated in his faux-empathic campaign of the conservative heart that Clintonism, being postmodern and post-ideological unto its innermost parts, works as deftly on the tax-cutting, privatizing right as it did within the often unruly union-and-activist ranks of the Democratic Party.

In much the same manner, *The West Wing* continues to renew the peculiar, powerful cultural brief by which Clintonism has thrived—and will continue to thrive in the aftermath of the Clinton years. In 1992 candidate Bill Clinton proudly acknowledged that he "always wanted to be in the cultural elite"; *The West Wing* has extravagantly granted his wish, by apostrophizing his administration (while, of course, airbrushing out its more embarrassing policy failures, crimes, and lapses of morality). But more than that, the enduring appeal of the show, in our popular and political cultures alike, is that it has performed a trick more powerful than probably even Clinton could have imagined. It has made him that most quintessentially American liege of that most desirable American dominion: as an archetype, a fable, a prototype for Jed Bartlet, Bill Clinton, through the good graces of Aaron Sorkin, has become the President of Television. We need some satire, and fast.

14 | The Liberal Imagination

JOHN PODHORETZ

The West Wing is the ultimate Hollywood fantasy: the Clinton White House without Clinton.

Of all those whom Bill Clinton has seduced and abandoned and then seduced and abandoned again, always with the promise of another seduction, the Hollywood elite has been almost as loyal as Monica was, and with about as much to show for it. Now Hollywood has taken its revenge, and a perverse but devastating sort of revenge it is, in the form of this season's prestige television drama, *The West Wing*.

This mildly successful show premiered last fall, but in the past month it has caught fire in the press, with cover stories in major magazines and articles in major newspapers. This is as it should be, because the media are liberal and *The West Wing* is an escapist fantasy for them. Creator and writer Aaron Sorkin has modeled his series on the glamorous early years of the Clinton White House. Nearly every character in *The West Wing* has a real-life parallel from Clinton's first term, Rob Lowe as George Stephanopoulos, Bradley Whitford as Paul Begala, Allison Janney as Dee Dee Myers, Richard Schiff as Gene Sperling, and Moira Kelly as Mandy Grunwald.

But the central character, the president himself, is nothing like the real man. And there's a good reason for that. *The West Wing*, you see, is nothing more or less than political pornography for liberals, made up of equal parts unrequited longing for and rage at Hollywood's not-so-obscure object of desire, William Jefferson Clinton.

♦   ♦   ♦

There's been a lot of talk about how meticulous Sorkin and team have been in recreating the charged atmosphere of the White House. But that's a lot of nonsense, given that you never see anybody in *The West Wing* on the telephone or in tedious meetings, which is how real White House aides spend their days and nights. Instead, it's full of endless shots of people walking down corridors, around corners, into offices and out of offices, all of which conveys a sense of terrible urgency. Exactly the same sort of urgency is on display in Sorkin's other show, the sitcom *Sports Night,* which is set in the offices of a cable television program.

The show's fans concede that some of the atmospherics are wrong. For instance, the glamorous working quarters depicted are far larger than the tiny spaces and narrow hallways of the real West Wing. Still, they say, *The West Wing* succeeds in speaking deep truths about politics and the people who work in politics. Former Clinton administration official Matthew Miller, in a cover story for *Brill's Content* titled "The Real White House" (2000), claims that the show "presents a truer, more human picture of the people behind the headlines than most of today's Washington journalists." Mike McCurry, Clinton's ex-press secretary, told Miller he watches *The West Wing* because it treats "those who work in politics as human beings."

Human beings? These characters aren't human beings—they're noble soldiers in a noble cause, and they have been washed clean of every impurity because of it. *The West Wing* makes Miller, McCurry, and others like them into American heroes. Sorkin's staffers are wonderful in almost every possible way, or at least in ways that Hollywood considers wonderful. In the first episode, the George Stephanopoulos character picks up a woman at a bar, goes home with her, and later discovers she is a high-priced call girl. Rather than fleeing in fear for his job and the reputation of his administration, he spends the rest of the season trying to save her. When the press starts to sniff around the call-girl story, the Dee Dee Myers character expresses outrage, not at her colleague's irresponsibility, but at this intrusion into his private life. And when she gives a lecture to the reporter who loves her, he agrees to stifle the story.

Meanwhile, the Paul Begala character gets into a fight on a *Crossfire*-type show with an officious minister from the Christian Coalition, because our Lochinvar is so honest he can't abide the supposed hypocrisy of a minister who opposes abortion and supports the death penalty. (Later, the pastor reveals he is not only an anti-Semite but so ignorant he doesn't know "Thou shalt not kill" is the sixth of the Ten Commandments.)

There are no staff conflicts of any consequence in Sorkin's *West Wing*, no turf battles between these White House aides. They love each other, admire each other, and support each other. No one is hungry for power, perks, or privilege. No one is motivated by ambition, anger, resentment, fear, or the hunger to run other people's lives. There's not even a stock villain or a comic foil with such ambitions and hungers. No, the characters have come to save America and the world.

And if you think they're wonderful, just wait until you meet the president. The occupant of Sorkin's Oval Office is an immensely thoughtful, infinitely wise, deeply caring, thoroughly monogamous, and unambiguously principled Nobel Prize-winning economist (yes, Nobel Prize-winning economist) named Josiah Bartlet, an appellation worthy of a signer of the Declaration of Independence.

◆   ◆   ◆

Bartlet means nothing but well. This is not a president whose conduct forces his aides to spend hundreds of thousands of dollars they don't have on personal defense lawyers. There's no Monica Lewinsky, no Kathleen Willey, no four-way phone-sex call with Dick Morris, no bouts of foul temper, no jokes about dating the mummified corpse of a fourteen-year-old Inca girl. In the Bartlet White House, you're not even allowed to curse. ("This is the White House, Seymour, not the Jersey Turnpike," the chief of staff says to a profane visitor. "Watch your mouth.")

Bartlet makes chili for his staff, and boy, is it good. He plays poker with them. He feels his staffers' pain, each and every one of them. Concerned that his young African American assistant isn't having enough fun, the president insists that the Paul Begala character take the kid out for a drink in George-town. "The man's like a camp counselor," the Begala character protests, but you know he loves the Big Guy.

His advisors do fret about the political consequences of various hot top-ics, but not Bartlet, who has yet to do a single thing wrong. He is good hu-mored, but also full of righteous anger. After an antiabortion group threatens his teenage daughter, he tells the Christian Coalition minister and his lackeys: "You'll denounce the Lambs of God and until you do, get your fat asses out of my office."

When trucking companies and Teamster officials won't compromise on a new contract, he informs them that at 12:01 A.M., "I'm using my powers to nationalize the trucking industry." He gets them to negotiate by saying, "Talk to me for five minutes apiece and we're going to settle this. Remain standing." And doggone it if they don't make a deal.

Bartlet is tough too. After his doctor is killed in a Syrian terrorist attack in Lebanon, he vows to strike back "with the fury of God's own thunder." His anger is so pure that his chief of staff must talk him down into an unsat-isfying "proportionate response," and his willingness to control his right-eous anger is yet another mark of his greatness as a man and a president. Bartlet's loving wife tells him he has "a big brain, a good heart, and an ego the size of Montana. You don't have the power to fix everything, but I do like watching you try."

For reasons known only to himself, Sorkin firmly denies that his show has a leftward bent. "I would disagree this is a liberal show," he told *Enter-tainment Weekly*. Why? Well, Bartlet wanted to bomb Syria, which isn't a very liberal thing to do, and "we know now he's not particularly vocal about gay rights."

Referring to the didactic but speedy debates that take place on the show about such scintillating matters as census sampling and human-rights viola-tions in Indonesia, coproducer John Wells told Matthew Miller, "Nothing goes into the show without a full pro and con." Wells did admit there are no two sides of the issue when it comes to gun control, "I don't think any of us really believes in the other side of the argument very much," he said. But in the end, that's the case with every political debate on *The West Wing*. The liberal argument always, always, always prevails.

If the same had been true inside the Clinton White House in its first term, there wouldn't have been a second term. But that's the pornographic appeal of *The West Wing* to liberals. The unholy fantasy of it.

Bill Clinton must have seemed like a fantasy come true back in 1991, when he and Hollywood began their long and rocky romance. The Arkansas governor wowed the biggest names in Tinsel-town with his comprehensive knowledge of popular culture. So what if he called himself a "new Democrat," supported the death penalty, and talked about welfare reform? He surely didn't believe all that right-wing stuff, he was only saying it to win, and Hollywood was hungry for a Democrat in the White House. Showbiz titans raised huge sums of money for him, with Barbra Streisand alone pulling in a cool $1 million; she even sang at his inauguration despite her notorious stage fright.

Remember that inauguration, a meticulously planned three-day function intended to suggest that a newer, younger, hipper, and more culturally aware generation was finally taking charge of America? Streisand serenaded Clinton with "Some Enchanted Evening." Michael Jackson, not yet the subject of pedophilia allegations settled out of court, was surrounded by little boys as he sang "Heal the World." Fleetwood Mac, the 1970s California pop super group, reunited to sing the campaign anthem, "Don't Stop Thinking about Tomorrow." Easy listening, boomer-style, was represented by the saxophonist Kenny G (who was said to be Clinton's favorite musician, in case you were wondering whether the pop-culture-crazed president's taste for pop culture is any more elevated than his taste in women).

Bit speaking parts were handed out by the dozens to Goldie Hawn and Sally Field and Geena Davis. Throughout the inaugural festivities, Warren and Annette, Barry Manilow and Macaulay Culkin, Cosby and Nicholson wandered around Washington as though they were the American army liberating Paris.

Yes, it seemed a new era had dawned. (For twelve years the only song performed at Republican functions had been Lee Greenwood's "God Bless the U.S.A.") And though Clinton had run as a moderate, in those heady early days he gave every indication that he was going to govern farther to the left. The Hollywood elite thought it had died and gone to heaven when the first major issue to arise in the Clinton administration was the president's wish to end the ban on gays in the military. None of them had actually been in the armed forces, though most of them had produced or written or starred in or directed movies in which American military men were villains, but they sure knew a lot of gays. Or were gay themselves. And they thought they had a true friend in the White House.

The Lincoln Bedroom, not yet up for sale on a nightly basis, was a home away from home for Clinton's earliest and closest Hollywood intimates, like sitcom producers Linda and Harry Bloodworth-Thomason and actress Markie Post, the star of the Bloodworth-Thomason program *Hearts Afire*. So many celebrities were traipsing through the White House that a star-struck Paul Begala kept a camcorder handy to record their presence. In April 1993, when Clinton was in Vancouver for a summit with Boris Yeltsin, he stayed up late with Sharon Stone and Richard Gere in Richard Dreyfuss's hotel room, and, according to *W* magazine, he "briefed" celebrities "on how they could help him 'rebuild America.' " This, confesses George Stephanopoulos in his memoir, *All Too Human* (1999), "inevitably and jus-tifiably led to clucks in the press for hobnobbing with Hollywood stars at a superpower summit."

Trouble in paradise. Around the same time as the president's consulta-tion with Sharon Stone, a gaggle of Clinton contributors from Hollywood were invited to the White House to share their ideas on how to promote health care reform with Hillary Clinton's task-force chairman, Ira Maga-ziner, and James Carville, among others. There were several emperors of Hollywood around the table in the Roosevelt Room, most prominently Tri-Star Pictures chief Mike Medavoy and MCA president Sidney Sheinberg.

These were men accustomed to being listened to, sucked up to, having their every idea praised, their every whim satisfied. But it was not to be, be-cause in the middle of the meeting, Carville lost it. He hurled imprecations at them for being rich dilettantes with no sense of the true woes of middle-class folk, using the language of the Jersey Turnpike. No one had ever said such things to these people; at least not since they were in the mailroom sucking up to the abusive superiors they would soon dethrone.

Carville behaved like "Anthony Perkins playing Fidel Castro on acid," said sitcom producer Gary David Goldberg, who hurled his notes at Carville and shouted, "How dare you speak to us this way?" After all, he and the others had been invited, and had gone to Washington on their own dime. They were a *task force*! Besides which, Goldberg said, his mother had "died because she didn't have adequate health care." (Goldberg had made $100 million from the syndication sales of his show *Family Ties*.)

The administration put out word that Carville was in the doghouse for his behavior, but the truth was very nearly the opposite. There was a method to Carville's madness, as there always is. The Clinton administration's intimacy with Hollywood had become a political liability for a New Democrat who claimed to be a spokesman for culturally conservative values and not the knee-jerk limousine liberalism of the Hollywood elite. Clinton was close to seeming like a star-struck swain, not the Leader of the Free World, and Carville provided his president the cover to keep his distance. This became especially important after the May 1993 flap on the tarmac of Los Angeles International Airport, when Clinton was said to have held up air traffic for ninety minutes by having his hair cut by coiffeur-to-the-stars Christophe on Air Force One.

Clinton avoided Hollywood for months, until December 1993, when he attended a fundraiser at the headquarters of Creative Artists Agency, then the most powerful institution in Hollywood. Barbra sang "Can't Help Lovin' That Man" to him. Then, after pocketing $250,000 in soft money, Clinton pulled a Sister Souljah by challenging Hollywood executives to consider the impact their mindlessly violent films and television shows were having on innocent children.

They initially swooned. "He's like a prophet because he speaks completely from the heart," said producer Brian Grazer. Echoed Mark Canton, then head of Columbia Pictures: "I'm going to really take Sunday to put things in perspective." But there was a certain irritation in the room. Screenwriter Gary Ross complained that Hollywood had been unfairly "whacked by the media" in the first months of the Clinton administration. And director Rob Reiner told the *Washington Post*, "I do think it's a little simplistic to say there's a cause and effect between TV and movies and violence."

♦   ♦   ♦

At the time, Reiner was preparing to film a romantic comedy about a widowed president and his new love, with Aaron Sorkin as his screenwriter. *The*

American President, which came out in 1995, features a Clinton-like Michael Douglas whose pragmatic politics has succeeded in getting him high approval ratings, but has made him a cautious and tentative leader. Through the love of environmental lobbyist Annette Bening, Douglas casts aside his centrism. He delivers a speech to a rapt press corps in which he says he will seek legislation to ban the ownership of all guns, proudly declares himself a card-carrying member of the ACLU, and says he will end global warming. The message to Clinton from Reiner, Sorkin, and the Hollywood they represented was unmistakable: *Don't be you. Be this man.*

The problem is that Clinton *was* that man, or as close to it as any president was likely to come, in his first two years in office. And it nearly destroyed him. His advocacy of gays in the military led to an embarrassing defeat at the hands of Colin Powell and Sam Nunn. Rather than offering the middle-class tax cut he had promised during the campaign, he pushed a significant tax increase through Congress. He saw to the passage of the Brady Bill forcing a waiting period before the purchase of a handgun. Most impressively, he advocated nationalizing one-seventh of the U.S. economy with his health care plan.

And in November 1994, the Republican Party ran over Clinton and the Democrats with a steamroller.

To save himself and his party, Clinton was forced to move to the right, in part with his aggressive support of the V-chip, a piece of equipment that allows parents to screen television shows they consider harmful for their children. Hollywood hated the V-chip with an anger both self-righteous (threat to free speech) and fearful (would harm ratings, lower profits). But again, Hollywood embraced Clinton. How could it not? What choice did it have? Well, it could have decided not to lift a finger for him, which is what Silicon Valley decided after Clinton's first term. But Hollywood felt itself under assault from Clinton's enemies. Newt Gingrich was on the prowl. Newt Gingrich, the enemy of all things progressive, the man who said that the revered actor-filmmaker Woody Allen's affair with his teenage stepdaughter "fit the Democratic platform perfectly." And Bob Dole delivered a much-discussed speech in 1995 condemning the entertainment industry for making movies and television shows of which he disapproved (though he had never seen any of them).

Never mind the V-chip, and forget Hollywood's disappointment with what it took to be Clinton's obstinate refusal to rule the way Rob Reiner would. Clinton raised something like $10 million in hard and soft money in Hollywood in 1996, by far the most lucrative fund-raising he did, if you leave out the Chinese Army.

Hollywood seemed to have come to a new, more sober understanding of Bill Clinton. He wanted to be one of them, but couldn't be, not really, not with the country the way it was. Then came Monica, a scandal that was immensely confusing for the showbiz elite, who work in an industry where sexual harassment is a behavioral norm. *He had sex with an intern? And the problem is: what could be the problem with that?* "When it comes to private matters," producer Sean Daniel said at the time, "Hollywood has made its peace with far more scandalous behavior."

It's also an industry where conspiracies are the norm and where the top dogs have achieved greatness by plotting against others. This is one of the reasons why political conspiracy movies are so popular and taken so seriously within the Hollywood community; because they assume everybody else schemes the way they do. Hillary Clinton's charge that the entire business was a right-wing conspiracy made perfect sense to them.

Once again the wolves were at the door, this time led by Kenneth Starr. "Starr should be tried for treason," cried Haim Saban, the creator of *Mighty Morphin Power Rangers,* who raised $1.5 million for Clinton in a single night at his house in September 1997. Clinton needed Hollywood, and Hollywood delivered. "There's no decline in support," said the octogenarian *eminence grise* Lew Wasserman. Far from it, in fact. For what Clinton pulled off in the wake of the Lewinsky business was a Washington version of a beloved Hollywood dream-come-true, the critic-proof hit. No matter how bad his press, no matter how many pundits and columnists said he was finished, Clinton's approval ratings just kept on climbing.

Once again, Clinton had proved himself a winner, and Hollywood, as we've said, loves a winner. But after Clinton triumphed over his impeachers, and over the departed Newt Gingrich and the defeated Bob Dole, what was left of his presidency for his most reliable donors and friends? He wasn't going to pursue the agenda Hollywood was so enthusiastic about. Even in the arena of gun control, Clinton's not-so-ringing rhetoric about "closing the critical gun-show loophole" doesn't have the pizzazz of Michael Douglas's plan in *The American President* to ban *all* guns.

In fact, it didn't look like he was going to pursue much of anything except Al Gore's election in the year 2000, and while Hollywood has gotten over Clinton's advocacy of the V-chip, it still hasn't quite forgiven Gore for his wife Tipper's crusade against dirty song lyrics back in the 1980s. That's why the entertainment industry split down the middle in 1999, half for Gore, half for Bill Bradley.

And really, when you come down to it, what *has* Clinton done for Hollywood aside from collecting tens of millions of dollars there? He saved the elite from the neo-Victorian monsters of the Republican Party, but precious little else. The Camelot-like "brief shining moment" that began with gays in the military and ended with the haircut on the tarmac must evoke a mix of feelings inside the Hollywood breast, nostalgic reverie for what might have been and bitter disappointment in what was.

Enter Aaron Sorkin. "Sorkin is not cynical," Matthew Miller writes, and, by the seemingly innocuous act of portraying politicians with empathy, *The West Wing* has "injected into the culture a subversive competitor to the reigning values of political journalism." But the show has no empathy for real politicians and their lackeys, only for fictional ones and their Knights of the Round Table. Sorkin wants to portray an elevated, spiritually superior White House in *The West Wing*, and too much has happened in the past seven years to make that a possibility with a character like Bill Clinton at the center.

And so Sorkin has taken the story of the Clinton White House and eliminated what he sees as its most troubling aspect. Sorkin has airbrushed Clinton from his own White House as crudely as Stalin airbrushed those he had killed from official Soviet photographs, and in his place has superimposed a paragon of virtue so unsullied by the wear and tear of politics that Parson Weems himself might feel a little abashed.

Republicans tried to impeach Clinton, and failed. The enthusiasm for *The West Wing* among liberals suggests that they have a fate in store for Clinton more horrifying than this legacy-obsessed president could have imagined in the depths of his troubles back in 1998: they are going to spend the rest of their lives erasing him and the support they gave him from their minds, and the nation's.

THE WEST WING

BIBLIOGRAPHICAL OVERVIEW

---

15 | The Transformed Presidency

People and Power in the Real *West Wing*

MYRON A. LEVINE

Much of the drama of NBC's much-celebrated *The West Wing* focuses on the actions of key senior members of the White House staff; these are the individuals who have a close working relationship with the president, who advise the president on key policy and political matters. *The West Wing* has capably captured the importance of this institution and the sense of excitement that accompanies work in the White House.

Indeed, the institutionalized White House has grown in size and gained in importance over the years. Staff members have assumed new functions and provided a president with much-needed assistance. But, in doing so, this more prominent staff also poses certain dangers and risks for the presidency, a matter that is less well presented in creator Aaron Sorkin's televised White House.

A vast literature, written by both presidential scholars and former White House insiders, has described the growth and transformation of the modern presidency. This essay reviews that literature, and thus helps us to gauge the degree of accuracy or inaccuracy of the portrait of the American presidency presented by *The West Wing*.

The Way Things Used to Be: The White House of FDR

The growth of the presidential staff is often attributed to the forces set in motion by World War II and the post-war era. A brief look back at the presidency of Franklin D. Roosevelt reveals a White House that is much smaller and, in important ways, quite different from the bureaucratized, institutionalized presidency of today.

In her Pulitzer Prize-winning *No Ordinary Time—Franklin and Eleanor Roosevelt: The Home Front in World War II* (1995), Doris Kearns Goodwin describes a White House with the informality of a "small, intimate hotel," where houseguests came and even stayed for years:

> The permanent guests occasionally had private visitors of their own for cocktails or for meals, but for the most part their lives revolved around the president and first lady, who occupied adjoining suites in the southwest quarter of the second floor. On the third floor, in a cheerful room with slanted ceilings, lived Missy LeHand, the president's personal secretary and longtime friend. The president's alter ego, Harry Hopkins, occupied the Lincoln suite, two doors away from the president's suite . . . Lorena Hickok, Eleanor's great friend, occupied a corner room across from Eleanor's bedroom. This group of houseguests was continually augmented by a stream of visitors—Winston Churchill, who often stayed for two or three weeks at a time; the president's mother, Sara Delano Roosevelt; Eleanor's young friend Joe Lash; and Crown Princess Martha of Norway. (9–10)

Roosevelt valued Hopkins, the frail secretary of commerce and former head of the Works Progress Administration, who wound up serving as the president's emissary to London, Moscow, Teheran, and Yalta:

> "Stay the night," the president insisted. So Hopkins borrowed a pair of pajamas and settled into a bedroom suite on the second floor. There he remained, not simply for one night but for the next three and a half years, as Roosevelt, exhibiting his genius for using people in new and unexpected ways, converted him from the number-one relief worker to the number-one adviser on the war. Later, Missy [LeHand] liked to tease: "It was Harry Hopkins who gave George S. Kaufman and Moss Hart the idea for that play of theirs, 'The Man Who Came to Dinner.' " (37)

Hopkins, the president's sounding board, occupied the Lincoln Study, just doors away from the president's bedroom.

By today's standards, the Roosevelt White House was relatively small, personal, and homey. A ritual evening cocktail hour, where the president himself mixed the drinks, offered "intimate gatherings" (Goodwin 1995, 34), a time for relaxation, gossip, and swapping jokes in an informal atmosphere. Cocktails, card playing, movies, and gossip all offered the president the opportunity to escape the burdens of the office and renew his energies (419). The FDR White House was so "un-imperial" that FDR and his guests even had to put up with drab, simple, and overcooked meals—oatmeal for breakfast—as the president could not bring himself to replace his housekeeper (198–99). Interpersonal relationships were often quite close, as seen in the anecdote told about the time the president approached Churchill with the idea of calling the treaty among the twenty-six Allies the "United Nations":

> By far the best story was told by Harry Hopkins, who claimed the president was so excited by his inspiration that he had himself wheeled into Churchill's bedroom early one morning, just as the prime minister was emerging from his bath, stark naked and gleaming pink . . . The president apologized and said he would come back at a better time. No need to go, Churchill said: "The Prime Minister of Great Britain has nothing to conceal from the President of the United States!" (312)

During Churchill's extended visits, the Rose Suite and nearby rooms served as the virtual headquarters for the British wartime government.

The FDR White House poses a stark contrast with the more layered, bureaucratized, and institutionalized presidency of today. Structured and hierarchical staff relationships, a businesslike atmosphere, and an earnestness of purpose all characterize the contemporary White House—as NBC's *The West Wing* so capably captures. By comparison, the Roosevelt White House, with its fluidity, informality of structure, and absence of large numbers of staff, seems almost antediluvian.

The West Wing also shows a professionalized White House press corps and an institutionalization of presidency-press relations that is quite different from the Roosevelt presidency. Roosevelt's relationship with the press was characterized by a "mutual respect and professional intimacy" (Kernell 1977, 78) that would seem quite remarkable if it were to occur today. Faced with growing press corps of two hundred reporters, FDR appointed the first presidential press secretary, Stephen Early (79). Still, Roosevelt met the press "frequently and routinely" (79) and maintained close, personal relationships with reporters: "For seven years, twice a week, the president had sat down with these reporters, explaining legislation, announcing appointments, establishing friendly contact, calling them by their first names, teasing them about their hangovers, exuding warmth and accessibility. Once, when a correspondent narrowly missed getting on Roosevelt's train, the president covered for him by writing his copy until he could catch up" (Goodwin 1995, 26).

By the second half of the century, advances in technology and a change in press corps norms (resulting from Watergate and Vietnam) would act to undermine the intimacy of presidency-press relations that characterized the Roosevelt era. John Kennedy was the first presidential master of the new medium of television. Television offered the president new opportunities to communicate directly with the public, bypassing reporters. Presidents no longer had to suffer the risks of being too available to the press. Presidential press conferences became less frequent; they also became less a means of providing hard answers to the press questions and more a stage from which the president could reach the American public directly. A press secretary and a communications director—and their burgeoning staffs—would also now stand as a buffer between an increasingly media-savvy president and a growing corps of increasingly investigative and adversarial reporters (Edwards 1983, 108–28; Grossman and Kumar 1981, 81–156; Kernell 1977, 65–94).

Presidents discovered the advantages of "going public" as part of their governing strategies (Kernell 1977, 11–48). As a result, they relied more heavily on the assistance of staffs of pollsters, media relations advisors, press spokespersons, speechwriters, and aides serving as liaisons to key political constituencies and interest groups (Edwards 1983; Grossman and Kumar 1981; Kernell 1977; Tulis 1987; Peterson 1992; Patterson 2000, 129–84, 193–218; Spragens and Terwood 1980).

The West Wing capably captures the institutionalized nature of much of the modern-day White House-press relations. The series devotes many of its story lines to the actions of White House officials charged with media responsibilities: communications director Toby Ziegler (Richard Schiff), deputy communications director Sam Seaborn (Rob Lowe), and press secretary C. J. Cregg (Allison Janney). Indeed, we even see C. J.'s colleagues excluding her from an inner White House decision circle to avoid putting her in a difficult position when she must attempt to fend off aggressive queries from the press on sensitive matters.

"The Swelling of the Presidency"

For most of the nation's existence, presidential staffs were extremely small—for a while, almost nonexistent. Jefferson had only one messenger and one secretary. Early presidents paid staff salaries out of their own pockets, oftentimes relying on the services of relatives. It was not until 1857 that Congress appropriated money for the first presidential staff member, a clerk. Even in the twentieth century, Woodrow Wilson had only seven full-time aides (Burke 2000, 417–19).

The growth of the White House is seen as the result of FDR's proactive efforts to meet the challenges posed by the Great Depression and fascism in Europe. The Executive Office of the Presidency (EOP) was created in 1939 to give the nation's chief executive new staff resources. Yet, by today's standards, the Roosevelt White House had very few staff members; in preparing his legislative initiatives during his first hundred days, Roosevelt had to rely greatly on personnel loaned to him from other government agencies (Burke 2000, 419).

Roosevelt sought to avoid staff institutionalization. He wanted to maintain close control over staff members, to keep his aides "on a very short leash" (Pfiffner 1998, 46): "FDR did not allow his White House staff to grow so large that he could not personally supervise each member's activities. As a result, even at the height of the war, his senior White House staff, not counting clerical aides, numbered no more than a dozen. And they had few assistants of their own; there was little of the staff layering so common today" (Dickinson 1997, 20).

FDR sought the assistance of generalists whom he could flexibly assign to tasks as needed; he feared that staff members would regard fixed jurisdictional assignments as "hunting licenses" for unsupervised policy initiatives. FDR also employed a competitive model of staffing where he used the work produced by one aide to check on the work done by another. Roosevelt did not have a chief of staff, an institutional innovation that would be introduced later by Eisenhower; instead, the president handed out staff work assignments himself. Often attacked for being disorderly and confusing, the Roosevelt managerial approach had clear advantages: "staff parochialism, closed-mindedness, and complacency were less likely to take root" (Dickinson 1997, 19; also see Neustadt 1990, 220–21).

The numbers clearly document "The Swelling of the American Presidency" (Cronin and Genovese 1998, 302). The White House had only 45 full-time employees in 1937; ten years later, under Truman, the number stood at 190. During the Nixon years, the number ballooned to 550 before peaking at 605 under George Bush, Sr., and falling back to 543 during Clinton's first year. Even these numbers may understate the true size of the White House staff as there is no easy way to document the exact number of personnel from other executive branch agencies who are detailed on temporary assignment to various presidential offices.

The EOP has mushroomed to the point that it fills not just the White House but also the next-door Eisenhower Executive Office Building (formerly known as the Old Executive Office Building), the New Executive Office Building, and various townhouses and other offices in Washington. New responsibilities led to new presidential advisory structures: the National Security Council (NSC) (begun under Truman); the Council of Economic Advisors; the Office of Policy Development (with both domestic policy and economic policy responsibilities); and the Office of Management and Budget (OMB) (a very valuable tool for setting presidential priorities and establishing centralized control over executive branch agencies). There are also lesser EOP offices: the Council on Environmental Quality; the Office of the U.S. Trade Representative; the Office for National Drug Control Policy; and the Office of Science, Technology, and Space Policy (Patterson 2000, 18, 49–95). Responsibilities for policy formulation and implementation, once lodged with cabinet members and their subordinates, are now increasingly lodged with the White House staff, aides whom the president more fully trusts.

There are important staff resources that help a president get his legislative program through Congress. Beginning with Eisenhower, an office of legislative liaison was set up to help maintain a two-way flow of communications with Senators and House members. The White House legislative affairs office functions, as Bryce Harlow has observed, as "[a]n Ambulatory Bridge Across a Constitutional Gulf" (Patterson 2000, 114).

In this aspect, *The West Wing* fails to present a full and balanced portrayal of the institutionalized presidency. Its focus on the actions of the president, the chief of staff, and certain top senior staff and media advisors gives a distorted view of the workings and influence of presidential staff. In short, *The West Wing* slights the influence of key institutional advisors. Viewers gain little insight, for example, into the importance of the OMB and its director, and are given only the briefest glimpses of the president's National Security Advisor, Nancy McNally (Anna Deavere Smith), who makes fleeting and intermittent guest appearances on the show when a foreign policy crisis arises. In Sorkin's televised White House, the highly influential elements of the modern institutionalized presidency are underplayed in favor of the more humanized stories of the White House inner circle.

Managing the Institutionalized Presidency

The contemporary president must be an institutional manager capable of giving direction to and overseeing the actions of the presidential bureaucracy as well as executive branch departments and agencies. Presidents have found that personnel decisions are critical to institutional management: "Second to none in importance and priority at the White House is the selection of the men and women whom the president wishes to have serve in policymaking positions in the administration—and serve at his pleasure, without tenure" (Patterson 2000, 219). The president fills approximately 635 White House positions and another 5,840 noncareer positions in the bureaucracy (220–21). The Office of Presidential Personnel (OPP), working under the direction of the White House director of personnel, screens applicants and insures that new recruits can be entrusted to deliver the president's policies (Weko 1995). The importance of the White House personnel operation is seen in its staffing numbers: The early Reagan administration had 100 persons who worked for the OPP; in 1993, under Clinton, there were 130 (Pfiffner 1998, 92–93). During its presidential transition, the Clinton personnel office optically scanned 160,000 resumes into its computer system (Patterson 2000, 226).

A president's chief of staff is a key figure in the managerial presidency, dispensing and coordinating the assignments dispensed to other staff aides and monitoring their work; in effect, the chief of staff exerts total control over the work of other staff. The chief of staff also controls the president's schedule and determines just who has the need to see the president; it is the chief of staff who determines "where to draw the line," that is, when an issue is to be taken to the president (Patterson 2000, 351–52).

Jimmy Carter, in a reaction against ills revealed by Watergate, tried to govern without a chief of staff. Carter wanted to fashion a more open presidency and did not want a chief of staff who would serve as a "stopper" at the Oval Office door, isolating him from other voices in his administration as had been the case with Nixon. The experiment, however, did not work. In the absence of a chief of staff, Carter soon found that he himself was burdened with the detailed work of supervising staff. Without the guidance of a chief of staff, there was such great confusion in staff assignments and so much competition for the president's ear that, toward the end of his term, Carter finally relented and named trusted advisor Hamilton Jordan as chief of staff.

The Office of Management and Budget offers a critical resource for presidential management. The OMB does much more than simply help the president prepare his proposed budget. Working under the direction of the president's appointed budget director, the OMB ensures "legislative clearance," that each department's legislative requests are screened by the White House and reflect the president's program priorities. In essence, the OMB assists the president in setting his priorities and his preferred levels of spending for every discretionary agency program. Since Ronald Reagan, the OMB has also been an important tool to ensure centralized control over the rule-making process, restraining departments and agencies from issuing administrative regulations that conflict with the president's policy priorities. Critics complain that recent presidents have exerted such great control over the operations of the OMB that the "neutral competence" and professionalism of the office's dedicated careerists is being jeopardized (Burke 2000, 434–34; Campbell 1986, 266–68). A politicized OMB risks losing its credibility when it underestimates program costs or overestimates expected revenues in an effort to help "sell" the president's proposed budget.

In foreign policy, the National Security Council plays a dominant role. The NSC was created under Truman in order to facilitate interagency coordination and to ensure that the expertise of all relevant agencies would be brought to bear on complex security decisions. The NSC seeks to assure the proper flow of paperwork, allowing the staff of each agency to comment on proposed courses of action. Under recent presidents, however, the NSC and the national security advisor (the president's appointed head of the NSC) have gained an importance beyond efforts at interdepartmental, collegial decision making. Under a number of presidents, the national security advisor has tended to serve more as a presidential advisor advocating his or her own policy preferences, enjoying the influence that can accompany a top White House staffer's close proximity to the president (Burke 2000, 426–28).

Displacing the Cabinet

Cabinet secretaries differ from presidential staff members in that the former do more than simply work directly for and advise the president; they also have line administrative responsibilities for the day-to-day operation of huge executive departments. These line responsibilities often draw departmental secretaries away from the White House; these departmental chiefs may also develop views on departmental matters that are somewhat different from those of the president. As a result, over time, a cabinet secretary may lose some of a president's confidence. White House staff members, in contrast, do not suffer such split loyalties. To a great degree, members of the White House staff have displaced the cabinet as the president's primary advisors (Warshaw 1996).

Unlike classic cabinet government in Britain, the modern cabinet in the United States does not serve as a collective decision making body. Presidents may choose to rely on the advice of individual cabinet members, but presidents have not found the cabinet as a whole to be a very useful collegial decision-making or consultative body. Lyndon Johnson press secretary and special advisor George Reedy (1987) observed: "The cabinet is one of those institutions in which the whole is less than the sum of the parts. As individual officers, the members bear heavy responsibilities in administering the affairs of the government. As a collective body, they are about as useful as the vermiform appendix—though far more honored" (73). The tradition of ignoring the cabinet even goes back as far as Andrew Jackson, who chose instead to meet with a "kitchen cabinet" of political cronies and friends.

For the contemporary president, the cabinet is simply too large and diverse to allow the targeted discussion and informed give-and-take that complex issues require. A cabinet member responsible for veterans' affairs, housing, or agriculture, for instance, may have little of substance to add in the midst of a foreign policy crisis. In responding to the Cuban missile crisis, John Kennedy convened the executive committee (ExCom) of the NSC, not the cabinet, to review alternative courses of action. In the executive committee work group, the president assembled a wide array of intelligence, diplomatic and defense experts, cabinet officials, and White House staff aides—including speechwriter Ted Sorenson and political associate Kenny O'Donnell—whose judgment JFK valued (Allison and Zelikow 1999, 110–11; Preston 2001, 97–136).

In today's "cabinet of unequals" (Cronin and Genovese 1998, 291–92), secretaries in the "inner" cabinet enjoy greater influence than do secretaries in the "outer" cabinet. The Departments of State, Defense, and Treasury constitute the inner cabinet; the president turns to them for advice on crucial foreign policy and economic policy matters that he must repeatedly face. The heads of the other departments—Agriculture, Interior, Transportation, Health and Human Services, Housing and Urban Development, Labor, Commerce, Energy, Education, and Veterans' Affairs—work on matters that are less central to the president. These secretaries form an outer cabinet; they enjoy less frequent access to the president and are generally called upon for advice only on those occasions when their jurisdictional concerns gain primacy on the president's agenda (292–93).

The Justice Department is sometimes in the inner cabinet and sometimes in the outer cabinet. Attorneys General Robert Kennedy and Edwin Meese were important *consigliores*, respectively, to JFK and Reagan. Janet Reno, in contrast, worked largely as an outsider, distrusted by Clinton and his staff.

Presidents generally choose cabinet members on the basis of their abilities. Yet, political considerations—the racial, ethnic, gender, geographical, and political balance an appointee can bring to an administration—are often also important, especially in the selection of members of the outer cabinet.

Just how far "out" can an outer cabinet member be when chosen for political considerations? At a reception during the early days of his administration, Ronald Reagan did not even recognize "Silent" Sam Pierce, his secretary for Houasing and Urban Development and the only African American in the cabinet; Reagan greeted his new department head with an it's-so-nice-to-meet-you, "Mr. Ambassador."

Even when individual cabinet members serve as presidential counselors, they compete with presidential staff for influence. Cabinet heads must spend the great bulk of their time outside the White House, running their departments and meeting with the representatives of various departmental constituencies (Hess 1988, 202); this means that cabinet secretaries are often absent from the White House when key matters are discussed. As a result, in the competition between White House staff and cabinet members, it is often the staff that emerges victorious. National Security Advisor Henry Kissinger, not Secretary of State William Rogers, dominated foreign policy during Nixon's first term in office. Cyrus Vance, Jimmy Carter's secretary of state, eventually resigned, having lost his power struggle with more hawkish National Security Advisor Zbigniew Brzezinski.

What explains the drift of influence from cabinet members into the hands of White House staff? The president does not always fully trust the perspective of departmental secretaries who risk "going native" as they spend so much time with departmental bureaucrats and their constituencies. A departmental secretary is no longer simply the president's representative; he or she also, to some extent, becomes the advocate of the department's point of view. White House staff, in contrast, work only for the president and pose no such problem of divided loyalties.

New presidents have regularly promised to lessen the dominance of White House staff and strengthen the role played by cabinet officials; but once in office, confronted with the difficulties of getting things done, presidents eventually come to see the advantages of drawing decision making into the hands of trusted White House advisors. Of all the modern presidents, Eisenhower paid the greatest respect to the authority of individual cabinet officials and to the cabinet as an advisory body. "General Eisenhower" respected lines of organizational hierarchy and the authority of his appointees: "Under the Eisenhower system the cabinet officers were expected to run the daily operations of their departments without presidential interference" (Hess 1998, 59). Eisenhower attended frequent cabinet meetings—an average of thirty-four a year over his two terms (Greenstein 1982, 113), a marked contrast to paucity of cabinet meetings convened by more recent chief executives.

Richard Nixon came to the presidency promising a return to a cabinet-centered government" (Pfiffner 1996, 41); but within six months departmental secretaries were ignored and cabinet meetings were virtually forgotten as White House staff aides drafted major domestic policy bills in relative secrecy (Nathan 1975, 42–43). Having failed to win legislative approval for much of his domestic agenda, Nixon adopted an "administrative presidency" strategy where White House officials were to exert strict control over the day-to-day actions of the executive departments (45). As part of the plan to give Domestic Policy Advisor John Ehrlichman greater power over agency affairs, Nixon, on the heels of his landslide 1972 re-election, asked for the resignation of all cabinet and subcabinet appointees: "They could keep their jobs only if they agreed to live by the cardinal rule: the White House was to call all of the shots" (Dean 1976, 153; also see DiClerico 1995, 183–88, and Nathan 1975). Only the intrusion of Watergate derailed the administrative presidency.

Jimmy Carter, reacting to the abuses of Watergate, promised to reverse the direction of White House power by revitalizing the cabinet. But, like his immediate predecessors, he too soon came to regard cabinet meetings as a waste of time; they were convened less frequently. Toward the end of his term, Carter sought greater White House review of agency actions and, like Nixon, even demanded the resignation of each cabinet member; he accepted five (Pfiffner 1996, 45–47; also see Campbell 1986, 59–61).

Ronald Reagan similarly sought to increase the involvement of cabinet members in policy by establishing a system of "cabinet councils" (Campbell 1986, 25–26, 150–52). These interdepartmental work groups met regularly with top OMB officials and other White House staff members, who assured the councils' fealty to the president's policy goals. While the system of councils did promote greater cabinet action in domestic policy, on the whole the cabinet councils dealt primarily with "secondary-level matters" (Newland 1985, 153–61); "many of the most important decisions were not made through the cabinet council apparatus" but by top-level White house officials, "who often ignored cabinet council decisions" (Pfiffner 1996, 52).

The West Wing capably captures the advantageous position of White House staff members relative to cabinet secretaries. Departmental secretaries are seldom presented in the show. In at least one episode, a White House staffer, Toby Ziegler, is shown dressing down a departmental head who has begun to push his own programs and political ambitions and not just those of the president. There is little doubt in *The West Wing*; as long as they enjoy the president's favor, senior White House staff members, not cabinet secretaries, are "top dog."

Risks and Dangers: Sycophancy, Isolation, and Competition

Individual departmental secretaries can be influential, but only if, like White House staff, they moderate their independent voice and subjugate their policy views to those of the president. As George Reedy (1987) explains, "The secretaries do not have a political status and it is considered bad form for any one of them to deviate in the slightest from the line laid down by their chief— so bad that deviation usually spells an end to a public career" (75–76). Modern cabinet members, like presidential staff, lack the political base necessary to express "the kind of dissent that a president should hear on a direct, personal basis if he is to remain in touch with reality" (78). The tradition of cabinet loyalty is so strong as to mute internal criticism. Bill Clinton was able to appeal to this tradition in convincing Secretary of Health and Human Services Donna Shalala, a former university president with considerable professional stature, to mute her outrage upon having discovered that Clinton had deceived her and other cabinet members in his earlier denials of his sexual relationship with Monica Lewinsky.

Of course, presidents look for more than mere loyalty when choosing a departmental secretary; they also seek a person with the ability to manage his or her department. As a result, individuals of stature with a reputation for independence—including James Schlesinger (under Gerald Ford), Jack Kemp and Alexander Haig (under Reagan), and Janet Reno (under Clinton)—can gain cabinet posts (Cronin and Genovese 1998, 279–81).

Presidents are also often constrained when dismissing a maverick cabinet member. Clinton, facing continued criticisms over Whitewatergate, travelgate, the Lewinsky episode, and other matters, allowed Janet Reno to remain in office despite the White House's view that the attorney general was not a dependable team player.

White House staffers, lacking such stature, are even more prone than cabinet members to a sycophancy and a yes-man relationship that risks distancing the president from reality. In the "American monarchy" (Reedy 1987, 3), the presidency takes on certain aspects of royalty: "No one thrusts unpleasant thoughts upon a king unless he is ordered to do so, and even then he does so at his own peril" (97). Staffers who gain their place in the administration as a result of their participation in the president's victorious election campaign are especially likely to see the president's priorities as their own.

The "one fixed goal in life" for a White House assistant "is somehow to gain and maintain access to the president" (Reedy 1987, 88). The result is a competition among White House staff members to curry the favor of the president and senior staff in order to gain increased responsibilities and status. The Nixon White House was so competitive that it was "in a state of perpetual internal flux" (Dean 1976, 20); offices were constantly being reassigned, altered, and redecorated, all serving as testimony to who was moving up and who was moving down the White House hierarchy. The most highly valued offices, of course, are those with proximity to the president and senior staff. The great danger is that a staff member may sacrifice his or her independent judgment and concern for ethics in the race for advancement. John Dean, the presidential counsel whose tell-all Watergate testimony led to Nixon's demise, recalled his own early White House experiences of "climbing towards the moral abyss of the President's inner circle, thinking I had made it to the top just as I began to realize I had actually touched bottom" (21).

The White House is a place where groupthink regularly occurs and where courses of action desired by the president are rarely subjected to the most complete and exacting scrutiny. The culture of deference in the White House even helps to explain such major presidential disasters as Truman's overextension of the war in Korea, Kennedy's approval of the absurdly unrealistic Bay of Pigs invasion scenario, Johnson's continued escalation of the war in Vietnam, and Nixon's pattern of continued deceit in the Watergate cover-up (Janis 1982, 14–71, 97–130, 198–241). Indeed, writing after Watergate, Richard Neustadt (1990) admitted that his classic formulation of presidential power had underestimated the power of loyalty and the ability of misguided staff loyalty to lead a presidency to disaster (191).

The dangers posed by White House isolation and groupthink are especially severe when presidents, acting on the basis of incomplete advice, initiate unwise military interventions. As the Vietnam War dragged on, Congress in 1973 passed the War Powers Resolution, with its requirement that the president notify and consult with congressional leaders in advance of committing troops into situations of "imminent involvement in hostilities"; the consultation requirement was an attempt by Congress to break the isolation of White House inner advisory circles an a critical policy area. But the attempt has largely failed; in crisis after crisis since Vietnam, presidents have largely ignored the War Powers Resolution and have failed to consult with Congress in any meaningful way (Fisher 1987, 134–206).

On occasion, rivalries among staff factions can wind up breaking the circle of groupthink by bringing competing points of view to the president's attention. But such factionalism poses new problems for the president: the inability to get staff to act as a team; paralysis of action as decisions are delayed by continued internal debate; and the considerable damage to an administration caused by "leaks" as each White House faction uses the press to undermine the other (Morris 1997, 101–3).

The Reagan presidency suffered from the conflict among various staff factions. Clinton's first term was marred by the "chronic conflict" (Morris 1997, 97) between two White House factions, one committed to the more moderate New Democratic policy positions that the president had expressed during the campaign, and a second, more liberal faction that saw a Clinton presidency and a Democratic Congress as offering an opening to pass bold policy initiatives consistent with Democratic party's traditions. Plagued by the internal conflict, Clinton soon came to express his regret that he did not devote the same time and care in recruiting and screening his staff that he did in selecting his cabinet (97).

The West Wing presents a quite rosy and positive portrayal of White House staff, a portrayal that in many ways is a healthy and necessary corrective to the anti-Washington impulse that has long dominated the American public culture. But this portrayal is too positive, too unreal. In the TV White House, as opposed to the real-world White House, there is no serious factionalism and no grave danger of staff groupthink and presidential isolation. The staff of the Bartlet White House may disagree with one another on details of policy or politics; but they are united as a team in their loyalty to the president and his ideals. Consequently, *The West Wing* cannot even recognize the political nature of many White House leaks, how one how staff faction in the White House may leak a story to the press in order to advance its policy desires. Instead, in the televised White House, as the third-season *West Wing* episode "War Crimes" naïvely presents, leaks to the press are apolitical; they occur when immature junior staff try to impress outsiders with their insider knowledge.

The Impact of Presidential Personality and Style

The exact relationship between a president and White House staff varies from president to president. The tendencies toward isolation and staff factionalism are inherent in the institutionalized presidency, but they are also dependent on a president's personality and managing style. Not all presidents suffer equally from the risks of groupthink and isolation. John Kennedy, for instance, encouraged the flow of a diversity of views. Speechwriter and Kennedy confidant Theodore Sorenson recalled that JFK wanted advisors to be "skeptical and critical, not sycophantic" (Preston 2001, 111). Secretary of State Dean Rusk similarly remembered that JFK "liked to have discussions that were more or less like seminars where various people around the table would be invited to speak up and present their views" (110–11). Kennedy did not want his advisors to serve as "filters to the president," but as a "debate team" that considered policy options from "multiple, conflicting perspectives" (George and George 1998, 211).

James David Barber's study of "presidential character" underscores the extent to which president-advisor relations are shaped by a president's personality. According to Barber (1992, 4–83), the dangers of isolation are most apparent in the case of ego-defensive *active-negative* presidents who are compelled to action in order to compensate for their inner demons. These presidents see themselves as surrounded by enemies and attribute all criticisms of their policies to the ill motives of their attackers. Lyndon Johnson did not even allow his war councils to examine his policies critically:

> Chester Cooper described how this process worked in a National Security Council meeting. "The President, in due course, would announce his decision and then poll everyone in the room—council members, their assistants, and members of the White House and NSC staffs. 'Mr. Secretary, do you agree with the decision?' 'Yes, Mr. President.' 'Mr. X, do you agree?' 'I agree, Mr. President.' (Kearns [Goodwin] 1991, 338)

These senior advisers would one-by-one give the assent that Johnson requested as he went around the table. LBJ had only a limited tolerance for dissenting points of view. He blamed scapegoats for the mounting protests against the Vietnam war and for his declining approval ratings; he saw intellectuals, the press, knee-jerk liberals, Kennedyites, crackpots, and other conspirators as all being out to get him (Kearns [Goodwin] 1991, 329; Barber 1992, 44). Johnson saw Robert Kennedy, whom he always referred to as "Sonny Boy," to be the main villain (Barber 1992, 44). In the Nixon White House, the distrust and the sense of being besieged by "ruthless" enemies was so great that it led to a quite unhealthy do-it-to-them-before-they-do-it-to-you attitude (161–64).

The *passive-positive* presidents, by comparison, are compliant figures who play to the audience in a search for approval and affection. Ronald Reagan hated confrontation, tried to "split the difference" to avoid offending competing advisors, and was slow to fire top aides even when it was necessary to do so (Barber 1992, 224–31; George and George 1998, 225–26). Reagan possessed a strong foreign policy vision, but its implementation suffered as the president was reluctant to establish discipline among competing staff factions (George and George 1998, 233). In the critical national security policy arena, Reagan was a delegator, and his presidency suffered from a lack of firm control: "the president distanced himself to a surprising and dangerous degree from both the substance and the process of foreign-policymaking" (230).

Barber's third type of president, the *passive-negative*, is an increasingly rare type of executive who dislikes politics but who accepts the call to public service out of a sense of civic obligation. This type is similarly characterized by excessive reliance on staff and a tendency toward drift.

The *active-positive* president, according to Barber, has the most healthy personality. Brought up in an atmosphere of unconditional love and affection, the active-positive—FDR, Truman, Kennedy—is sure of who he is. He does not take criticism of his policies as criticism of himself as a person; he can learn from his mistakes, grow in office, and adapt flexibly to changing situations. Kennedy learned from the Bay of Pigs fiasco; in the Cuban missile crisis, he sought out a diversity of opinions and questioned agencies' estimates as to their capabilities (Barber 1992, 364–79; Janis 1982, 14–47, 132–58).

Barber's typology is provocative but not well grounded in personality theory (Hargrove 1993, 95). Presidents are complex figures whose behavior does not easily fall within one of Barber's four boxes (George 1974; George and George 1998, 181; Nelson 2000, 210–11). Recent scholarship, for instance, has pointed to Eisenhower's successful leadership, including his more assertive command of the advisory process (Greenstein 1982; Henderson 1988), a portrayal that is quite at odds with Barber's characterization of Ike as "passive." Even the evidence on Kennedy is more mixed than Barber conveys. Kennedy revisionists charge that JFK often took conflict (especially with Castro) personally, that he exacerbated Cold War crises, and that he was not truly open to advice contrary to his tough, pragmatic foreign policy interventionism (Fairlie 1973; Miroff 2000, 273–307; Miroff 1976; Wills 1994).

Thomas Preston (2001) does not seek to classify a president's character; instead, Preston simply tries to assess the variety of ways that modern presidents have utilized their advisory systems in different policy areas (5–31). A president's relationship with his cabinet and staff will vary with his need to assert his power, his personal ability to see the complexities of issues, and his expertise or familiarity with a policy area. Eisenhower, Kennedy, and George H. W. Bush, for instance, all came to the presidency with considerable foreign policy experience and chose to rely on their own judgments in foreign affairs; in domestic policy, however, these executives were more reliant on the suggestions of advisors. Bill Clinton acted as his own "navigator" in domestic affairs, having had considerable experience as governor and having earned a considerable reputation for being a policy "wonk"; in foreign policy, however, he was less experienced, and his course of action was more dependent on the dominant views expressed in his advisory group (14–16). As Clinton grew in office and gained familiarity with the issues, he became more active in foreign policy making (31, 243–50).

A president's ability to see the "complexity" of an issue has both benefits and drawbacks. Presidents who have a greater tolerance for complexity seek out more extensive contextual information and advice, including criticisms of potential courses of action. But such an extensive information search and deliberation can also slow down action. In contrast, low-complexity leaders, like Truman, who see the world in terms of "black-and-white" policy problems, are more likely to act decisively, relying on the recommendations of a few trusted experts without feeling the need to seek a wider discussion that explores every possible scenario (Preston 2001, 9–10, 32–63).

George W. Bush, in the early days of his presidency, exhibited the characteristics of a low complexity leader, who had a low cognitive need for information and who saw issues in simple black-and-white terms. Bush had no intense need to personally dominate the decision-making process; he allowed a large policy role for advisors. The White House advisory system was hierarchically structured, in corporate-like fashion, with chief of staff Andrew Card jealously guarding the president's time. Policy memos written for the president were kept quite brief, and staff presentations were mandated to be short and to the point; there was little tolerance for extended and free-ranging discussion, which were seen as a waste of the president's time. Staff members were expected to assume the role of loyal team players.

Having served as governor of Texas, Bush possessed much greater familiarity with domestic issues, especially school reform, than with foreign policy. In the wake of the deadly attack on the World Trade Center, the president's tendency toward black-and-white thinking allowed him to deliver a relatively swift and decisive response against the Al Qaeda organization in Afghanistan. Sure of the correctness and the morality of the United States' cause, he did not unduly delay or limit the strike while advisors explored and debated innumerable complexities and ramifications of American action: the possible destabilization of the region, the impact that the bomb-ings could have on American relations with the Muslim world, and the impact that American action could have on both the Israel-Palestine conflict and India-Pakistan relations. Lacking intimate knowledge of the national security arena, the president turned to key inner circle advisors—Secretary of State Colin Powell, Secretary of Defense Donald Rumsfeld, National Security Advisor Condoleezza Rice, and Vice President Richard Cheney—testifying to the importance of key foreign policy advisors to inexperienced presidents.

The Changing Roles of the Vice President and the First Lady

The vice presidency and the first lady have assumed a new importance in the modern presidency that was not at all typical in the past. Such traditional wisdom as that voiced by "Cactus" John Nance Garner, FDR's first vice president, that his office was not "worth a warm pitcher of spit" is simply dated.

Even as late as the 1960s and 1970s, vice presidents like Hubert Humphrey and Spiro Agnew were often excluded from key decision-making councils. But today, vice presidents tend to play the role of valued staff members. Vice presidents now enjoy considerable staff; they also have an office in the West Wing and access to key briefings and presidential meetings. To a great extent, the vice presidential office was transformed as Presidents Carter and Reagan gave heightened prominence to their Veeps, respectively Walter "Fritz" Mondale and George Bush. Clinton utilized Al Gore even more extensively. In each case, these vice presidents demonstrated their competence and earned the trust of the president, showing that they would subjugate their policy views and political ambitions to those of their chief and that they would never contradict or embarrass the president in public (Cronin and Genovese 1998, 328–38).

In return for their fealty, they were rewarded with increasingly substantial policy responsibilities: Bush, for instance, served as Reagan's point man on regulatory reform and paperwork reduction; Gore was made responsible for the "reinvention" of government and also acted as a key presidential advisor on foreign policy. Bush Vice President Dan Quayle, largely ridiculed by the press, did not fully pass the test of winning the president's trust; but he too grew in office and was given considerable responsibilities, attesting to the transformation of the vice presidential office (Pika 2000, 547–52).

Vice presidents today are picked for their abilities to govern and not just for the political assets they may bring to an electoral ticket. Compare the selection of Agnew and Cheney: Nixon chose Maryland's Spiro Agnew as his running mate, having little knowledge of the man other than that the relatively unknown governor of Maryland would allow Nixon to bridge relationships with the more moderate Rockefeller wing of the Republican party. George W. Bush's selection of Richard Cheney, in contrast, was obviously more the result of Cheney's extensive Washington experience and credentials in foreign policy, Bush weaknesses, than of any concern for the three electoral votes from Cheney's home state of Wyoming.

Reflecting the changing role of women, the first lady has gained a new primacy as a presidential advisor, most conspicuously in the public stage occupied by Hillary Clinton. An active spouse can be the "First Special Counselor" (Patterson 2000, 281), no longer just the wifely adjunct who devotes her time solely to hospitality duties and such tertiary policy matters as Lady Bird Johnson's efforts to beautify America by removing unsightly billboards and used car dumps from the nation's highways. The heightened role of the first lady is clearly evident in the transformation of the East Wing office. Hillary Clinton had a full-time speechwriter (which grew to two writers); her personal staff numbered twenty and was supplemented by fifteen interns and another fifteen volunteers; additional staff worked for the White House Social Office (Patterson 2000, 292).

Still, as Hillary Clinton found out and as Eleanor Roosevelt had similarly discovered at an earlier time, the role of an activist first lady is fraught with danger. Little wonder, then, that Barbara Bush and Laura Bush, who devoted their time to such traditional "caring" policy areas as mental health and education, were less divisive figures who gained more unmixed public approval for their efforts.

Eleanor Roosevelt was a valuable complement to FDR, acting as the "eyes and ears" for the disabled president as she toured the nation. Eleanor's social policy convictions balanced Franklin's political pragmatism; she pushed him to act on behalf of the poor and excluded (Goodwin 1995). She also wrote a syndicated daily newspaper column. Widely popular, though,

Eleanor Roosevelt also often received public scorn for her failure to play a more traditional wifely role. She was eventually forced to give up the formal governmental position she had accepted as assistant director of the Office of Civilian Defense, as her actions in that office became the target of merciless criticism from Congress and journalists (Goodwin 1995, 280–81, 323–26).

Like Eleanor Roosevelt, Hillary Clinton was an activist leader who gained newfound popularity but who also was a polarizing figure. She suffered for overtly violating traditional gender expectations, as when she announced that she would be known as Hillary Rodham Clinton, not just Hillary Clinton. During the election campaign, Bill Clinton had promised a new activist "partnership" fit for modern times, that when you voted for one you got two dynamic leaders. Yet, in retrospect, it was clearly a political mistake for Bill as president to put Hillary in command of the cabinet-level task force charged with developing his national health care initiative, his number one domestic priority. Hillary became a high-visibility lightening rod who attracted attacks that undermined the entire health reform effort. The appointment was also unwise as it muted the normal give and take of policy development; ordinary aides would not willingly challenge the positions advocated by the president's wife (Patterson 2000, 284–85).

It is not only liberal, activist Democrats like Eleanor Roosevelt and Hillary Clinton who have seized greater influence beyond the confines of their East Wing offices. Nancy Reagan, too, played an important political role, but did so largely behind the scenes. She suffered greatly as the press ridiculed her love of fashion, her concern for the furnishings of the White House, the inadequacy of her "Just say 'No!' " approach to drugs, and even her willingness to consult an astrologer. But, devoted to "Ronnie," she also served her husband well, seeking to protect his interests and even his place in history. In fact, Nancy may have been the only "disinterested advisor" (Neustadt 1990, 313) in a highly factionalized White House. Nancy policed White House personnel, urged the president to oust disloyal aides, kept White House chief of staff Donald Regan in check, and alerted the president to threats to his public standing (312–14).

Overall, the president's spouse has gained a new primacy as a presidential advisor but still must be somewhat circumspect regarding traditional gender roles. Eleanor Roosevelt and Hillary Clinton at times were effectively punished for going too far and violating expectations. The lessons are simple: First ladies cannot hold formal positions of responsibility. First Ladies can be active and will enjoy as much influence as the president allows; but the politically wise first lady will find it useful to shield the full degree of her influence from the American public and to pay at least some respect to traditional role expectations.

If *The West Wing* has totally missed the transformation of the vice presidency,[1] it at least has captured, somewhat, the rise of the new first lady. Vice President John Hoynes (Tim Matheson) is no loyal advisor to the president who earns the president's trust and thereby gains substantial policy responsibilities. Instead, Hoynes seems to come from another era, if not from another political world. Chosen purely for his ability to strengthen the November ticket, Hoynes is a strong-willed maverick, a man of unremitting political ambition who is marginalized (indeed, he is seldom seen) in the Bartlet White House, as he will not bend his policy convictions to the wishes of the president. Abby Bartlet (Stockard Channing), the president's wife, is a physician, a modern woman with her own career. She is also an unofficial presidential advisor. She presses (unsuccessfully) for the mention of the Violence Against

---

1. It should also be noted that *The West Wing* also presents a totally antiquated version of that venerable institution, the Senate filibuster. In the second-season episode "The Stackhouse Filibuster," C. J. Cregg describes a filibuster as if the Senate had not changed since the days of *Mr. Smith Goes to Washington* (1939): "The rules of a filibuster are simple enough. You keep the floor as long as you hold the floor. What does that mean? It means you can't stop talking ever. You can't eat and you can't drink which is fine because you can't leave the chamber to use the bathroom either. But all that's nothing compared with this: You aren't allowed to sit down. You aren't allowed to lean on anything . . ." But today, no filibuster is that dramatic. Instead, filibusters have become relatively routine and involve the introduction of various procedural delaying devices and the threat of unlimited debate; unlike Jimmy Stewart, no one senator alone tries to hold the floor. Filibusters today do not require great physical stamina and fortitude. As the number of filibusters has increased over the years, cloture votes to shut off filibusters have also become relatively routine. If a filibuster occurs, Senate leaders will call for a cloture vote to end debate; if that vote fails, they will seek to negotiate a compromise with the filibusterers. If that fails, the leaders cannot win, and they simply move on to other important agenda items; there is no sense allowing a team of filibusterers to stall action forever. It seems that both C. J. Cregg and Aaron Sorkin have spent more time watching old movies than in watching the contemporary Senate in action.

Women Act in the State of the Union message; she helps direct "damage control" and keep embarrassing information from the media; concerned for the president's health (the president suffers from multiple sclerosis), she also pressures him not to run for re-election.

A Transformed Presidency

The White House has grown greatly and been transformed as the national government has assumed new domestic and foreign policy responsibilities. The growth of the EOP has provided presidents with important assets for leadership, but the growth of presidential staff also poses new problems of isolation and factionalism. Presidents must demonstrate considerable managerial abilities if they are to gain effective control of the institutionalized presidency and maximize their leadership potential.

But the contemporary Washington environment, with its extreme dispersion of power, does not lend itself easily to leadership. Ironically, those presidents who are most recognized as "great" leaders are more often than not executives who sought to "preserve" order and minimize the potential of threatening change. The presidency has been transformed; but a transformed presidency is no guarantee of transformational leadership (Riley 2000, 435–40).

The many episodes of *The West Wing* point to a number of difficulties and in the presidential job. Nonetheless, in its overall portrayal of an idealized, heroic, liberal, transformed presidency, where the president is aided by a team of energetic, loyal, and caring staff, *The West Wing* may still overestimate the potential for presidential leadership.

WORKS CITED

INDEX

Works Cited

Episodes of *The West Wing* (NBC)

"And It's Surely to Their Credit." Season 2, episode no. 5, first broadcast Nov. 1, 2000. Written by Aaron Sorkin, story by Kevin Falls and Laura Glasser, directed by Christopher Misiano.

"Celestial Navigation." Season 1, episode no. 15, first broadcast Feb. 16, 2000. Written by Aaron Sorkin, story by Dee Dee Myers and Lawrence O'Donnell Jr., directed by Christopher Misiano.

"Crackpots and These Women, The." Season 1, episode no. 5, first broadcast Oct. 20, 1999. Written by Aaron Sorkin, directed by Anthony Drazan.

"Dead Irish Writers." Season 3, episode no. 15, first broadcast Mar. 6, 2002. Written by Aaron Sorkin, story by Paul Redford, directed by Alex Graves.

"Documentary Special." Season 2, first broadcast Apr. 24, 2002. Interview material prepared by William Couturie, Eli Attie, and Felicia Willson.

"Election Night." Season 4, episode no. 7, first broadcast Nov. 6, 2002. Written by Aaron Sorkin, story by David Gerken and David Handelman, directed by Lesli Linka Glatter.

"Ellie." Season 2, episode no. 15, first broadcast Feb. 21, 2001. Written by Aaron Sorkin, story by Kevin Falls and Laura Glasser, directed by Michael Engler.

"Enemies." Season 1, episode no. 8, first broadcast Nov. 17, 1999. Written by Ron Osborn and Jeff Reno, story by Rick Cleveland, Lawrence O'Donnell Jr., and Patrick Caddell, directed by Alan Taylor.

"Game On." Season 4, episode no. 6, first broadcast Oct. 30, 2002. Written by Aaron Sorkin and Paul Redford., directed by Alex Graves.

"H.Con-172." Season 3, episode no. 10, first broadcast Jan. 9, 2002. Written by Aaron Sorkin, story by Eli Attie, directed by Vincent Misiano.

"He Shall, from Time to Time." Season 1, episode no. 12, first broadcast Jan. 12, 2000. Written by Aaron Sorkin, directed by Arlene Sanford.

"In Excelsis Deo." Season 1, episode no. 10, first broadcast Dec. 15, 1999. Written by Aaron Sorkin and Rick Cleveland, directed by Alex Graves.

"In the Shadow of Two Gunmen: Parts I and II." Season 2, episodes no. 1 and 2, first broadcast Oct. 4, 2000. Written by Aaron Sorkin, directed by Thomas Schlamme.

"In This White House." Season 2, episode no. 4, first broadcast Oct. 25, 2000. Written by Aaron Sorkin, story by Peter Parnell and Allison Abner, directed by Ken Olin.

"Isaac and Ishmael Special," Season 3, Oct. 3, 2001. Written by Aaron Sorkin, directed by Christopher Misiano.

"Let Bartlet Be Bartlet." Season 1, episode no. 19, first broadcast Apr. 26, 2000. Written by Aaron Sorkin, Peter Parnell, and Patrick Caddell, directed by Laura Innes.

"Lies, Damn Lies and Statistics." Season 1, episode no. 21, first broadcast May 10, 2000. Written by Aaron Sorkin, directed by Don Scardino.

"Lord John Marbury." Season 1, episode no. 11, first broadcast Jan. 5, 2000. Written by Aaron Sorkin and Patrick Caddell, story by Patrick Caddell and Lawrence O'Donnell Jr., directed by Kevin Rodney Sullivan.

"Manchester: Parts I and II." Season 3, episodes no. 1 and 2, first broadcast Oct. 10 and 17, 2001. Written by Aaron Sorkin, directed by Thomas Schlamme

"Mandatory Minimums." Season 1, episode no. 20, first broadcast May 3, 2000. Written by Aaron Sorkin, directed by Robert Berlinger.

"Midterms, The." Season 2, episode no. 3, first broadcast Oct. 18, 2000. Written by Aaron Sorkin, directed by Alex Graves.

"Night Five." Season 3, episode no. 13, first broadcast Feb. 6, 2002. Written by Aaron Sorkin, directed by Christopher Misiano.

"Noel." Season 2, episode no. 10, first broadcast on Dec. 20, 2000. Written by Aaron Sorkin, story by Peter Parnell, directed by Thomas Schlamme.

"Pilot." Season 1, episode no. 1, first broadcast Sep. 22, 1999. Written by Aaron Sorkin, directed by Thomas Schlamme.

"Posse Comitatus." Season 3, episode no. 21, first broadcast May 22, 2002. Written by Aaron Sorkin, directed by Alex Graves.

"Post Hoc, Ergo Propter Hoc." Season 1, episode no. 2, first broadcast Sep. 29, 1999. Written by Aaron Sorkin, directed by Thomas Schlamme.

"Proportional Response, A." Season 1, episode 3, first broadcast Oct. 6, 1999. Written by Aaron Sorkin, directed by Marc Buckland.

"Shibboleth." Season 2, episode no. 8, first broadcast Nov. 22, 2000. Written by Aaron Sorkin, story by Patrick Caddell, directed by Laura Innes.

"Short List, The." Season 1, episode no. 9, first broadcast Nov. 24, 1999. Written by Aaron Sorkin and Patrick Caddell, story by Aaron Sorkin and Dee Dee Myers, directed by Bill D'Elia.

"Six Meetings Before Lunch." Season 1, episode no. 18, first broadcast Apr. 5, 2000. Written by Aaron Sorkin, directed by Clark Johnson.

"Stackhouse Filibuster, The." Season 2, episode no. 17, first broadcast Mar. 14, 2001. Written by Aaron Sorkin, story by Pete McCabe, directed by Bryan Gordon.

"Stirred." Season 3, episode no. 17, first broadcast Apr. 3, 2002. Written by Aaron Sorkin and Eli Attie, story by Dee Dee Myers, directed by Jeremy Kagan.

"Take Out the Trash Day." Season 1, episode no. 13, first broadcast Jan. 26, 2000. Written by Aaron Sorkin, directed by Ken Olin.

"Take This Sabbath Day." Season 1, episode no. 14, first broadcast Feb. 9, 2000. Written by Aaron Sorkin, Paul Redford and Lawrence O'Donnell Jr., directed by Thomas Schlamme.

"Twenty Hours in America." Season 4, episode no. 1 and 2, first broadcast Sep. 25, 2002. Written by Aaron Sorkin, directed by Christopher Misiano.

"Twenty Hours in L.A." Season 1, episode no. 16, first broadcast Feb. 23, 2000. Written by Aaron Sorkin, directed by Alan Taylor.

"Two Bartlets, The." Season 3, episode no. 12, first broadcast Jan. 30, 2002. Written by Kevin Falls and Aaron Sorkin, story by Gene Sperling, directed by Alex Graves.

"Two Cathedrals." Season 2, episode no. 22, first broadcast May 16, 2001. Written by Aaron Sorkin, directed by Thomas Schlamme.

"War Crimes." Season 3, episode no. 6, first broadcast Nov. 7. 2001. Written by Aaron Sorkin, story by Allison Abner, directed by Alex Graves.

"What Kind of Day Has It Been?" Season 1, episode no. 22, first broadcast May 17, 2000. Written by Aaron Sorkin, directed by Thomas Schlamme.

"White House Pro-Am, The." Season 1, episode no. 17, first broadcast Mar. 22, 2000. Written by Aaron Sorkin, Lawrence O'Donnell Jr., and Paul Redford, directed by Ken Olin.

Books, Articles, Interviews, and Other Sources

Alexander, Herbert E. 1992. *Financing Politics: Money, Elections, and Political Reform.* 4th ed. Washington, D.C.: CQ Press.

Allison, Graham, and Philip Zelikow. 1999. *The Essence of Decision: Explaining the Cuban Missile Crisis.* 2d ed. New York: Addison-Wesley/Longman.

Althusser, Louis. 2001. *Lenin and Philosophy, and Other Essays.* Translated by Ben Brewster. New York: Monthly Review Press.

Anderson, Roger. 2000. " 'The West Wing' Is a Hit—Even If It's Not Always True to Life." *Detroit News,* Apr. 19, no-dot ed., O5.

Arendt, Hannah. 1958. *The Human Condition.* Chicago: Univ. of Chicago Press.

"Audiences Fragmented and Skeptical: The Tough Job of Communicating with Voters." 2000. *Pew Research Center.* Feb. 5. Report available at: www.people-press.org.

Auster, Albert. 2001. *"The West Wing:* To An Outsider, It Celebrates the Importance of Public Service." *Television Quarterly* 32, no. 1: 39–42.

Bachrach, Judy. 1978. "The View from the White House Ground Floor." *The Washington Post,* Aug. 2, B1.

Bailyn, Bernard. 1992. *The Ideological Origins of the American Revolution.* 1968. Reprint. New York: Belknap.

Barber, James David. 1992. *The Presidential Character: Predicting Performance in the White House.* 4th ed. Englewood Cliffs, N.J.: Prentice-Hall.

Baudrillard, Jean. 1988. *Jean Baudrillard: Selected Writings.* Edited by Mark Poster. Stanford, Calif.: Stanford Univ. Press.

Bell, Derrick. 1987. *And We Are Not Saved: The Elusive Quest for Racial Justice.* New York: Basic.

———. 1992. *Faces at the Bottom of the Well: The Permanence of Racism.* New York: Basic.

Benhabib, Seyla. 1992. *Situating the Self: Gender, Community, and Postmodernism in Contemporary Ethics.* New York: Routledge.

Berens, Jessica. 2001. "Groomed for High Office: Wild, Funny and No Stranger to the Barricades, Martin Sheen is Nobody's Idea of a President." *Calgary Herald,* Feb. 5, final ed., B6.

Berger, Rose Marie. 2000. "Scripted Hope in *The West Wing.*" *Sojourners,* May 29, 61.

Bianco, Robert. 2001. " 'West Wing' Lectured More Than Entertained." *USA Today,* Oct. 4.

Birnbaum, Jeffrey H. 1996. *Madhouse: The Private Turmoil of Working for the President*. New York: Random House/Times Books.

Bolter, Jay David, and Richard Grusin. 1999. *Remediation: Understanding New Media*. Cambridge, Mass.: MIT Press.

Branegan, Jay. 2000. "You Could Call It the Wonk Wing." *Time*, May 15, 82–85.

Brantlinger, Patrick. 1977. *The Spirit of Reform: British Literature and Politics, 1832–1867*. Cambridge, Mass.: Harvard Univ. Press.

Brauer, Carl. 1988. "Lost in Transition." *The Atlantic Monthly*, Nov.: 74–80.

Brill, Steven. 2000. "Truth or Fiction: Pick One: Fictional *West Wing* Bests Many Reporters in Depicting a Nuanced Washington." *Brill's Content* 3, no. 2.

Burke, John P. 2000. "The Institutional Presidency." In *The Presidency and the American Political System*, 6th ed, edited by Michael Nelson, 417–42. Washington, D.C.: CQ Press.

Calvo, Dana. 2000. "Politics—But Not as Usual." *Los Angeles Times*, Aug. 7, F1.

Campbell, Colin, S. J. 1986. *Managing the Presidency: Carter, Reagan, and the Search for Executive Harmony*. Pittsburgh: Univ. of Pittsburgh Press.

Carey, James W. 1986. "Why and How? The Dark Continent of American Journalism." In *Reading the News*, edited by Robert K. Manoff and Michael Schudson, 146–96. New York: Pantheon.

Chang, Yahlin. 1999. "TV's Top Dogs." *Newsweek* 134, Oct. 11, 80–81.

Clark, Heather. 2002. "Remember, *West Wing* Is Fictional—New Mexico." AP. Accessed Apr. 3: cnn.com.2002.Showbiz/TV/04/03/westwing.newmexico.ap/index.html.

Combs, James. 1984. *Polpop: Politics and Popular Culture in America*. Bowling Green, Ohio: Bowling Green Univ. Popular Press.

Connolly, William. 1991. *Identity/Difference: Democratic Negotiations of Political Paradox*. Ithaca, N.Y.: Cornell Univ. Press.

Converse, Philip E. 1964. "The Nature of Belief Systems in Mass Publics." In *Ideology and Discontent*, edited by David Apter, 206–61. New York: Free Press.

Cooper, Chester. 1970. *The Lost Crusade: America in Vietnam*. New York: Dodd, Mead.

Cronin, Thomas E. 1980. *The State of the Presidency*. 2d ed. Boston: Little Brown.

Cronin, Thomas E., and Michael A. Genovese. 1998. *The Paradoxes of the American Presidency*. New York: Oxford Univ. Press.

Dean, John. 1976. *Blind Ambition*. New York: Simon and Schuster.

de Jonge, Peter. 2001. "Aaron Sorkin Works His Way Through the Crisis." *New York Times*, Oct. 28, late ed., sec. 6, 42.

Derrida, Jacques. 1995. *Archive Fever: A Freudian Impression.* Translated by Eric Prenowitz. Chicago: Univ. of Chicago Press.

Dickinson, Matthew J. 1997. "Uprooting the Presidential Branch? The Lessons of FDR." In *FDR and the Modern Presidency: Leadership and Legacy,* edited by Mark J. Rozell and William D. Peterson, 13–35. Westport, Conn: Praeger.

DiClerico, Robert E. 1995. *The American President.* 4th ed. Englewood Cliffs, N.J.: Prentice-Hall.

DiMaggio, Madeline. 1990. *How to Write for Television.* New York: Prentice-Hall.

Disch, Lisa. 1997. " 'Please Sit Down, But Don't Make Yourself at Home': Arendtian 'Visiting' and the Prefigurative Politics of Consciousness-Raising.' " In *Hannah Arendt and the Meaning of Politics,* edited by Craig Calhoun and John Mc-Gowan, 132–65. Minneapolis: Univ. of Minnesota Press.

Edwards, George C., III. 1983. *The Public Presidency: The Pursuit of Public Support.* New York: St. Martin's.

Elazar, Daniel J. 1984. *American Federalism: A View from the States.* 3d ed. New York: Harper and Row.

"Election 2002 Results." CNN Online. Accessed Nov. 9: cnn.com.

Endrst, James. 2000. "Executive Privilege: Do It In Your Own Way. 'West Wing' Ignores the Actual Election." *The Bergen County Record* (N.J.), Oct. 25, Y10.

Fairlie, Henry. 1973. *The Kennedy Promise: The Politics of Expectation.* New York: Doubleday.

Fallows, James. 1979. "The Passionless Presidency." *Atlantic Monthly,* May, 33–48.

Feinberg, Richard. 1999. *"West Wing:* TV's New Political Realism." *Straits Times,* Nov. 20, 85.

Feuerherd, Peter. 2000. "A 'Wing' and a Prayer." *Commonweal* 127, Mar. 10, 47.

Field, Syd. 1982. *Screenplay: The Foundations of Screenwriting.* New York: Dell.

Finn, Patrick. 2001. E-mail posted to WestWing@uvm.uvic.ca listserv.

Fiore, Faye. 2001. "Politicians Covet a 'West Wing' Connection." Los Angeles Times Wire Services, published in *The Bergen County Record* (N.J.) Jul. 25, F6.

Fishbein, Leslie. 1983. *"Roots:* Docudrama and the Interpretation of History." In *American History/American Television: Interpreting the Video Past,* edited by John E. O'Connor, 279–305. New York: Ungar. Also available on *Film and History* 1999 CD-ROM.

Fisher, Louis. 1987. *Presidential War Power.* Lawrence Kans.: Univ. Press of Kansas.

Fiske, John. 1987. *Television Culture.* New York: Routledge.

Franklin, Nancy. 2000. "On Television: Corridors of Power." *New Yorker* 76, Feb. 21–28, 290–94.

Frantzich, Stephen. 1998. "Considering the Use of Public Affairs Video in the Classroom." Presentation, made at *C-Span in the Classroom Seminar for Professors*, **DATE**, Washington, D.C.

Freeman, Michael. 2002. "'24' is No. 1; Fox Newcomer Knocks Out Perennial Heavyweight 'West Wing' in Electronic Media Critics Poll." *Electronic Media*, Jan. 7, 24.

"Future of the Public Intellectual: A Forum, The." 2001. *Nation*. Originally published Feb. 12, accessed Oct. 30: www.thenation.com/doc.mhtml?i= 20010212&s=forum.

Gallagher, Catherine. 1985. *The Industrial Reformation of English Fiction: Social Discourse and Narrative Form, 1832–1867*. Chicago: Univ. of Chicago Press.

Gans, Curtis. 1993. "Television: Political Participation's Enemy #1." *Spectrum: Journal of State Government* 66, no. 2: 26–30.

Gans, Herbert. 1979. *Deciding What's News*. New York: Pantheon.

George, Alexander L. 1974. "Assessing Presidential Character." *World Politics* 26: 234–82.

George, Alexander L., and Juliette L. George. 1998. *Presidential Personality and Performance*. Boulder, Colo.: Westview.

George, Alexander L., and Eric Stern. 1998. "Presidential Management Styles and Models." In *Presidential Personality and Performance*, edited by Alexander L. George and Juliette L. George, 204–12. Boulder, Colo.: Westview.

Gergen, David. 2000. *Eyewitness to Power: The Essence of Leadership, Nixon to Clinton*. New York: Simon and Schuster.

Gianos, Phillip L. 1998. *Politics and Politicians in American Film*. Westport, Conn.: Praeger.

Giglio, Ernest. 2000. *Here's Looking at You: Hollywood, Film, and Politics*. New York: Peter Lang.

Giroux, Henry A. 2000. "Cultural Studies and the Culture of Politics: Beyond Polemics and Cynicism." *JAC: A Journal of Composition Theory* 20: 505–40.

Gladstone, Brooke. 2000. "Politics in Movies." *Morning Edition*. Washington, D.C.: National Public Radio, Sept. 7.

Glasgow University Media Group. 1976. *Bad News*. London: Routledge & Kegan Paul.

———. 1980. *More Bad News*. London: Routledge & Kegan Paul.

Glasser, Theodore L. 1992. "Objectivity and News Reporting." In *Philosophical Issues in Journalism*, edited by Elliot D. Cohen, 176–85. New York: Oxford Univ. Press.

Goldfarb, J. C. 1991. *The Cynical Society*. Chicago: Univ. of Chicago Press.

Goodman, Tim. 2001. "Political Quagmire: Left-Leaning 'West Wing' Is Losing Its Relevance." *San Francisco Chronicle*, May 13, final ed., 60.

Goodwin, Doris Kearns. 1991. *Lyndon Johnson and the American Dream*. New York: St. Martin's.

———. 1995. *No Ordinary Time—Franklin and Eleanor Roosevelt: The Home Front in World War II*. New York: Touchstone/Simon and Schuster.

"Government Goes Down the Tube: Images of Government in TV Media." 1999. Center for Media and Public Affairs, May 4. Executive summary and full text available at cmpa.com/archive/ExecSummTvStudy5499.htm.

Graham, Jefferson. 1999. "1 Good Man Trying to Handle 2 Good Shows: Writer Sorkin Adds 'Wing' to His 'Night.' " *USA Today*, Aug. 10, final ed., 3D.

Greenberg, Bradley S. 1980. "Conclusions." In *Life on Television: Content Analyses of U.S. TV Drama*, edited by Bradley S. Greenberg, 183–90. Norwood, N.J.: Ablex Publishing.

Greenstein, Fred I. 1982. *The Hidden-Hand Presidency: Eisenhower as Leader*. New York: Basic Books.

———, ed. 1988. *Leadership in the Modern Presidency*. Cambridge: Harvard Univ. Press.

Grossman, Michael Baruch, and Martha Joynt Kumar. 1981. *Portraying the President: The White House and the News Media*. Baltimore: Johns Hopkins Univ. Press.

Guillory, John. 1993. *Cultural Capital: The Problem of Literary Canon Formation*. Chicago: Univ. of Chicago Press.

Habermas, Jürgen. 1968. *Knowledge and Human Interests*. Translated by Jeremy Shapiro. Boston: Beacon.

———. 1984. *The Theory of Communicative Action*. 2 vols. Translated by Thomas McCarthy. Boston: Beacon.

———. 1986. "Hannah Arendt's Communications Concept of Power." In *Power*, edited by Steven Lukes, 75–93. New York: New York Univ. Press.

———. 1990. *Moral Consciousness and Communicative Action*. Translated by Christian Lenhardt and Shierry Weber Nicholson. Cambridge, Mass.: MIT Press.

Hadley, Elaine. 1995. *Melodramatic Tactics: Theatricalized Dissent in the English Marketplace, 1800–1885*. Stanford: Stanford Univ. Press.

Hale, John F. 1993. "A Different Kind of Democrat: Bill Clinton, the DLC, and the

Construction of a New Party Identity." Paper presented at the annual meeting of the American Political Science Association, Sep. 2–5, in Washington, D.C.

———. 1995. "The Making of the New Democrats." *Political Science Quarterly* 110: 207–32.

Hargrove, Erwin C. 1993. "Presidential Personality and Leadership Style." In *Researching the Presidency: Vital Questions, New Approaches,* edited by George C. Edwards III, John H. Kessel, and Bert A. Rockman, 69–109. Pittsburgh: Univ. of Pittsburgh Press.

"Harper's Index." 2001. *Harper's Magazine,* June, 13.

Heith, Diane J. 2000. "Presidential Polling and the Potential for Leadership." In *Presidential Power: Forging the Presidency for the Twenty-First Century,* edited by Robert Y. Shapiro, Martha Joynt Kumar, and Lawrence R. Jacobs, 380–407. New York: Columbia Univ. Press.

Henderson, Phillip G. 1988. *Managing the Presidency: The Eisenhower Legacy—From Kennedy to Reagan.* Boulder Colo.: Westview.

Hess, Stephen. 1988. *Organizing the Presidency.* Rev. ed. Washington, D.C.: Brookings Institute.

Hinds, Julie. 2000a. "All About Bartlet." *Detroit Free Press,* Oct. 1. Accessed Nov. 4: www.freep.com.

———. 2000b. "Bartlet 2000: The Fictional President from 'The West Wing' has Real-life Appeal." *Detroit Free Press,* Oct. 1. Accessed Nov. 4: www.freep.com.

Hollywood Reporter. 2000. Web and Television Ratings. Accessed Nov. 00: www.hollywoodreporter.com/hollywoodreporter/television/index.jsp.

Honig, Bonnie. 1993. *Political Theory and the Displacement of Politics.* Ithaca and London: Cornell Univ. Press.

Humphrey, Hubert H. 1976. *The Education of a Public Man: My Life and Politics.* Edited by Norman Sherman. Garden City, N.Y.: Doubleday.

Ignatief, Michael. 1998. *Isaiah Berlin: A Life.* Toronto: Viking.

———. 2001. *The Illuminati.* Five-part radio broadcast. Transcript accessed Oct. 30: www.radio.cbc.ca/programs /ideas/ideas.html.

Jacoby, Russell. 1987. *Last Intellectuals: American Culture in the Age of Academe.* New York: Basic Books.

———. 1994. *Dogmatic Wisdom: How the Culture Wars Divert Education and Distract America.* New York: Doubleday.

———. 2000. *The End of Utopia: Politics and Culture in an Age of Apathy.* New York: Basic Books.

James, Caryn. 1999. "Does the Mush Keep Brains Afloat on TV?" *New York Times* 15 Dec., late ed., D1.

Jameson, Frederic. 1997. *Postmodernism; or, The Cultural Logic of Late Capitalism.* Durham, N.C.: Duke Univ. Press.

Jamieson, K. H. 1988. *Eloquence in an Electronic Age.* New York: Oxford Univ. Press.

Janis, Irving L. 1982. *Groupthink.* 2d ed. Boston: Houghton Mifflin.

Johnson, Brian. 2000. "The White House Hustle: Liberal Fantasy Thrives in *The Contender* and *The West Wing.*" *Maclean's* 113, no. 42: 70–73.

Johnson, Ted. 2000. "Spencer's Gift." *TV Guide* 48, Jan. 22–28, 48–50.

Johson, Martin Philip. 1999. *The Dreyfus Affair: Honour and Politics in the Belle Époque.* New York: St. Martin's.

Kant, Immanuel. 1965. *Groundwork of the Metaphysics of Morals.* Translater by H. J. Paton. New York: Harper and Row.

Kantorowicz, Ernst. 1957. *The King's Two Bodies: A Study in Medieval Political Theology.* Princeton: Princeton Univ. Press.

Kearns [Goodwin], Doris. 1976. *Lyndon Johnson and the American Dream.* New York: Signet.

Kernell, Samuel. 1977. *Going Public: New Strategies of Presidential Leadership.* 3d ed. Washington, D.C.: CQ Press.

Kiesewetter, John. 1999. "For a Pacifist, Martin Sheen Plays a Pretty Good President." *Cincinnati Enquirer,* Oct. 17. Accessed Nov. 3, 2000: enquirer.com

———. 2000. "The 'Acting' White House: From Its Hallways to Its Scripts, NBC's 'The West Wing' Stays Entertainingly Correct." *Cincinnati Enquirer,* Jan. 26, all ed., E1.

Kohut, Andrew. 2000. "Getting Voters to Engage." *Columbia Journalism Review* 39: 28.

Langbauer, Laurie. 1999. *Novels of Everyday Life: The Series in English Fiction, 1850–1930.* Ithaca, N.Y.: Cornell Univ. Press.

Lee, Patricia-Ann. 1990. "Teaching Film and Television as Interpreters of History." In *Image as Artifact: The Historical Analysis of Film and Television,* edited by John E. O'Connor, 96–107. Malabar, Fla.: Krieger.

Lewis, Ann F. 2001. "*The West Wing:* An Insider Calls It the Insider's View of Democracy." *Television Quarterly* 32, no. 1: 36–38.

Lieberman Joseph, I., with Michael D'Orso. 2000. *In Praise of Public Life.* New York: Simon and Schuster.

Light, Paul C. 1984. *Vice Presidential Power*. Baltimore: Johns Hopkins Univ. Press.

Lindlaw, Scott. 2001. "Setting Politics Aside,'West Wing' Cast Gets White House Tour." *Associated Press*, Apr. 29, BC cycle.

Littleton, Cynthia. 2001a. "Wells Queried About Handling of 'Wing' Deals." *The Hollywood Reporter*, Jun 29, 1.

———. 2001b. " 'West Wing' Rises to Occasion. Terrorism Themed Episode Pulls in Show's Highest Numbers Ever." *The Hollywood Reporter*, Oct. 5, 1.

Littwin, Susan. 1999/2000. "Going to the Wells." *Written By*, Dec./Jan. Accessed Nov. 3, 2000: www.wga.org/WrittenBy/index.

Long, Tom. 2000. " 'West Wing' Fiction Wins over Reality with Idealism." *Detroit News*, Oct. 5. C1.

Matthews, Christopher. 1999. *Hardball: How Politics Is Played—Told by One Who Knows the Game*. New York: Simon and Schuster.

McBride, Allan. 1998. "Television, Individualism, and Social Capital." *PS: Political Science and Politics* 31, no. 3: 542–52.

McBride, Allan, and Robert K. Toburen. 1996. "Deep Structures: Polpop Culture on Primetime Television." *Journal of Popular Culture* 29, no. 4: 181–200. (For chap. 10, retrieved via EBSCOhost, Mar. 24, 2001.)

McKissack, Fred. 2000. "The West Wing Is Not a Wet Dream." *The Progressive* 64, no. 5 (May): 39.

Mead, George Herbert. 1934. *Mind, Self, and Society*. Chicago: Univ. of Chicago Press.

Miga, Andrew. 1999. "White House Drama More Colorful than the Real White House." *Boston Herald*, Sep. 23, AI ed., 3.

Mill, John Stuart. 1993. *Utilitarianism; On Liberty; Considerations on Representative Government*. 1861. Reprint. Edited by Geraint Williams. London: Dent.

Miller, Matthew. 2000. "The Real White House." *Brill's Content*, Mar., 88–95, 113.

Miroff, Bruce. 1976. *Pragmatic Illusions: The Presidential Politics of John F. Kennedy*. New York: Longman.

———. 2000. *Icons of Democracy: American Leaders as Heroes, Aristocrats, Dissenters, and Democrats*. Lawrence: Univ. Press of Kansas.

Morris, Richard. 1997. *Behind the Oval Office: Winning the Presidency in the Nineties*. New York: Random House.

Morrow, Lance. 2000. "How the Loser Can Be a Winner." *CNN*. Nov. 27: www.cnn.com/2000/ALLPOLITICS/stories/11/27/morrow11_27.a.tm/index.html.

Nathan, Richard P. 1975. *The Plot That Failed: Nixon and the Administrative Presidency*. New York: John Wiley and Sons.

Nelson, John S., and G. R. Boynton. 1997. *Video Rhetorics: Televised Advertising in American Politics*. Urbana, Ill.: Univ. of Illinois Press.

Nelson, Michael. 2000. "The Psychological Presidency." In *The Presidency and the Political System*, 6th ed., edited by Michael Nelson, 199–222. Washington, D.C.: CQ Press.

Nelson, Ted. 2001. Home page. Accessed Oct. 30: www.sfc.keio.ac.jp/~ted/.

Neustadt, Richard E. 1990. *Presidential Power and the Modern Presidents: The Politics of Leadership from Roosevelt to Reagan*. New York: Macmillan.

Newcomb, Horace. 1974. *TV: The Most Popular Art*. Garden City: Anchor-Doubleday.

Newland, Chester A. 1985. "Executive Office Policy Apparatus: Enforcing the Reagan Agenda." In *The Reagan Presidency and the Governing of America*, edited by Lester M. Salamon and Michael S. Lund, 135–80. Washington, D.C.: Urban Institute.

O'Connor, John E. 1987. *Teaching History with Film and Television*. Washington, D.C.: American Historical Association.

O'Connor, John E., and Martin A. Jackson. 1974. *Teaching History with Film*. Washington, D.C.: The American Historical Association.

Oppenheimer, Jean. 2000. "The Halls of Power." *American Cinematographer* 81, no. 10 (Oct.): 74–83.

Orszag, Rica Rodman. 2001. "Do You Recognize the Clinton West Wing in *The West Wing?*" *The Atlantic Monthly*. Web-only sidebar: www.theatlantic.com/issues/2001/03/lehmann-rorszag.htm.

Owen, Rob. 2000. " 'West Wing' Elects to Keep Its Idealistic Platform." *Pittsburgh Post-Gazette*, Oct. 4, E1.

Oxfeld, Jesse. 2000. "Census Consensus: *The West Wing* Covered It Better." *Brill's Content* 3, no. 2: 94.

Patterson, Bradley H., Jr. 2000. *The White House Staff: Inside* The West Wing *and Beyond*. Washington, D.C.: Brookings Institute.

Payne, Rebecca. 2000. "Good Stories Come from Expanding News Values." *Civic Journalism Interest Group News* 5 (summer).

Pennington, Gail. 2000. "Hail to the *West Wing*." *St. Louis Post-Dispatch*, Oct. 4. E1.

Perloff, Richard M. 1998. *Political Communication: Politics, Press, and Public in America*. Mahwah, N.J.: Lawrence Erlbaum.

Peterson, Mark A. 1992. "The Presidency and Organized Interests: White House Patterns of Interest Group Liaison." *American Political Science Review* 86: 612–25.

Pfiffner, James P. 1996. *The Strategic Presidency: Hitting the Ground Running.* 2d ed. Lawrence, Kans.: Univ. Press of Kansas.

———. 1998. *The Modern Presidency.* 2d ed. New York: St. Martin's.

Poniewozik, James. 1999. "Capital Ideas: A Speechwriter's—Sorry, Scriptwriter's—D.C. Series." *Time* 154, Oct. 4, 96.

Preston, Thomas. 2001. *The President and His Inner Circle: Leadership Style and the Advisory Process in Foreign Affairs.* New York: Columbia Univ. Press.

"Question of Color, A." 000. *TV Guide* 48, Jan. 22–28: 36–40, 52.

Rawls, John. 1971. *A Theory of Justice.* Cambridge: Harvard Univ. Press.

———. 1996. *Political Liberalism: The John Dewey Essays in Philosophy.* New York: Columbia Univ. Press.

Reader, Keith, and Khursheed Wadia. 1993. *The May 1968 Events in France: Reproductions and Interpretations.* New York: St. Martin's.

Reedy, George E. 1987. *The Twilight of the Presidency: From Johnson to Reagan.* Rev. ed. New York: New American Library.

Reeves, Richard. 2000. "Days and Nights with Bill Clinton." *Talk*, Sept., 130–37, 185–90.

Reich, Robert B. 1997. *Locked in the Cabinet.* New York: Knopf.

Riley, Jeff. 2002. "FindLaw Entertainment," review of *The West Wing*, written by Aaron Sorkin, directed by Clark Johnson. *FindLaw.* Apr. 5: //e.findlaw.com/reviews/westwing/000405.html.

Riley, Russell L. 2000. "The Limits of the Transformational Presidency." In *Presidential Power: Forging the Presidency for the Twenty-First Century,* edited by Robert Y. Shapiro, Martha Joynt Kumar, and Lawrence R. Jacobs, 435–55. New York: Columbia Univ. Press.

Robins, J. Max. 1999. "The Robbins Report." *TV Guide* 47, May 1–7, 53–54.

Rochelle, Warren. 1999. "The Literary Presidency." *Presidential Studies Quarterly* 29, no. 2: 407–21.

Rossiter, Clinton. 1960. *The American Presidency.* 2nd ed. New York: Harcourt Brace.

Rush, George and Joanna Molloy with Lola Ogunnaike and Kasia Anderson. 2001. " 'West Wing' Cast in a Liberal Mood." *Daily News*, Aug. 29, final ed., 18.

Said, Edward. 1996. *Representations of the Intellectual: The 1993 Reith Lectures.* New York: Vintage Books.

Schlesinger, Arthur M., Jr. 1973. *The Imperial Presidency.* Boston: Houghton Mifflin.

Schram, Sanford. 1991. "The Post-Modern Presidency and the Grammar of Electronic Electioneering." *Critical Studies in Mass Communication* 8: 210–16.

Schudson, M. 1982. "The Politics of Narrative Form: The Emergence of News Conventions in Print and Television. *Daedalus* 111, 97–112.

Scott, A. O. 2000. "Hail to the Chief: From TV to Hollywood, the Demystification of the American President." *New York Times,* Nov. 6, E1.

Sepinwall, Alan. 2000. " 'West Wing' Won't Bask in Glory as Season Opens with Two-Parter." *San Diego Union-Tribune,* Jul. 31, 1st and 3d ed., E7.

Shales, Tom. 2001a. " 'The West Wing' Assumes the Role of Moral Compass." *Washington Post,* Oct. 5, C1.

Shales, Tom. 2001b. "TV, Making 9–11 Its Business; After Showing Life-Changing Events, the Medium Buys In to the New Order." *The Washington Post,* Dec. 30, G2.

Shister, Gail. 2000. "Real-Life Cabinet Secretary Is Hooked on NBC's 'The West Wing.' " *Knight Ridder Newspapers,* Apr. 18. Accessed Nov. 4: www.robertfulford.com/WestWing.html.

Shister, Gail. 2001. " 'West Wing' Doesn't Welcome Real Politicians." *The Bergen County Record* (N.J.), Jan. 14, all ed., Y2.

Smith, Lesley.2000. "Reigning Men." *Pop Matters,* fall 1999. Accessed Nov. 4: popmatters.com/tv/reviews/w/west-wing.html.

Snierson, Dan, and Caroline Kepnes. 2002. "Best in Shows: A By-the-Numbers Look at the Ups and Downers of Fall TV." *Entertainment Weekly,* Jan. 25, 7.

Sorkin, Aaron. 1995. *The American President.* Final draft screenplay. Accessed Oct. 17, 2000: plaza18.mbn.or.jp/~happywel /script/apresident.html.

———. 2000. *PBS NewsHour.* Television interview by Terence Smith. Sep. 27. Transcript available at: www.pbs.org/newshour/media/ west_wing/sorkin.html.

Spragens, William C., and Carole Ann Terwood. 1980. *From Spokesman to Press Secretary: White House Media Operations.* Washington, D.C.: Univ. Press of America.

Starn, Randolph. 1996. "The New Erudition." *Representations: Special Issue,* (fall): 1–15.

Stephanopoulous, George. 1999. *All Too Human: A Political Education.* New York: Little, Brown.

Stock, Brian. 1983. *The Implications of Literacy: Written Language and Models of*

Interpretation in the Eleventh and Twelfth Centuries. Princeton: Princeton Univ. Press.

Storey, John. 1993. *An Introductory Guide to Cultural Theory and Popular Culture.* Athens, Ga.: Univ. of Georgia Press.

Sylvester, Shari. 2000. "Aaron Sorkin Profile: 'West Wing' Creator Surprised by TV Success." *CNN.com.* Sep. 7, accessed Oct. 6 at: www.cnn.com/2000/SHOW-BIZ/TV/09/07/sorkin/index.html.

Tarloff, Erik. 1999. "West Wing: True or False?" *TV Guide* 47, Oct. 23, 6.

"Television's Top 50." 2001. *Houston Chronicle,* May 20, 2 STAR ed., 26.

Tuchman, Gaye. 1978. *Making News.* New York: Free Press.

Tucker, Ken. 2000. "Meet the Prez." *Entertainment Weekly.* Feb. 25: www.ew.com.

Tugwell, Rexford G. 1960. *The Enlargement of the Presidency.* Garden City, N.Y.: Doubleday.

Tulis, Jeffrey K. 1987. *The Rhetorical Presidency.* Princeton, N.J.: Princeton Univ. Press.

"TV's 'West Wing' Is Not a Good Replica of the Real Thing." 1999. *Detroit News* 29 Sep., final ed., E5.

Villa, Dana. 1996. *Arendt and Heidegger: The Fate of the Political.* Princeton: Princeton Univ. Press.

Wallace, Amy. 2000. "Hollywood's Gift to the Political Process." *Los Angeles Times Magazine,* Aug. 13.

Walsh, Edward. 1978. "The White House Office Shuffle." *Washington Post,* May 20, A1.

Warshaw, Shirley Anne. 1996. *Powersharing: White House-Cabinet Relations in the Modern Presidency.* Albany, N.Y.: SUNY Press.

Waxman, Sharon. 2000. "Inside *The West Wing's* New World." *George,* Nov., 54–59, 94–96.

———. 2001. "Will 'West Wing' Go Up in Smoke?" *The Washington Post,* Jul. 20, C1.

Weinraub, Bernard. 2000. "In Its Second Season, 'The West Wing' Is Turning into a Certified Hit." *New York Times,* Oct. 17, E1. Accessed at: nytimes.com.

Weintraub, Joanne. 2000. "Winging It." *Milwaukee Journal Sentinel,* Mar. 9, all ed., 1E.

Weko, Thomas J. 1995. *The Politicizing Presidency.* Lawrence Kans.: Univ. Press of Kansas.

"West Wing Creator Criticizes Brokaw Special." 2002. CNN.com. Accessed Feb. 28: www.cnn.com/2002/SHOWBIZ/TV/02/26/west.wing.ap/.

"West Wing Honcho Blasts Bush." 2002. CBSNews.com. Feb. 26.

White, Mimi. 1992. "Ideological Analysis and Television." In Channels of Discourse, Reassembled, 2d ed, edited by Robert C. Allen, 161–70. New York and London: Routledge.

Wills, Garry. 1994. The Kennedy Imprisonment. Boston: Little, Brown.

Wolff, Michael. 2000. "The Other Political Drama." New York, Dec. 4, 42–47.

Wren, Celia. 1999. "The Inside Dope(s): NBC's West Wing." Commonweal 126, no. 21 (Dec. 3): 17–19.

Index

In this index, *The West Wing* is abbreviated throughout as *WW* and *The American President* as *AP*.

Other titles in The Television Series

Bonfire of the Humanities: Television, Subliteracy, and Long Term Memory Loss
David Marc

"Deny All Knowledge": Reading the X Files
David Lavery, Angela Hague, and Marla Cartwright, eds.

The Gatekeeper: My 30 Years as a TV Censor
Alfred R. Schneider, with Kaye Pullen

Gen X TV: *The Brady Bunch* to *Melrose Place*
Rob Owen

Lou Grant: The Making of TV's Top Newspaper Drama
Douglass K. Daniel

Prime-Time Authorship: Works about and by Three TV Dramatists
Douglas Heil

Prime Time, Prime Movers: From I *Love Lucy* to *L.A. Law* America's Greatest TV Shows and
the People Who Created Them
David Marc and Robert J. Thompson

Rod Serling's *Night Gallery:* An After-Hours Tour
Scott Skelton and Jim Benson

The Story of Viewers for Quality Television: From Grassroots to Prime Time
Dorothy Collins Swanson

Teleliteracy: Taking Television Seriously
David Bianculli

Television's Second Golden Age: From *Hill Street Blues* to *ER*
Robert J. Thompson

TV Creators: Conversations with America's Top Producers of Television Drama,
Volumes 1 and 2
James L. Longworth, Jr.

The View from Highway 1: Essays on Television
Michael J. Arlen